# THE TEAM THAT CHANGED
# RUGBY FOREVER

# THE TEAM THAT CHANGED
# RUGBY FOREVER

## THE 1967 ALL BLACKS

### ALEX McKAY

First published in 2017 by New Holland Publishers
London • Sydney • Auckland

The Chandlery 50 Westminster Bridge Road London SE1 7QY
United Kingdom
1/66 Gibbes Street Chatswood NSW 2067 Australia
5/39 Woodside Ave Northcote, Auckland 0627 New Zealand

www.newhollandpublishers.com

ISBN: 9781869664725

Group Managing Director: Fiona Schultz
Managing Director: David Cowie
Publisher: Christine Thomson
Project Editor: Pete Malicki
Designer: Andrew Quinlan
Production Director: James Mills-Hicks
Printer: HangTai Printing Company Limited

10 9 8 7 6 5 4 3 2 1

Keep up with New Holland Publishers on Facebook
www.facebook.com/NewHollandPublishers

# CONTENTS

# PROLOGUE

*The idea of the team is an ancient one. Long, long ago, in search of a little peace and quiet, the old men of the tribe sent the young men off to hunt. If there were too many young men they'd split into smaller groups and fight each other. But as many as fifteen of them could band together under a single leader, and might even hunt something worth eating. Of course, the tribe would have starved if they had really depended on their young men. Women, who knew about these things, grew crops because nature made tasty animals very shy and very fast.*

*But that idea of a small band of men took root. Under a good leader, the differing skills and personalities of each man might complement the whole and form a sum greater than the parts. And because young men became old men who sat and embroidered tales of wondrous deeds long gone by, as old men are wont to do, these bands, these teams, became memorable. Some, whose deeds were mightier than most, or whose tales were best told, became legends.*

\*\*\*

In 1967 the world changed forever. It was one of those explosively crowded years when each new day seemed to herald some fresh sensation. Events and consequences tumbled forth in youthful vigour and confusion. Even novelties that then seemed trivial later proved momentous. It was a year of turmoil, a year of chaos, a year that twisted everything familiar into some new and alien form. It was the end and it was the beginning.

Just three days into 1967, former B-movie actor Ronald Reagan was sworn in as Governor of California, beginning his journey to the American presidency. The next day the Doors, a southern Californian gothic rock band that were the antithesis of everything Reagan stood for, released their first album. Its raunchy hit single *Light My Fire* gained more poignant meaning a few weeks later when a launch-pad inferno incinerated the crew of Apollo One – an inauspicious beginning for a programme that put men on the moon little more than two years later.

The Cultural Revolution raged in China as the Red Guards orchestrated chaos at Chairman Mao's behest. In Vietnam, the war reached its peak as 15,000 Americans and tens of thousands of Vietnamese died. Far more were slaughtered or starved in an obscure conflict in Biafra, while the Six Day war rewrote the map of the Middle East. In April, Muhammad Ali refused induction into the American Army and was stripped of his world heavyweight title. In October, guerrilla leader Che Guevara was killed in Bolivia. Both men became revolutionary icons, their faces shining from posters as social protests raged in Europe and race riots turned American cities like Detroit into combat zones.

But 1967 wasn't just about war and conflict. Some preferred to make love, not war. In June, 400 million people watched the Beatles sing *All You Need is Love* on the first live global television link. The times were, as Bob Dylan had predicted, "a'changing". Hippies flooded into San Francisco for the Summer of Love as psychedelic guru Timothy Leary called on people to "Turn on, Tune in and Drop out." Iconic 60s band Pink Floyd released their first album, as did Jimi Hendrix and David Bowie. The Beatles trumped them with their classic *Sgt. Pepper's Lonely Hearts Club Band.* The Rolling Stones countered with two albums, somewhat overshadowed by their arrest and conviction on drug charges. On October the 8th, the musical *Hair* premiered off Broadway.

In New Zealand history, October the 8th was a big day too. A new law allowed licensed premises to stay open later than six every evening. The 'Six O'clock Swill', wherein workers finished their day at five, raced to the nearest pub and then drank as much as humanly possible in the remaining minutes, passed un-mourned into memory. But while that radical change dominated the front pages of the newspapers for weeks, the back pages were as always dominated by the great New Zealand obsession: rugby football. Within days of the relaxation of licensing laws, the national team, the All Blacks, departed for the northern hemisphere, where they were scheduled to play eighteen games in the British Isles, France, and Canada. So eventful was that tour to be that over the next two months patrons drinking long into the evenings were never short of rugby matters to discuss.

The team no sooner reached the northern hemisphere than some of its players witnessed a fatal gun-fight on the streets of San Francisco, while other players chatted to the Flower Children sleeping in the parks. In England, an opposition player mistimed a tackle and was paralysed for life. In Scotland, Colin Meads, already a legend, was sent off for reckless play, the first All Black to suffer that fate in more than forty years. Several times the team had to change their itinerary at the last moment. One change was forced by heavy snow in Wales. Another by the modern equivalent of a medieval plague, an outbreak of foot-and-mouth disease that lead to the cancellation of the Irish section of the tour. Yet despite all those distracting incidents, and without injury replacements, psychoanalysts, dietary technicians, personal trainers, video analysts, media coaches, motivational specialists, legal advisors, or even tattoos, the team returned home unbeaten.

In keeping with the era, that 1967 All Black side was the most extraordinary team in the game's history. Not because it was the best, although it is among the contenders for that title, nor because of the incredible events that shaped it on and off the field. What made it so extraordinary was that it changed the game and it changed the men who made up the team and the lives they lived. Of that 32-man squad – 30 players, a coach, and a manager – three were to be knighted (as was a New Zealand journalist who covered the tour). Four others were later to be elected to Parliament and a fifth died before he would have been. One of those politicians also became New Zealand High Commissioner to Zimbabwe and, in effect, to Southern Africa. Of course, there are many measures of success and other members of the team succeeded in business, the professions, and in that tough and most New Zealand of occupations: farming.

In that amateur age, around half the players were involved in farming in one sense or another, and most were more familiar with the paddock than the paved road. It is unthinkable today, when the urban centres quickly procure the rising stars of New Zealand rugby, but the captain of the team played for Wairarapa and its most famous player was a lock forward from King Country. That player, Colin – now Sir Colin – Meads, transcended them all. He was unquestionably the player of the century, perhaps the only automatic choice for an all-time Best Ever World XV. The 1967 tour added a new chapter to the legend of Meads, but he was already the archetypal New Zealander of that generation. He embodied all the virtues Kiwi males liked to identify in themselves: modest, hard-working, adaptable, honest in word and deed, laconic, tough yet kind to the less fortunate, and utterly reliable in a tight spot. As a Kiwi icon and an example of how a humble and egalitarian New Zealander could rise to world stature, his only equal was that other great knight: Everest summiteer Sir Edmund Hillary.

Yet Meads was just a player and not a leader– at least in any official sense. Leadership, and the greatest credit for the team's unique character and status, was in the hands of three other men. The manager Charlie

Saxton and the coach Fred Allen were both former All Blacks. What is more, they had both seen active service in World War Two. That meant they knew the difference between war and sport, but also its similarities in terms of character requirements.

Most significantly, Saxton had captained, and Allen played in, the 'Kiwis': the NZ servicemen's team that in the cold northern winter of 1945-46 had captivated war-weary European crowds with their spectacular brand of attacking rugby. Reunited at the head of the All Black team in 1967, they were determined to resurrect that style after two grim decades in which New Zealand rugby emphasised forward play and relentless kicking rather than running and passing. The new leadership wanted– although they would not have seen it in such terms–a game that matched a bold, more colourful era.

Joining Saxton and Allen in the leadership triumvirate was an inspired choice as the team captain: Brian – now Sir Brian – Lochore. He may well have been the greatest of many fine All Black captains. A man of quiet dignity who inspired great loyalty in his men, Lochore was the epitome of the natural leader. He led the team that changed New Zealand rugby. They re-orientated its approach, added lustre to its traditions, and advanced the All Blacks into the modern world. They were the bridge between the old era and the new.

Lochore's men were not as All Blacks are today, living in a professional bubble from their teenage years. They were amateur footballers, spending most of their Saturday afternoons playing for local clubs alongside their less-talented neighbours. None were wealthy, indeed most were far from it and they all had to earn a living in the wider world. Unlike modern All Blacks, many had gathered real life experiences. One had been on the big 'overseas experience' Several had undergone the then compulsory military service, one spent two years as a Mormon missionary in Canada. Others drifted across the country in search of work and experience, as young Kiwis do. In short, they were typical New Zealanders in everything but their excess of sporting talent.

Let it be clear. These men were not, with perhaps the odd exception long after sundown and in very select company, '60s children' in the sense we understand that term today. Their politics were conventional, not radical, and their culture was more inclined to rugby, racing, and beer than sex, drugs, and rock and roll. No obvious line can be drawn connecting them to Andy Warhol or Tom Wolfe, Bob Dylan or Malcolm X. They were short-haired men who played serious rugby. Yet collectively they signalled the end of one era and the beginning of another just as surely as the Pink Floyd signalled a new era in popular music and Germaine Greer brought a new era in gender relations. The 67 All Blacks were the team that changed the game in a year that changed the world. That was what made them fit perfectly into the 1960s.

This is the story of that great All Black team and what became of them, and it is the story of leadership that bound 30 individuals of distinct character into a team great enough to transcend the limitations of the past and allow a shining future for their chosen field of expression. It is also the story of the changing world around them, in another New Zealand.

\*\*\*

The past is notoriously hard to capture. We remember events, not processes. Change, being incremental, slips by almost unnoticed except perhaps in the mirror. Last year the offside law changed. This year the players began returning to the dressing room at half-time instead of staying on the field. Over decades these changes mount up until what was once commonplace becomes almost forgotten.

Hardest of all for the historian to capture is the *spirit* of the times, that indefinable something in the air that shapes the world-view of a generation, that binds it to a cause or frees it to remake the world anew. It is with that *spirit* that a generation sees and understands things. We can find it in their songs. In the 1950s, the original rock-an-roller Chuck Berry wrote songs about girls and cars because they were what most interested young men who bought records. Cars meant freedom, escape, the open road. But if girls still mean pretty much the same things in the 21st century as they did then, cars mean something very different. Today they mean traffic jams and global warming. Their generational meaning has changed even more than their styling. No-one sings about cars anymore.

Memory – at least for spectators – is not quite the same as history, either. Our memories of rugby in 1967, like our memories of World War Two, are in black and white. Vietnam in 1967 was a war in colour because most of our memories of it actually come from movies like *Apocalypse Now* or *Forrest Gump*. But New Zealanders never saw Lochore's men in anything but black and white newsreels, so we remember it in monotones which now date it to a long-gone era.

What is certain is that 1967 was the end of one era and the bridge to the new. Of course we didn't know that then, anymore than the British had known in 1940 that Dunkirk was a victory. But everything was about to change, even rugby, which seemed to be set in stone. Monotones were about to be coloured in, skirts to rise, and, as the cliché has it, the old to give birth to the new.

To properly understand the 1967 All Blacks today, we need to unmake change, to go back to when not just rugby, but New Zealand society was very different. A time before foody culture, for example. Eating out meant the same food that you had at home, it was just that someone else cooked it for you and you didn't have to worry about the washing up. Restaurants were unpretentious; the waiter called you "mate", a reminder that in an egalitarian land he was neither inferior nor superior to you. The waitress was usually a friend of your sister's, not an Irish backpacker. Graham Kerr was on television, but not everyone had such a novelty and the Galloping Gourmet was two years away. And there were few of those things that are today considered basics. There was no yoghurt, no energy drinks, and margarine was only available on a doctor's prescription, for to actually prefer it to butter was to challenge the economic basis of the nation.

Unless there was a budget, the financial news was buried somewhere in the middle of the paper. Near the back were pages of real jobs, ones with award wages and pension plans. Unemployment was almost unknown, usually measured in dozens. Politics was a series of storms in teacups. The amount of real passion it created could be judged by the fact that the Prime Minister's home address and telephone number were in the Wellington phone book.

It was a very safe society, if one avoided certain drinking establishments. You could put your nine-year-old kid on the overnight train from Auckland to Wellington and just ask some old folks nearby to keep an eye on them. The kid could sleep softly head against the wooden seats all the way to Paekakariki, slowly waking as the train rolled along with the sea beside it on the run into Wellington and its waiting trolley-buses.

This was a land of Maoris and British immigrants. The dominant culture was British; *pakeha* as the Maoris called the Europeans. Maoris were respected in theory and sometimes in practice. I didn't really know what *tapu* land was, but I knew you didn't go onto it. Maori rugby was actually at a low ebb in 1967, with few players in the All Blacks. Most notable was crowd favourite Waka Nathan. Newspapers called him "the Black Panther" as they had the great George Nepia, for Political Correctness had not been invented and it was a compliment at the time.

The legendary fullback Nepia had played all 28 games on the 1924 northern hemisphere tour. But his fame obscured the fact that few Maoris had been prominent in the black jersey. They weren't permitted to tour South Africa and many, like Keith Davis, the sole Maori in the 1953-54 team, were said to be "half-caste and Europeanised." But there were many questions that were never asked in the New Zealand of that time.

Certainly the genders rarely blurred. Men smelled like men, something best appreciated by sheep dogs, but there was no men's deodorant then. Men knew how to fix things, especially cars, because New Zealand, like a latter-day Cuba, was the land of the 'old bomb'. Sky-high import duties meant new cars were restricted to bookmakers, publicans, and politicians. But there was nothing mechanical that couldn't be fixed with Number Eight wire, a pair of old stockings, and a particular combination of oaths and hammer blows.

The breathalyser had not yet cut its swathe through the nation's social habits. Men drank beer from large brown bottles then threw them out the car window to shatter on the roadside verges. On certain roads it was said to be possible to navigate at night entirely by following their glittering shards in the headlights.

Women, by and large, stayed home. They knew how to make scones and sponges. They could knit, sew, and play netball, and if they really wanted to be rocket scientists or lumberjacks there was nothing actually stopping them, but why would they? There was a simple phrase that summed up their world. It was always at the bottom of the tickets to a dance or an after-match function in the country; it read: *Ladies a plate.* So while the men drove, the women sat beside them nestling a plate of sponge cake they had baked that afternoon. They got the recipe from the *Women's Weekly* and added extra cream or some coconut flakes to make it their own. But there was a change coming. We had a cousin who toured with the Kiwi league team. He bought his wife home a hot-water bottle as a present from Paris. She threw it at him.

Everyone had a story like that: how they told the boss what they thought of him, that killer comeback that put their spouse or their foreman in their place. But those stories only meant something because they upset the natural order. The natural order was that you did what you were told, told by your parents, told by your teachers, told by your boss, told by your coach. You could grow up and never hear anyone question authority.

Hanging over the nation was the giant shadow of two World Wars, wars that had given authority its power. Society was judged by two generations who had served in overseas conflicts. Their offspring grew up expecting the call to come again. Going off to war was just what you did. Every town had its war memorial, inscribed with the names of those who had not returned. Those who had returned talked only obliquely about combat, but war had shaped the way they saw the world and how they judged people. It inured them to violence, made them suspicious of human weakness, and left them unable to express emotions except through a haze of alcohol. Their outlook shaped New Zealand society in the 1950s and 60s. It seemed natural that the former commander of New Zealand's wartime army should become Governor-General. The war was still there. Heroes like Upham, Elliot and Ngarimu were honoured for their medals of valour in the second war. Gallipoli was still remembered from the first war; name-checked at dawn service on ANZAC day.

Yet the actual Gallipoli was not yet a place of pilgrimage for flag-draped young Kiwis. Nationalism was unfashionable then, for the soldiers had seen its logical conclusions. They were proud of the peaceful society their flag represented, but reluctant to wave it like Americans. They preferred, in their understated culture, to wear little badges on their lapels, the insignia of the Returned Services Association. It said they belonged, they had served; whether humbly or heroically mattered not. Even in 1967, All Black supporters wore them in London. By that time, as Kiwi exile journalist Wallace Reyburn waspishly noted, other nations had "moved on".

War service created its own networks of trust and mateship. When my father needed a bale of hay from Eric Courtney, the laconic farmer next door, he offered to pay for it. "Ohhh, *buksheesh* eh?" was all Eric said, obliquely acknowledging that having both served in North Africa they knew there were things more important than money. And if a boy listening did not yet understand such things, he sensed they existed.

Of course there were always alternative currents in New Zealand society, for there was a certain Scottish tolerance to difference and English celebration of eccentricity, spiced with a touch of Irish and Maori rebellion. There were known to be homosexuals, for example. They joined dance companies and went into the arts, or became stewards on ocean liners. Apparently you could tell them by the way they put their hands on their hips. They mostly lived in Auckland. .

There were certain rituals that marked New Zealand culture. Summer lawns were mowed on Saturday mornings, the drone of a thousand motor-mowers was the sound of the suburbs. So too there were national fashions. At one point they produced a sweet and watery orange drink in a thin opaque plastic globe. It was the size of cricket ball and had a small neck on it. Someone discovered that neck fitted neatly onto the radio aerial of a car, and within weeks virtually every car in the country had a plastic ball on its aerial.

But there was never any doubt about the central ritual of New Zealand culture: rugby. During the summer there were cricket and tennis, fine games both, but neither stirred passions nor defined the nation. Then there was racing and the beach and the mountains that produced Hillary, perhaps the most famous Kiwi of them all.

But really, beaches and mountains or cricket and tennis, indeed summer itself, was what happened when you were resting from rugby. Rugby was the sport that defined the nation, that enabled conversation with strangers. On Saturday, around 2:30 in the afternoon, the whole country fell silent and waited for kick-off. You played, you watched, you listened, you reminisced, or you were left out. The nation was at prayer.

\*\*\*

For a player, New Zealand rugby was a straightforward pyramid of merit that reached up through school, club, and province before culminating in the All Black team. If you were good enough, and determined enough, you moved up to the next level, and the next, and the next until eventually you found out how good you were. Then you knew, and so did everyone else. And everyone had their tales of those who were good enough but not determined enough. That Hora Hora fullback who scored four tries in a club game but turned down the rep team. That Christchurch sporting natural who enjoyed good-fellowship more than the solitary training runs. It's not true that every New Zealander wants to be an All Black, although it is true that many climb high on the pyramid before they realise that.

Befitting an egalitarian land, the champion provincial team was always open to debate. No knock-out competition or simple league table decided the title of New Zealand's Best Team. The Ranfurly Shield ruled at provincial level. Its unique format required you beat the holders on their home ground to win the Shield. A provincial side unbeaten through a season or more could only claim supremacy if they beat the holders at their ground. Teams might lose the Shield in their first defence, or keep it for several seasons. Thus it moved around; Hawke's Bay, Otago, Taranaki, Auckland… each had their dynasty. If you were lucky, you were young when it happened to your team, then the memory lasted a lifetime. To be in a side that won the Shield was as much as most provincial players ever hoped for. Even to play in a Shield game was something special, with two or three times as many spectators as a game might otherwise attract.

Nations and cultures must have their proud myths and rugby was at the centre of New Zealand's. The pantheon of heroes was filled by ancients like Jimmy Duncan and Billy Wallace, Bert Cooke and George Nepia. Post-war greats like Bob Scot and Don Clarke were lauded as fit to 'join the immortals'. Many were the tales told of these heroes and their deeds. So too of great teams; the 1905 'Originals', the 1924 'Invincibles', and the mighty 1956 juggernaut that overwhelmed the Springboks.

But myth must have its tragedies. New Zealand had Bob Dean's try-that-wasn't in the 'Originals' only defeat at Wales' fabled fortress, Cardiff Arms Park. It had Cyril Brownlie's sending off against England in 1924, and defeats by South Africa in 1937 and most comprehensively in 1949 when the series was lost 4-0. Out of that last tragedy came another: the belief that a winning team must comprise a mighty forward pack allied to a great goal kicker and inside backs who could drive the opposition back with long raking kicks into touch. The belief was sustainable, but the cost was high, no more so than a 1959 test when the Lions scored three tries but lost to Don Clarke's six penalty goals. New Zealand rugby was – and not only according to the scribes of the northern hemisphere – monolithic, predictable, and boring to watch. But that was as true of Kiwi society as it was of their rugby, for sport is only a reflection of a wider culture.

True, like David, who slew Goliath when the biggest and bravest had failed, there was a spectacular alternative on the bench. New Zealand had actually played attacking rugby for much of its history. But as the 1950s turned into the 1960s, the All Blacks steamrollered on. In 1963-64 the much revered Wilson – later Sir Wilson – Whineray lead his team to the northern hemisphere. They played ten-man rugby and returned with 34 victories from 36 games. It was business as usual. It was not just rugby that was colourless. The whole country seemed to be stagnant as it slept on the verge of change it could barely detect coming. The safe world the returning soldiers had built was egalitarian, friendly, and free. It was also conservative, unimaginative, and extremely boring.

\*\*\*

The winds of change came slowly. In 1967, as we have seen, many things happened in the world, some that were important then and some that are important now, which are not necessarily the same thing. But New Zealand was at the end of the line. Momentous changes were something

Kiwis read about in newspapers or, if they had a television, something they watched in black-and-white on the one available channel. The *Avengers*, with the divine Miss Peel, was the highlight of the week along with *The Man From U.N.C.L.E.* Still, hints of the expanding minds of the psychedelic 60s were coming over the radio. The first Number One in the 1967 hit parade was the Beach Boys' *Good Vibrations*, the epitome of early 60s surf sound, all sunshine and clean-cut good looks.

But as the All Blacks headed across the Pacific, Scott McKenzie ruled the New Zealand pop charts, telling us to wear flowers in our hair if we went to San Francisco. The All Blacks ignored his advice. Their hair was too short to host flowers. Not even a moustache graced their rugged faces, which mirrored John Wayne not John Lennon.

In any case, the All Blacks had another song: *Ten Guitars*, fast becoming the anthem of a generation of New Zealanders. It was the B-side of Engelbert Humperdinck's great lament *Please Release Me*, another All Black favourite because the more you drank the better you could sing it (although critical audiences might not agree). But it was *Ten Guitars* that Nathan would always play on his guitar, or Mac Herewini on his ukulele, with Jack Hazlett and Alister Hopkinson singing along.

Yet if that was a song everyone could sing music, like fashion, was becoming part of a generational divide. It is hard to remember today just how much the older generation *hated* longhair and everything associated with it, especially 'pop music'. The generation gap was real and has never been so real before or since. Hairstyles signposted the fundamental issue of the generational divide: the Vietnam war. Generations shaped by World Wars now found the next generation questioning a very different conflict. A complex Third World anti-colonial nationalist struggle took on extreme meaning in the context of the Cold War. New Zealand, true to its old allies, followed America into that war. In the simplest understanding, and thus that of the great majority, that complex struggle could be reduced to a game. Not rugby, but dominoes. According to the inevitable sequence of falling dominoes, if Vietnam fell to the communists then Thailand would follow suit. That meant, apparently, that Malaysia, Singapore, and Indonesia would quickly follow, leaving the ANZACs to face the yellow hordes, millions of faceless fanatics bent on applying the principles of dialectic materialism to the dairy farmers of Hokitika and Invercargill.

The vast majority of Kiwi youth actually held fast to the teachings of their elders. Serious radicals and hippies were few and far between. But suddenly there was a choice. The young did not have to follow the old. They could remake the world, conjuring one less authoritarian, less patriarchal, less grey. And where would rugby fit in that brave new world?

For a time rugby was a bridge between generations. But out on the perimeters of society there were growing numbers of young men who thought rugby was a dull and pointless combat reflecting a dull and pointless culture. They found other sports they could take up which didn't involve violence. There was surfing and its harmony with the waves, or Frisbee, that most non-competitive of sports that even the dog could enjoy. There was also the logical extension of Frisbee, which was doing nothing at all.

Remember that being a member of a subversive subculture is an awful lot of fun, especially when you're young. Like any other culture it brings community, identity, and the certainty that you are entirely superior to all who do not belong to your group. Religions, indie bands and fashion houses all depend on that feeling.

So at this moment in history when the vast majority of Kiwis drank around the fire in the backyard and sang *Pokare Kare Ana* and *Ten Guitars* in communal harmony, their certainties were being questioned, their world view challenged. Rugby would not necessarily prosper in a new world. If it was going to remain a bridge between generations and the centre of Kiwi identity, it needed to change.

Studies of popular revolutions reveal an odd fact: their leaders do not come from the downtrodden classes they claim to speak for. Leaders of workers or slaves are always steeped in the values of the ruling class. Apartheid ended when a true-blue (or perhaps true-white) Afrikaner called time. The USSR collapsed when Gorbachov, born and raised within the communist system, admitted the game was up. Karl Marx was more at home in the British Library than he ever was in a factory, and Che Guevara was a doctor, not a labouring *lumpenprolitariat*. That fact is crucial to the transformation of the All Blacks in 1967. At the wave of their leaders' wand, the national side abandoned the sterility of two decades of grinding defensive play. In a year of change, the All Blacks changed and because they changed they stayed at the centre of New Zealand culture.

There is no obvious link to what was going on in society, no cause and effect. This was not a reaction to growing disenchantment with rugby or some hippy no-hoper's preference for a surfboard over a rugby ball. It was just the spirit of the age. It came out of the blue, or at least out of a dream of beating South Africa's best. But it happened right in the same time wave as revolutions in art and music, love, politics, film, and all the other aspects of human culture that make life worth living.

What happened was a palace coup.

***

—

# IN THE BEGINNING THERE WAS JIMMY DUNCAN: AN ARCHAEOLOGY OF THE 1967 ALL BLACKS

Historians have a saying – 'if you want to understand the 18th century, study the 17th' – and to really understand the '67 tour we do need to go back a long way. Back to the days before cars and televisions and sliced bread. Back before the All Blacks were a product. Back to a time when Otago, thriving in the wake of the late 1800s gold rush, was the centre of wealth and power in New Zealand. In those boom times, the gold-panner's restless spirit and determined fortitude combined with a certain blend of Scottish prudence to give the southerners an independent character they have never quite lost. One such Southern Man of considerable renown was 'Jimmy' Duncan, and it is with him that our story really begins.

Duncan was a saddler by trade and when any man of means rode a horse, the trade was a good one. But in those formative years of the New Zealand game, the Dunedin-born Duncan earned wider renown as a rugbyman. Debuting in 1889, he represented Otago for fourteen years. In the old photos he stands out, or more precisely his bushy black moustache stands out. Whenever he could, Duncan wore a cap to cover his premature baldness. He wouldn't look out of place in Dunedin today.

At half-back, 1st 5/8 or in the long forgotten wing-forward position, Duncan represented New Zealand from 1897-1903 and was captain in the later years. A noted tactician, he invented the backline system of two 5/8ths that New Zealand teams have used ever since. Such tactical innovations saw him made the first official All Black coach and he took the 1904-05 'Originals' to the UK. He was reportedly sidelined by the team's Auckland contingent, though he denied it. After the tour he turned to refereeing, completing a unique treble when he became a test referee in 1908.

Yet there was more to Duncan's legacy than his pioneering coaching, his tactical innovations, or his colourful career. Coaching Otago Boys' High School First XV in 1931-32, the master found his disciple: a talented young half-back named Charlie (no-one ever called him Charles) Saxton. Duncan taught the young man the tricks and traditions of the trade, not least the dive-pass, that most sublime expression of the art of half-back play. Saxton is at the centre of our story, but there was another lad who had absorbed Duncan's wisdom a few years earlier. His influence on New Zealand rugby also lived on. His name was Victor Cavanagh, like his father before him.

The young Cavanagh first came to prominence as a cricketer. He made it as far as twelfth man for NZ against Doug 'Bodyline' Jardine's England side and for several seasons he and Saxton opened the batting together for Otago. But it was to be rugby that brought both men greater fame. 'Young' Vic's brief rugby-playing career with Otago was ended by injury in 1931. But then the young man took up coaching, which is like saying the young Mozart took up music; what really happened was that they found the expression of their genius.

'Young Vic' coached the Southern club in Dunedin, while his father 'Old' Vic coached University. A tremendous rivalry developed between the two sides – immortalised in A.P. Gaskell's short story *The Big Game*. Matches between them drew crowds of five or even ten thousand. Both Cavanaghs were excellent tacticians. The father, having coached sides with lightweight forward packs, countered their weaknesses in the scrum with a rucking game. The son refined that tactic by having the 2nd 5-8 deliberately run into the opposition ranks to set up a ruck for his forwards. 'Show me a forward pack and I'll run into it' became the 2nd 5-8's creed. That tactic that was still fundamental in 1967.

In 1935, Old Vic was coaching Otago and gave Saxton his debut against Wairarapa. Saxton scored tries in his first three games and starred in the victory over Canterbury that brought the Ranfurly Shield to Dunedin for the first time. Saxton was on his way up. The following year, in a unique move, the Cavanaghs, father and son, became co-coaches of the Otago Shield team. Saxton's old cricket mate – just four years his senior – was now his rugby coach, and we can begin to see a pattern in Saxton's life where his personality and talents gained him influential friends and patrons. Yet Saxton was not born to the purple and his path was not paved. In 1920, when he was just seven, his father had died in the contemporary equivalent of a car-crash – a fall from a horse. Responsibility was thrust on him at that early age and he took on hard work as a virtue.

The need to make a living took Saxton to South Canterbury in 1937, the year the touring Springboks shook New Zealand's rugby world. They hammered Shield-holders Otago 47-7, wounding the Cavanagh brand. Saxton's new province fared similarly, going down 43-6. Saxton – now captaining his team – was singled out by Springbok legend Danie Craven, then a young half-back himself. Craven nominated Saxton as the best half-back the tourists had seen in New Zealand. The national selectors didn't agree. Saxton made the trials, but not the All Blacks. Still, his luck was holding in a sense: the All Blacks were comprehensively beaten. It was a good series to miss.

Saxton went on to play for Southland and captained them when they took the Shield from Cavanagh's Otago. He continued to make friends as upwardly mobile as he was. At South Canterbury he became great mates with their star three-quarter, Tom Morrison, of whom more later. After a Shield defence against Bush, he befriended the opposition centre, one Keith Elliot. Years later they both served in the Middle East. Elliot, with all the social authority of one who'd earned a Victoria Cross, became a prominent campaigner against the exclusion of Maoris from All Black tours of South Africa. He and Saxton stayed friends.

Defeat at the hands of the 1937 Springboks had an earth-shattering impact on New Zealand rugby. Occasional defeats on tour might be forgiven, but for the first time the All Blacks had lost a home series. No longer could they claim to be the rugby world's best, or even first among equals. They now ranked below South Africa, and perhaps even Australia and Wales who had both recently beaten them.

Excuses could have been made. The country was deep in the Depression years. Rugby was secondary to survival. Jobs were scarce. People went hungry. Families were split as their men-folk tramped the country in search of work. Tens of thousands were reduced to living on charity, sleeping rough, scrounging food and tobacco. They scrambled for assignment to government relief camps that were little more than chaingangs, often driven by brutal overseers drunk with power. Many men grew bitter, none more so than war veterans. For men like my grandfather, who had fought at Gallipoli and whose brother had died there, the sight of former comrades reduced to beggary was a heartbreaking betrayal of everything they had fought for. Laughter and frivolity were in short supply. The future seemed bleak. Even communism and religion promised nothing that was not hard-earned.

There was also a more technical excuse for New Zealand rugby's decline. The nation had clung to an outdated scrum formation into the 1930s while the Springboks mastered a more powerful technique that made their scrum entirely superior. But pioneers don't make excuses, they endure and they trust in the future. So New Zealand rugby looked forward. With a tour to South Africa planned for 1940, the chance of redemption was close.

The build up to that tour began in 1938, when the All Blacks headed to Australia with a group of new players. On their previous tour there in 1934 they had lost a two match series. The 1938 tour offered the chance both to avenge that defeat and to establish the foundation for the Big One: away victory over the Springboks on the scheduled 1940 tour.

No-one with a life remembers the 1938 All Black team today. Its radiance is eclipsed by Philip Nel's 1937 South Africans and Adolf Hitler's 1939-45 Germans. But actually the '38 side was something special. In retrospect, they were one of the most influential teams in All Black history, bringing together a group of men who were to shape the future of New Zealand rugby, not least the 1967 tour. Five of the 1938 team— Saxton, Morrison, Jack Sullivan, Jack Griffiths, and Les George — were serving on the fourteen man New Zealand Rugby Football Union (NZRFU) Council when Saxton was appointed manager of the 1967 team. Tom Morrison, as chairman of both the Council and the core seven-man Executive, was then the most powerful man in New Zealand rugby. You didn't get to manage the All Blacks without his approval.

As a player, Morrison had been the Jeff Wilson of the 1930s, a charismatic, try-scoring, goal-kicking wing or fullback. Born in Gisborne in 1913, he debuted for South Canterbury as an eighteen-year-old and was soon the star of the side. Seven tries in the first three games of 1935 gave him national prominence. The 1947 *New Zealand Rugby Almanack*, making him one of its five Players of the Year, recalled he was "a shade unfortunate" to miss selection for the 1935-36 northern hemisphere tour.

Morrison also missed the 1937 provincial and All Black games against South Africa with injury, while the selectors left out 1936 national captain, Wellington's Jack Griffiths. In 1938 however, Griffiths was back and Morrison was an automatic selection. He debuted in Australia, as did

Saxton and Southland forward Les George. Saxton in particular played to the manor born, scoring four tries in seven games, including one in the second test. The team, coached by Otago and 1905 'Invincibles' forward Alex McDonald, returned undefeated. Winning all three tests against the strong Wallaby side suggested New Zealand were well on track to beat the Springboks in 1940, even if South Africa's apartheid laws meant that players like Hawke's Bay Maori prop Everard Jackson would not be eligible for selection.

The selection panel that picked the losing 1937 All Blacks included no less than seven men. For the 1938 side they went to the other extreme. Former Wairarapa and North Island full-back Ted McKenzie became the only sole-selector New Zealand have ever appointed. The well-respected McKenzie kept the job for the 1940 tour. This had an unexpected consequence. McKenzie selected the touring side after trials in 1939, but before he submitted his team to the Rugby Union the tour was cancelled due to the outbreak of war. McKenzie, with the discretion characteristic of the time, never revealed the team he had picked. He did, however, later confirm to Morrison that he'd made the side, and that Saxton was to have captained them. It wasn't to be the last time Saxton missed a tour to South Africa.

While we will never know who else McKenzie selected, we can turn to Winston McCarthy, who proposed the 'Team That Never Was' in his book *Haka! The All Black Story*. In the early 30s McCarthy played for Bush – the province that combined with Wairarapa in 1971 – before finding fame as a radio broadcaster in the early 40s. That was a time when it was radio that brought the All Blacks into New Zealand living rooms, and McCarthy's ability to make any game sound exciting made him a media star. As the voice of New Zealand rugby, he was in close contact with the game's upper echelons. His guess as to the 1940 team is thus as good as any. His team included 1938 All Blacks Morrison, Sullivan, Saxton, and George (Griffiths having retired). He also selected Wellington forward

Ernie Todd, yet another member of the 1967 NZRFU Council. Those young players dreamt of victory on the high veldt in 1940. But only Sullivan ever wore the black jersey against the Springboks, with the then strong-running centre having distinguished himself by scoring both tries in one test of the 1937 series.

For most young Kiwis, the outbreak of war in Europe meant that personal dreams and plans were shelved. Britain, or 'Home' as so many *pakeha* still called it, was at war. As in 1914, that meant that New Zealand was at war. The generation that had grown up in the Depression - men whose fathers bore the memory of the Western desert, Gallipoli and the trenches of the Western Front - now followed their fathers into uniform and conflicts on faraway shores.

Like so many of their generation, most of the 1938 All Blacks enlisted. So too did Ernie Todd, whose hopes of national selection disappeared with the war. Most of them saw action and Griffiths won a Military Cross. Aucklander Ron Burk, no great player but another member of the 1967 NZRFU Council, earned a Distinguished Conduct Medal. The cost was high: when the war ended, three of the 1938 side had been killed.

At least one other member of the team was badly wounded. 1936-38 All Black Everard Jackson's father toured New Zealand with the 1908 Anglo-Welsh side but was sent home when they found he'd played professionally some years before. He later migrated to New Zealand and represented his new country at rugby league. He also married a local girl, a Maori. That meant their son Everard was ineligible to tour South Africa. Everard fought as a Lieutenant in the Maori Battalion but lost a leg to a short round during a training exercise.

The men who administered New Zealand rugby in the mid-60s were therefore products of the Depression, their rugby-playing a release from grim reality. Their early life was tough, favours were hard to come by, and even those whose families were better off were surrounded by destitution. The stature of the national rugby team reflected those depths. In 1934-

37, the All Blacks won just five of their eleven test matches. Those later administrators were men who had hoped to restore New Zealand's rugby to its earlier heights with a victorious tour of South Africa in 1940. Instead, after the promise of the 1938 tour, 1940 brought war and the mutilation and death of their teammates. Inevitably, they were deeply affected by their experiences.

Everard Jackson's son Moana recalled how those men lived with their experiences and how that later shaped the post-war world of their children:

> *For my generation, the Second World War took a long time to end. But in a sense, for our fathers who fought ... it never ended at all. Their experiences shaped the rest of their lives – and those of their children. Like many of my friends, therefore, I grew up to a certain extent with the legacy of war...the names of uncles buried in North Africa whom we would never meet. The faded photographs in family albums... the musty smell of uniforms in an old tin trunk.*

That kind of experience was characteristic of growing up in post-war New Zealand. We could never waste food in our house because our father had seen children starving in Italy. At the time, I failed to appreciate the relevance of that. But I liked the badges and the bayonets and the idea that Alf Voss, a courtly old gentleman about our town, had once attacked a German tank with a pick-axe and had a string of medals for bravery.

Away from the battles, rugby had been a cathartic release for those who could still enjoy it. Tournaments for soldiers were organised in the Middle East, and Tom Morrison, a Captain in the 27th Machine Gun Battalion, played there before returning to New Zealand in 1944. He quickly found form for Wellington, becoming, as the *Almanack* put it, "The idol of the crowd... a real personality, whose exploits will not be forgotten."

Yet Morrison no longer sought the black jersey. In 1946 and again in

1947 he declined the All Black captaincy on the grounds of his age. But he was given a place on the NZRFU Executive, an extraordinary honour for a current player. Morrison was clearly something special. McCarthy wrote of how, "He had so pleasing a personality that I have yet to hear an adverse word in connection with his name. His sense of humour, coupled with his high giggling laugh, made him a much-sort-after companion." Morrison radiated sincerity and a love of rugby. Testament to his character is given by '67 All Black Chris Laidlaw, a trenchant critic of rugby administration in that era. If there were knighthoods for service to the game, he wrote, Morrison was "My first and only choice."

Four years after joining the Executive, Morrison became All Black coach. Now resident in Wellington and managing a menswear business in partnership with 1955 All Black prop Ivan Vodanovich, Morrison could not afford the time off to coach the All Blacks on tour. But he coached them at home in 1950, 1952 and 1955-56. In his final year he was joined on the selection committee by 1938 teammate Jack Sullivan, who succeeded him as All Black coach. Morrison meanwhile moved on up the administrative ladder, becoming Chairman of the NZRU Executive in 1962.

***

Many New Zealanders who joined up in 1939 and formed the earliest battalions sent overseas later returned to guard their country against the threat from Japan. That was how Morrison came to play domestic rugby in 1944. But the 2nd New Zealand Expeditionary force (2NZEF), who served in North Africa and Italy, were still in and around Europe when the war ended. Among them were many top rugby players, not least Charlie Saxton, now Major Saxton of the 19th Armoured Division. He was already a veteran of the Long Range Desert Group, a behind-the-lines commando-type force.

Saxton was in Trieste when the war ended. That was an *interesting* time and place. Everyone wanted it and they were all heavily-armed. Kiwi soldiers, British naval forces, German renegades, Italian fascists, Italian communists, and Yugoslav partisans - royalist or communist- formed alliances that shifted by the hour. The young men drank heavily and waited expectantly for an almighty battle that never came.

There was another New Zealand Major in Trieste then who is part of this story: 22nd Battalion Intelligence Officer Terry McLean. He is better remembered today as the journalist who covered Saxton's '67 tour for the NZ Press Association, describing it in one of his best books: *All Black Magic*. There was another 22nd Battalion soldier there as well, my father, then Sergeant Colin McKay, a journalist whose career seemed a curious mirror of McLean's, but more of that later.

Leading the New Zealand Division in Trieste was General – later Lord – Bernard Freyberg VC, a charismatic Anglophile Kiwi with a taste for rugby and war. A short career in dentistry and playing rugby for Horowhenua in 1912-13 preceded a stellar military career. At Gallipoli he swam ashore alone in the darkness to guide the landings and on the Western front; his leadership in battle, while twice-wounded, won him a Victoria Cross. Decisive and confident in the military manner, he was immensely popular with his troops. He was also well-connected. A confidant of Winston Churchill among others, he was the obvious choice to command New Zealand's forces when war broke out in 1939.

Like so many of his men, Freyberg was a keen sportsman. He ensured his soldiers had opportunities to play rugby and appointed Jack Griffiths as his ADC, promoting him from Private to Major along the way. As early as 1940, he planned a rugby tour on the model of an NZ Army side that played in Britain after the First War. With his Government's approval, Freyberg ordered the side selected even while the war was still going on. A series of trials were held in England and Austria (which otherwise features but little in rugby history). 29 players were then chosen for the 1945-46 team, popularly remembered as the 'Kiwis'. No less than fifteen Kiwis later became All Blacks, although only one had represented them before the war. That was the man appointed captain and who acted as coach: Major Charlie Saxton.

Freyberg decreed one of the tour's main aims was to "Play bright, open football with the winning of the game the least important factor." Freed from the shadows of war, grateful to be alive, the team did play open, attacking, fifteen-man rugby that delighted players and spectators alike. Under Saxton's enlightened captaincy and with their shared experiences of conflict, they were a team united on and off the field. 1967 All Black coach Fred Allen, who made his name on this tour, remembered them being, "As happy a band of brothers as the game has ever known." Saxton's coaching skills were made clear as well, with the forwards' rucking abilities quickly improving under his influence.

The black-jerseyed Kiwis won 29 of their 33 games in Europe. International sides from England, Wales [!], and France were beaten – the latter twice – and only Scotland proved too strong. There was no Irish test, though Leinster held them to a draw. The Irish republic had remained neutral in the war and presumably suspicions of its turbulent politics cost them the fixture.

Later All Black teams in the U.K. were constantly reminded of the popularity of the Kiwi side by those who had watched them. But the Kiwis' impact was not only felt in Britain. Broadcaster McCarthy accompanied the team. He was now a soldier; indeed, he was made a commissioned officer to give him the necessary status to deal with the oh-so-formal BBC officials. His radio commentaries were broadcast back to New Zealand and had a considerable impact there. After all, the Kiwis beat Wales. But they also played fifteen-man rugby and here things get complicated, for that was not necessarily greeted with universal joy and rejoicing in their homeland. McCarthy, clearly a smart man, followed up his broadcasts with a book on the tour. This contained an impassioned foreword by none other than Charlie Saxton, which sheds light on the paradoxical reaction to the Kiwi side in their homeland. To understand it, we need to remember the 1937 Springboks' convincing series win and consider the rather sorry postscript that ended the Kiwi tour.

The team's popularity offered the chance to re-ignite rugby in peacetime New Zealand as it had in the northern hemisphere. So four months after the tour in Europe ended, its players reassembled in New Zealand to play five matches against provincial sides. It was clearly a poisoned chalice, and Saxton recognised that their reputation could suffer. Players who had been overseas for years were enjoying the experience – and the hospitality – of family and friends. Saxton for example, had met his five-year old son for the first time when he returned to New Zealand. Fitness levels had inevitably dropped. The result was that, as McCarthy lamented, "the 'Kiwi' team in New Zealand were not within 20 points of the overseas 'Kiwis'".

The team was resurrected against Auckland in a match refereed by the appropriately named Mr Lazarus, who presided over a 20-all draw. Wairarapa-Bush, Canterbury, and Otago were then defeated. Otago, now coached by Young Vic Cavanagh, certainly recognised weaknesses in the Kiwi forwards they could have exploited. But with the Kiwis lead by his old friend Saxton, Otago entered into the spirit of open rugby and were outplayed. At that point the Kiwis had racked up nineteen tries in four games including eight against Canterbury. 5-8 Fred Allen was in brilliant form, having contributed four tries and two dropped goals, so the tour was going as well as could be expected. But in the final match Wellington took a very different approach to the sporting intent of Otago.

Wellington were coached by '38 All Black coach McDonald. Coach of Otago before the Cavanaghs, he had recently moved to Wellington. Something else moved to Wellington around this time too: the indefinable sense of centrality. Travel was slow in those days and the country needed a centre. New Zealand's pioneering days were gone and the Depression had enhanced the power of central Government, for only the highest authorities could deal with such problems. The outbreak of war in 1939 hastened the process by which the capital city became the place where the decisions were made and the job vacancies multiplied. Otago's aura faded. Ambitious men moved to Wellington.

Macdonald had no intention of emulating Cavanagh's generosity of spirit. He had a point to make. His Wellington side, with big men like Ernie Todd up front, hit the Kiwis hard from the kick-off. As Saxton admitted, "We did not have the fitness nor the keenness to fight back." Saxton himself was a prime target, he took, McCarthy reported, "A terrible thrashing… Everything hit him but the goalposts … How he stayed on the field after it, I don't know" [but he did.] Wellington won the match 18-11. The wounded Saxton never played again.

This was an enormously significant game, one that shaped New Zealand rugby's future over the next two decades. The aura of the Kiwis' style of play was tarnished by the Wellington defeat. The '37 Springboks' victory had lead many of New Zealand rugby's most influential thinkers to conclude that fifteen-man rugby – the style the All Blacks had played for most of their history – would never beat South Africa. For New Zealand to win, they concluded, it needed a pack of similar if not larger size than the massive Springbok eight, with mobility sacrificed for bulk. They must also eliminate the mistakes that open backline play could produce. Only with ten-man rugby – eight forwards and half-backs driving them forward with accurate kicking – could New Zealand win the toughest tests. Wellington's victory was considered proof of that.

The Kiwis' style was the antithesis of ten-man rugby and so, as Terry McLean recorded, "The Kiwis had no sooner completed a most successful tour than a campaign of depreciation of their methods was waged against them." Saxton's foreword to McCarthy's book was his public response to that critique. While acknowledging the Kiwis made mistakes in the New Zealand post-script, he argued passionately that only with the attacking style of his Kiwi side could New Zealand rugby again reach the top.

Perhaps we can see the division as a reflection of the experience of war. Some men returned with a proper appreciation of the place of amateur sport in society. It was an escape, a joyous expression of physical energy, a hard contest between strong men, but ultimately it was a game, played for enjoyment. Other men, however, had had the humour drained out of them. "The tough experiences of his own upbringing, followed by the Depression and then the Second World War, " as McLean's biographer put it, "meant that there was no frivolous side to his personality." While McLean openly championed the Kiwis style, many others found no place in their thinking for anything but victory through strength, whatever the cost.

This debate over style, which was really an argument over which style would defeat South Africa, dominated New Zealand rugby for three decades and was only resolved by the 1967 All Blacks. Central to the debate was Young Vic Cavanagh's post-war Otago side. While successful before the war, Otago were even more so after it. There was never doubt that Cavanagh deserved much of the credit. To his supporters Cavanagh was the master, the greatest coach New Zealand never had.

With the war over, New Zealand rugby was again looking to the ultimate challenge. On the horizon was a South African tour in 1949, replacing the cancelled 1940 tour. While there was a new generation of players – no pre-war All Blacks wore the jersey in the post-war years – victory over South Africa remained the New Zealand obsession. But how victory was to be achieved was the question, and it looked like Cavanagh had the answers. In 1946-48, his Otago side reigned supreme en route to a then record nineteen Ranfurly Shield defences.

In retrospect it seems obvious that Cavanagh should have coached the 1949 All Black tour. They headed to South Africa with no less than eleven of his Otago players. But Cavanagh was a tough disciplinarian with strong views, a 'my-way-or-the-highway' type of guy. He was not universally popular. McLean noted national rugby administrators were among those who "actively disliked" him.

So they made McDonald All Black coach again. He'd first coached them as long ago as 1921 when they drew a home series against the Springboks. Perhaps most importantly in many eyes, he'd coached the Wellington side that beat the Kiwis. He certainly had a vast knowledge of the game and was liked and respected by his players. But McDonald was 66 when he set off for South Africa. That made him an old man in those days and his best years were behind him.

The 1949 tour was a sporting disaster, the tour from hell. The All Blacks won just fourteen of their 24 games and lost all four tests. Half-fit after a long sea voyage and generous Afrikaner hospitality, fatigued by frequent overnight train journeys and penalised for everything short of breathing by home town referees, they never got going. Despite taking as big a forward pack as possible, the Springbok eight were still superior and, as ever crucially, they kicked their goals and the All Blacks did not.

The humiliation of suffering a series whitewash made 1949 worse than 1937. Adding to the gloom was that New Zealand played two tests against Australia while the tour was going on. A virtual third XV – though bolstered by the availability of Maori players excluded from the South African tour – lost both tests to the Wallabies. Four more Otago players were included in that side, but still Cavanagh was overlooked. Instead aging Hawke's Bay rugby legend Norman McKenzie coached the side from the sideline, wearing his suit.

Though his tactical innovations live on, Cavanagh never did coach the All Blacks. There are still old timers who consider that the worst decision since Jesus selected Judas in his squad. They weren't alone in admiring the crusty southerner. When the soon-to-be triumphant 1971 British and Irish Lions side arrived in Dunedin, their celebrated coach Carwyn James called on Cavanagh. Ironically James was similarly neglected by his rugby establishment and never coached Wales.

Whatever the political machinations behind the selections of the 1949 coaches, the belief that the 'powers that be' would never appoint Cavanagh All Black coach seemed confirmed in 1950 when he was dropped from the South Island selection committee. Cavanagh retired to his newspaper business, abdicating his coaching position to his assistant. That assistant was Charlie Saxton, who coached Otago for the next seven years. But the demands of Saxton's business career and perhaps his ideas for fifteen-man rugby ruled out a national coaching position. Yet his talents weren't ignored; in 1956 he joined the NZRFU Council.

Physically Saxton was a small, dapper man, standing just 5ft 5 (1.65) and his playing weight was only 10st 7lbs (67kgs). Like Morrison he made his living in menswear. But he had a 44 inch chest and an air of brisk efficiency. The French didn't call him *Le petit Napoleon* for nothing. McCarthy described him as "One of nature's gentlemen", and he spoke plainly but tactfully. He was clearly blessed with the qualities of a man others would naturally follow. He also carried the teaching lineage from the Cavanaghs and from Jimmy Duncan and thus the earliest era of New Zealand rugby – the years even *before* the 1905 'Originals'.

Cavanagh passed into legend, his testament a series of articles in Dunedin's *Evening Star*. Like Saxton's earlier epistle in McCarthy's book, these were part of the debate about how to beat the Springboks. Cavanagh deplored the idea that the Kiwis approach was "an insidious threat to our national game." He argued for attack as the best form of defence, although his sides were more cautious than the Kiwis. Indeed there were those with the belief – not mentioned in Otago by those who valued their personal welfare – that Cavanagh's teams were robotic units devoid of flair. But Otago backs claimed 72 of the 84 tries his team scored in their record Shield defences.

Rugby is a simple game, though easily complicated. Essentially the aim is that fourteen men create the opportunity for the fifteenth to score. Anything else is decoration, if not ostentation. Cavanagh developed an attacking style that had the great virtue of simplicity and there is much of the modern game in the style he developed, much that has remained the basic New Zealand rugby approach ever since. The *Rugby Almanack* certainly saw Cavanagh's reign as a worthy one: in 1948 it concluded that:

> *There does not appear to be very much wrong with New Zealand rugby... we have at last gone back to the sound principles of the game... Due credit for the awakening must go, firstly, to the recent "Kiwis" side, who showed what could be done if Rugby was played as it was originally intended it should, and secondly, to Otago... Otago's success proved the method right... Yes, we must say "Thank You" to Otago for "showing us how".*

But again, all was not necessarily as it seemed. From its inception in 1935, *The New Zealand Rugby Almanack* was the accepted historical record of the first-class season, the *Wisden* of New Zealand rugby. Every game, every player, every official was faithfully recorded in the appropriate form. It was a statistician's heaven. But it also included an editorial, and nominated not only five Players of the Year and five Promising Players of the Year, but a New Zealand team. To be included as one of the five in either capacity was an acknowledged honour that was almost official. Yet the editorials could be waspish, and the team nominated and the brief comments on the abilities of the candidates could implicitly criticise the All Black selectors. Such matters verged on the subversive. Of course, like an artist or a film director in a one-party state, there were ways of getting around that accusation. Here it was insured against by emphasising that the *Almanack* team was judged looking back over the season rather than during it. Further insurance came from the editor's occasional tendency to leftfield, if not downright eccentric choices.

But the editors' post-war contemporaries had – in their eyes – good reason to detect a subversive tone to the *Almanack*. One of its editors was Arthur Carman, a lay preacher and conscientious objector in World

War Two who had been imprisoned for his beliefs. Morrison liked him, but most ex-servicemen despised such men, and plenty would have had them shot. I met him when he was a kindly old man among his treasure piles of books. He quietly let slip that as the Lions had won the series, three of their players – rather than the usual touring side's allocation of two – would be honoured as Players of the Year. As a boy, this subversion of the natural order seemed to me a secret of considerable importance, indeed something revolutionary. That was certainly how many read his opinions.

*** 

In the wake of the humiliating '49 tour, the proponents of attacking rugby were overwhelmed by the believers in ten-man rugby. There could be no further dispute about the style of play New Zealand adopted. Everything had to be sacrificed to the goal of beating the Springboks when they toured New Zealand in 1956. Uniting the country behind this crusade was not difficult. Men were accustomed to discipline by the years of war and the experience of military order. Those too young to have fought had not yet begun to challenge that culture. There was national service to be carried out and young men now had their own war in Korea. So rugby moved onto a military footing in preparation for the 1956 campaign, building up its reserves, training its men in different conditions, inspiring and unifying them with the fervour of the cause. It was all basic Management 101. Potential participants in the series prepared with unprecedented dedication to the cause.

True, the memory of the Kiwi team and its playing style cast a warm glow in the consciousness of New Zealand rugby for a generation, like the memory of a first love. But it did not set a precedent. The court of public opinion in that military-soaked society ruled that the Kiwis' style of rugby might have worked in that time and place, but it would never beat the

Springbok ogre, and that was what really mattered. New Zealand had never beaten them in a series. Correcting that clearly unnatural, if not entirely obscene, anomaly became an obsession. Like all obsessions, it blinded its holders to the wider world.

The Holy Grail was finally reached in 1956 by a – for its time – massive pack, backed up by the equally massive Don Clarke, a fullback whose goal-kicking was at the heart of New Zealand rugby's triumphs for the next decade. They won the series 3 – 1. New Zealand breathed again.

In one sense Clarke's goal-kicking obscured a certain truth: that the results of the 1949, 1956 and later the 1960 series against the Springboks largely depended on goal-kicking. They could easily have been reversed. Perhaps winning against and particularly in South Africa wasn't really about playing style at all. Perhaps it just came down to finding a better goal-kicker than they had – and getting neutral referees, although that was barely even on the horizon at that time.

Ten-man rugby now ruled the nation's sporting fields. Victory over the 1959 British Lions, with their brilliant backs, seemed to prove the supremacy of a forward-orientated approach. It was no accident that two of the three leading try-scorers in tests for New Zealand in the 1957-66 decade were the forwards Colin Meads and Kelvin Tremain. New Zealand rugby was winning rugby; dour, dull, but successful.

Of course there were always exceptions. Coach Ted Griffin and the Maori influence ensured that North Auckland played a more open game than most, and most teams would open up play if victory was ensured. But against the '59 Lions even the NZ Maoris played the ten-man game. So just as Kiwis today regard British rugby as obsessed with forward struggles to the point of tedium, so too was the New Zealand style then regarded by the outside world – except perhaps for the South Africans, whose appreciation of a scrum is as characteristic as their *brae* and their *biltong*.

Jack Sullivan coached the 1960 All Blacks' tour of South Africa. Victory eluded them but a close defeat –2-1 with one game drawn –seemed a fair effort and Whineray's men moved monolithically through the 60s. The Whineray years ended in victory over the Springboks in the home series in 1965. New Zealand was content. It looked forward with some confidence to the next tour of South Africa, scheduled for 1967. 1964-66 coach Neil McPhail, once of Saxton's Kiwi's, stood down. His reign was burnished by victory, but despite admiring Saxton's coaching principles, McPhail's teams never really broke out of the ten-man style. McPhail and Whineray handed on, however, not just a successful (if one-dimensional) team, they also left their successors to deal with international rugby's equivalent of a ticking bomb: South Africa's *apartheid* policy.

There was something special about the rivalry with South Africa, beyond even that with the great northern rival, Wales. The cancelled 1940 tour had elevated it to realms beyond the purely rational. Instead of meeting on the field, Kiwis and South Africans had met in the desert battlefields. They found in their endless arguments about rugby that they shared many things beyond the field. That meeting is crucial to understanding how a generation of New Zealanders, shaped by their war service, supported the continuance of ties with apartheid South Africa regardless of its inherent evil. To them it had nothing to do with Maori and Pakeha, it was about the shared experiences of New Zealanders and South Africans. There were deep and abiding friendships formed in that arena, and respect was mutual. That mutual admiration spread throughout the rugby game in both countries. And of course South African rugby was proudly undefeated at home, indeed not until 1974 did the Springboks lose a full four match series in South Africa. The result, as Sir Brian Lochore put it, was that, "Only the high-level rugby player can really understand the attraction of a tour of South Africa. Only he can appreciate the deep-seated urge to try and conquer there for the first time."

Planning for the 1967 tour began as soon as the '65 series was won.

A whole cavalcade of talent was being put together on and off the field. But outside the enclosed walls of New Zealand rugby the world was changing. Most Kiwis held to the position that sport and politics should not be mixed, that New Zealand should not concern itself with the internal politics of a country that it met on the sporting field. That was a respectable position, even a logical one. New Zealand businessmen dealt freely with countries where human rights were non-existent, and Kiwi Olympians inevitably competed against sportspersons from such lands. The outside world was a pretty nasty place when you got down to it. Even Australia's treatment of its indigenous people was shocking enough to Kiwis who ventured into the outback to witness it. Being black in the Deep South was not exactly a dream ticket in history, either.

But a logical position is not necessarily politically sustainable in the face of emotion. Aside from the fact that 'No politics in sport' was as realistic a slogan as 'No swearing in the bar', the emotional appeal of a grand gesture like banning sporting contact with the apartheid regime was unstoppable even before Nelson Mandela decorated a single T-shirt.

There were certainly Maori who were angry as well as sad about their people's exclusion from teams to tour South Africa. But New Zealand rugby accepted that nations had the right to make their own laws and that South Africa's apartheid policies meant Maori players could not tour there. Opposition to this appeasement policy grew steadily. By 1960,the 'No Maoris No Tour' camp had nationwide profile. Parliament was presented with a petition against the tour that had been signed by an extraordinary 200,000 people.There were demonstrations at the trial matches and a few placard-carrying protestors at the airport when the team left. It was all very civilised.

The arrival of the Springboks in 1965 attracted bigger protests, although for the majority of New Zealanders the demonstrators remained a strange and eccentric phenomena. While they included a good few churchmen and Maoris, whose opinions, while wrong, might at least be respected, they also included leftist and even communist unionists and students, the latter increasingly distinguished by a frightening new dress code. Their motives seemed more questionable. To some New Zealanders they were simply an alien and hostile threat to all that was good and decent about the Land of the Long White Cloud.

No-one articulated that position better than Auckland's Tom Pearce. If they made a TV mini-series about the period, Pearce would be the show's cardboard cut-out villain. Combative, outspoken, quick-tempered yet amusing, the populist Pearce had come close to All Black selection, warming the bench as reserve prop in all three tests against the 1937 Springboks. Moving into administration, he managed the 1960 All Blacks in South Africa and was NZRFU President in 1965, when the Springboks toured New Zealand. There were those in the Rugby Union who remembered that Pearce had been in a reserved occupation, one that prevented him being conscripted, and thus he had avoided 'doing his bit' in the war, but he had a hard core of admirers.

To Pearce the protestors were "long-haired bastards". "If we can let in drug-addicted pop singers we can certainly let in clean living white Springboks," he announced. The emphasis was on the *white*. In a statement that would not have looked out of place in Hitler's *Mein Kampf* he declaimed that, "Where the white man has been, he has brought law and the establishment of his regime for the benefit of mankind. If these go, we are lost." That position was mainstream a century before, and many an English gentleman still held that view in the 1930s, but by the mid-60s Pearce's views were starting to embarrass everyone to the left of Genghis Khan.

Brighter minds on the New Zealand and South African rugby unions officially maintained the 'No politics in sport' position while recognising the need for change. That South Africa should allow Maoris in visiting All Black sides was the obvious compromise solution. But even before the 1965 South African team departed New Zealand, their hard-line Prime

Minister, Dr Verwoerd, ruled out that solution.

In February 1966, the NZRFU declined South Africa's invitation to send an all-*pakeha* side to South Africa in 1967. France, whose team was then entirely of European blood, agreed to tour South Africa instead of the All Blacks. In March, at a meeting of the International Rugby Board in Edinburgh, New Zealand asked the Home Unions to arrange a northern hemisphere tour to replace the cancelled South African tour. In August, Chairman Morrison announced the itinerary for the 1967 northern hemisphere tour. New Zealand players now had a new goal, at least in the short term.

Northern hemisphere tours had their own special magic. Until now they had been once-in-a-generation events. Only long-serving forward Ian Clarke, brother of the mighty Don, had enjoyed a long enough career to make two such tours. Now most of Whineray's '63-'64 side were still available. Players who had missed that tour had a second chance to enjoy the famed atmosphere at Twickenham, at Murrayfield, and most particularly at Cardiff Arms Park. New Zealand sides there were assured a contest as hard as any in a swirling atmosphere of song and passion unmatched at any other ground. It was a place of hard-earned wins and legendary defeats.

The South African tour was only postponed until 1970 in the hope that by then social and political developments would allow Maoris to tour. The northern hemisphere tour thus offered the incentive that a successful tour on the resume would stand a player – or a coach – in good stead when it came to selecting the 1970 team. The postponement also meant that New Zealand's rugby leadership could explore a different style of play, for experience had shown that it was one thing to beat the Springboks at home, quite a different matter entirely to beat them in South Africa. Questions of tactics were more properly the domain of tour manager and coach, but it would be naive to think that the 'old hands' on the Rugby Union were not concerned with such things. Indeed their choice of manager could indicate the style they favoured, whether 'steady as she goes' or 'hard a port'.

In that amateur age, the appointment of the All Black manager for a major overseas tour was akin to the selection of a Pope, although smoke emerging from the chambers was tobacco-grey rather than heavenly white. But the process was entirely about nepotism; an insider was chosen from among insiders. It was a job-for-the-boys. During the process, all the administrators' political skills – arm-twisting, horse-trading, nods and winks – could be deployed elegantly or otherwise. Provincial bias and age-old vendettas were rarely far from the surface. While long-serving committee men from minor unions might be appointed for tours to Australia, the plum jobs of managing the All Blacks on tours to South Africa or the northern hemisphere were reserved for men from the major unions with a powerful presence in the national chambers.

The manager's position was crucial. Laidlaw described how "his attitude can inspire either enormous effort or generate an unconscious disinterest in the players." Frank Kilby, 1934 All Black captain and manager of Whineray's 1963-64 tour, remained on the Union's Executive Committee, the real circle of power. At the centre of that circle was Chairman Tom Morrison. With him on the seven-man committee were 1938 teammates Sullivan and Griffiths; his theoretical 1940 teammate Ernie Todd; 'All Black who never was', another former Wellington forward in '45-46 Kiwi Maurice Ingpen; and administrative kingpin Cec Blazey.

These men also served on the wider Council, which again Morrison chaired. Its fourteen members included the likeliest candidates for a manager's job. The 1967 Council included Duncan Ross, later a popular manager on the 1968 Australian tour, Ron Burk, a less than successful manager of the 1970 South Africa tour, as well as Todd, who would manage the 1972-73 U.K. tour. Bill Craddock, the Buller representative, had had his tour already – to Australia in 1958.

The Council also included Maori representative Ralph Love, Otago's

Saxon, and fellow '38 All Black Les George. Nominally above them were the President, C.G. Gibbons, and the Patron of the Union, the Governor-General Brigadier Sir Bernard Fergusson, but those posts were primarily ceremonial.

The administrators certainly didn't all get on; Sullivan once punched Ingpen and he and men like Burk and Todd were strong and serious-minded characters, little given to compromise or raucous laughter. Yet collectively these men represented a vast well of rugby – and military – experience and they brought together three strands of New Zealand rugby history. The first was the Otago tradition. We have seen the centrality of Otago men to the development of a New Zealand rugby style: Duncan and the two 5-8ths system, the Cavanagh's rucking game, and the stylistic experiments of Alex Macdonald with his brilliant 1938, aggressive 1946, and wretched 1949 sides. Yet each ground-shifting Southern innovation was associated with a touch of Shakespearean tragedy. None of the innovators are remembered as a great All Black coach; indeed the reputation of each is touched with failure.

The second strand of history was the 1938 All Black team, now at the centre of Rugby Union power. These were the men whose dreams of victory in South Africa in 1940 had been replaced by the nightmare of war. They were combat soldiers, indeed mostly officers, who had what the British so delightfully call 'a good war'. They had returned to administer rugby, to continued involvement in the game they loved. In the intervening years, the search for victory over the Springboks meant that they oversaw a conservative style of play, believing the end justified the means. But still there had been no victory in South Africa. Perhaps they were beginning to question their legacy. Or perhaps they were just beginning to think that they had to find another way to beat those damn Boks, and found themselves listening to the voices in the wilderness.

Those sirens were calling up the memory of the third strand of New Zealand rugby, the legendary Kiwi side that focused on all-out attack. If there was to be a change of direction, a recognition that ten-man rugby wouldn't succeed in South Africa and that a new style of play was needed to overcome them, then the Kiwis' style was the official opposition. It had to take over.

A major change of approach by any power can be signalled, and inspired, by a dramatic gesture in endowing new leadership upon a commander equipped by personality and belief to suit the hour – a Churchill replacing a Chamberlain. To change, the All Blacks required such a leader. And there was one man, a natural leader, straight, sincere, still young and vigorous, respected and liked by all. The man to whom Duncan, Macdonald and the Cavanaghs had passed the baton of the Otago tradition. A man who had debuted on the '38 tour with his friend Tom Morrison and later enjoyed a 'good war'. A man who now sat on the Council alongside seven or more men he had played rugby with. The apostle of fifteen-man rugby who had led the Kiwi team and coached it in the principles of attacking play that he preached in his official NZRFU coaching manual. A man who had – with the help of good friends like McCarthy and McLean in the media – consistently promoted the idea of fifteen-man rugby.

That man was Charlie Saxton, and he was appointed manager of the 1967 All Blacks.

***

—

# THE DRILL SERGEANT AND THE GENTLEMAN OFFICER

Fred Allen's early years were even tougher than those endured by Charlie Saxton, for sometimes having your father around is worse than losing him. Born on the wrong side of the tracks in Oamaru in 1920, Allen was one of six children to a violent alcoholic father. When the old man finally quit the family home, Fred had to leave school to support his kin. He found work in a Christchurch department store, but he never made it to high school and his prospects didn't look too bright. Like Saxton, however, Allen had two tickets out of a life of privation. He was prepared to work hard and he was blessed with a talent that would be his salvation. He was a brilliant rugby player.

Turning out for the Linwood club, he displayed all the skills of the top-class inside back, not least the side-step off either foot. He turned out to have another innate skill: that of leadership. Picked for Canterbury at nineteen, he was captain of the province within a year. But by then New Zealand was at war and his leadership abilities were needed elsewhere. Allen saw serious action in the Pacific as an infantry lieutenant, including fighting behind the lines in the Solomon Islands. Later he fought with the infantry in Italy before a shoulder wound ended his war. Allen recovered just in time to be flown from Rome to London to play in the trials for the 1945-46 Kiwi rugby team.

Allen made that team and was one of its stars. He played in 28 of the 38 games including the internationals and captained the side several times. More importantly for the future, Allen met his half-back partner and the team's captain-coach, Charlie Saxton. The senior officer won Allen's complete respect as a leader and as a man. The 'Position, Possession, and Pace' creed of attacking rugby Saxton espoused became Allen's own. Not only was it successful, it produced the most enjoyable of games for players and spectators alike. Saxton's way, Allen decided with the fervour of a convert, would be the style of rugby he would henceforth champion.

Later in 1946, with neither Morrison nor Saxon available to captain the first post-war All Black side, former *Lieutenant* Allen was chosen to lead the team against Australia – despite the presence in it of Kiwi teammate, *Major* Jack Finlay MC. Now playing for Auckland where he was expanding a belt-making business into a womens' fashion house, Allen was then chosen as one of the *Almanack*'s Players of the Year. The following season he captained the All Blacks again on a successful tour of Australia. Allen had reached the top of the tree.

The qualities that had taken him there were heavily influenced by his military years. He demanded the highest standards of those under him, nothing but the best was good enough. The need for things like punctuality and good grooming were as much a given as the need for sustained hard work. Discipline, both self-discipline and team discipline, was central to his thinking. As a person, Allen was committed, dynamic, and imbued with the charisma of those accustomed to the spotlight. As Wallace Reyburn put it in 1967:

*If it were necessary to invent the complete extrovert Freddie Allen would be the ideal prototype... he abounds in breezy camaraderie. He is outspoken, blunt, unequivocal. He says anything that flashes into his mind in front of anyone... Short and stocky, he is very dark... He laughs frequently. He has a ready wit.*

Not everyone was quite so enamoured of Frederick Allen though, and in 1949 his bubble burst. Allen captained the team which lost the series 4-0 in South Africa. Hampered by an injury he picked up in the first game, he never found his best form and stood down from the test side for the two final tests. But with Macdonald ailing he had to take on much of the coaching. Like most New Zealanders, Allen had favoured Cavanagh as coach, indeed he had recommended him when asked. Now Allen had to fill the master's role and unsurprisingly he failed.

Allen's playing career effectively ended in South Africa. Defeat in South Africa was an ignominious end to his top-class career and as captain he had to take more than his share of the mud thrown at his losing team by its critics. Allen was devastated by his demotion from hero to zero, finding solace in his growing business career. But his restless energy and love of the game soon found an outlet when he was invited to coach his Auckland club side, Grammar Old Boys.

In 1957, Allen was a surprising choice as sole selector-coach of the Auckland provincial side and initially he found it tough going. By the end of the 1959 season, the knives were being sharpened when an unexpected chance to challenge for the Ranfurly Shield brought success. After a brief hiccup against North Auckland, his side regained the Shield soon after and held it for a record 25 defences down to 1963. Allen was back on top.

By 1964, when he joined the then five-man New Zealand selection panel, Allen the coach was already becoming a legend. He was the strictest of disciplinarians. Greymouth in the 50s wasn't exactly Paris, but you could get a drink there anytime you wanted, even, as I discovered long ago, if you were a sixteen-year-old on a motor scooter. When some of Allen's visiting Auckland side partied on there later than he'd allowed, he had the team on the training ground at 6.30am on a wet, freezing morning after, and he ran them into the ground. After that the players thought twice about breaking his boundaries.

Allen was a psychologist too. He'd read out telegrams supposedly received from the public, complaining that "Meads is too old" or "So-and-so's not tough enough", using them to motivate players. Sensing his team a touch complacent before a Ranfurly Shield defence against Canterbury, he hid the Shield. When his players asked where it was, he told them that Canterbury were confident of winning it. So they wanted a photo of themselves with the 'Log of Wood' in order to get it in the Christchurch papers before the deadline for Sunday publication. Allen had therefore dutifully lent it to Canterbury so the southern team could be photographed with it – or so he claimed. His outraged team duly hammered the apparently presumptuous challengers, only to realise Fred had conned them again.

There were other stories. They were calling him Fred 'the Needle' and it wasn't a reference to the growing success of his clothing business. He didn't do warm and fuzzy on the training ground. He did Drill Sergeant. One man giving orders, the rest obeying as one. Famously Allen was also proving a master of the art of challenging a player to respond through relentless, provocative, brutal verbal denigration of their ability. The better the player, the more Allen tore into them, relentlessly seeking to needle them into new heights of performance to answer his challenge. Perhaps he was harder on the forwards too. At a certain point in his team talks he addressed each player in turn, starting with the fullback who, as '67 custodian Fergie McCormick recalled, tended to get off fairly lightly. But by the time he reached the forwards he was fired up and ruthlessly harsh.

One thing many – though not all – his old players agree on is that Allen's methods wouldn't have worked today. The modern professional would simply get up and walk out of such a verbal assault, with or without adding a very basic but probably anatomically impossible suggestion as to what the coach might go and do. Allen's methods worked because New Zealanders in the 60s were brought up on such assaults. Words of praise were pretty spare on the ground for young men then. The most they hoped for was a nod of acceptance – and that meant a lot. You were supposed to respond to criticism by improving. But even in those days it didn't always work like that and Allen knew that approach wasn't for everyone. Denigrating a player's ability was "potentially demoralising" and he did vary his approach according to the individual – sometimes. He'd tear into Waka Nathan, but gee up Nathan's more sensitive friend Mac Herewini with a few unstinting words of praise. Kember was another who tended to get off fairly lightly. Yet few players missed out on a tongue lashing at one time or other and some never forgave him.

Allen's training sessions were seriously tough, not overly long, but physically and mentally intense. As he told *Sunday Times* writer and former Welsh fullback Vivian Jenkins in 1967, the sessions were intended to bring the players to the point of exhaustion. For some they were too hard, too frequent, too tiring, but they gave the team the fitness that won games in the last ten minutes. Saxton fully supported this approach. Reviewing the '67 tour for the *New Zealand Weekly News* Christmas edition Saxton observed that:

> *The constant movement in Freddie Allen's training sessions… was exactly the sort of thing we aimed at when he and I were together in the Kiwi Army team… It was also exactly the sort of thing I was taught in pre-war days by the great All Black, Jimmy Duncan, and by the two almost equally famous Victor Cavanaghs, father and son, in their days as coaches in Otago.*

Critics pointed out that Allen's training was repetitive, with a few basic moves repeated time and again at increasing pace. But that was the point and it was common to many great sporting coaches. Liverpool football great Bill Shankley similarly favoured endless repetition of simple moves in training. Practice makes perfect or, as the old Greek coach Aristotle put it, "We are what we repeatedly do. Excellence is not an act, but a habit." Allen knew that great rugby wasn't about complicated moves. It wasn't rocket science. Doing the simple things better than your opponent was winning rugby, and mastering those simplicities was the basis of his approach.

Allen moved smoothly on the path from Auckland to All Black coach and it didn't take long for him to win the respect of established national players. In the foreword to Allen's 2011 biography, Colin Meads reflected that his old coach was "The most dynamic and inspiring individual I have known in 60 year's involvement in sport." He recalled Allen's motivational skills, his "loyalty and integrity", and singled out Allen's "remarkable ability to bond men from all walks of life into one closely knit unit." There was another quality of Allen's he stressed as well:

*He is, without a doubt, the strongest disciplinarian ever to coach the All Blacks. The black jersey was, for him, a privilege for which you were expected to meet certain standards – to train hard, to give of your best, to respect your opposition, and to uphold the traditions of the game both on and off the field.*

In his book *Fred Allen on Rugby*, Allen described the art of successful coaching as "A question of personality, communication and dedication." Perhaps Chris Laidlaw got closer to the truth. In his book *Somebody Stole My Game*, he described coaching as "...a mix of technical know-how, astute man management and plain good luck." Luck is a much underrated virtue. Some people seem born lucky. Indeed, Tibetans consider it an innate aspect of a person, like good looks or intelligence. Napoleon, asked what sort of Generals he wanted, shrewdly replied, "Lucky ones." Victory requires luck.

Allen had his share of good luck in life. In Italy he bent down just as an artillery shell passed over and killed the man above him, and his Auckland team got an unscheduled crack at the Shield when his job was on the line. He also had his share of bad luck, mostly connected to South Africa. But he was particularly fortunate to rise to the top of the coaching ladder just as changes in the laws of rugby made an attacking style of rugby more feasible. His Auckland teams had played attacking rugby, but on a restricted licence. Law changes in 1964 gave the backline more room to manoeuvre. Once Allen took charge of the All Blacks in 1966, he began to take advantage of those changes; not wholly, but in good measure. Initially the change was almost unnoticed, with Neil McPhail's last test as coach and Allen's first both ending in comprehensive victories, 20-3.

By 1967, Allen knew he had the best forward pack in the world and a backline of considerable quality. Now he wanted to take the team forward, lift it to a new level, deploy a style of attacking rugby that would, he believed, ultimately beat the Springboks on the *veldt*. Yet it was the actually the selection of his friend and guru Charlie Saxton as team manager that made the transformation possible, for it ensured his support at national level. To a great extent Saxton got the manager's job because a majority of Council members recognised the need to move away from ten-man rugby and Saxon represented fifteen-man attacking rugby, 1945-46 Kiwi-style. And Saxton had one other great thing going for him, he could control Fred Allen.

Allen certainly meant well. He kept himself fit despite being a chain-smoker, gave freely of his time, and was happy to help children get his players' autographs, knowing they were the players and supporters of the future. He actively sought self-improvement. But for all his virtues, Allen had his faults. He didn't always achieve the standards he set himself. He saw things in black and white, spoke his mind and was no great diplomat. His style was often confrontational. On occasion he drank more than was wise for a man in his position. Late in the evening after Meads was sent off at Murrayfield, he had to be dragged off a British journalist who had suggested Meads should have been sent off years ago.

In one sense that is a tribute to Allen's loyalty to his players, but in another it was clearly a position he should never have got himself into. There were certainly powerful men on the NZRFU who disliked him – Frank Kilby and Jack Sullivan were among those who never joined his fan club. But it was known that Allen still jumped at Saxton's command. Some of those who chose him must have considered that having the fiery Allen as coach required the calming influence of Saxton as team manager.

Allen became a legendary All Black coach. His 1966-68 teams were unbeaten in 37 games, the best record of any national coach before or since. 1967 was to be his absolute peak, the touring side his masterpiece. Then within a year he was gone, lost in the political arena where his skillset was poor. And just as the 1949 side would have beaten the Boks if they'd had Cavanagh as coach – or so the legend goes – the 1970 All Blacks would have been victorious if Allen had still been coaching them. No doubt both teams would have done better if the acknowledged masters had coached them.

Yet while the great majority of the surviving members of the '67 side continue to revere Allen, or at least to acknowledge him as the outstanding coach of their experience, there were reservations. One player, as we will see, despised him. Several others suggested that perhaps the '67 team was such a strong one that the identity of the coach didn't matter greatly. Invariably they mentioned Wellington's Bill Freeman as another coach who would have done as well (and they weren't all former Wellington players!) Yet Freeman's personality and coaching style were very different to Allen's. He was not shaped by the military and had more of the modern consensual style. He even let wives join their husbands for rugby dinners, a revolutionary step in the times.

There were plenty of good coaches in New Zealand. Ted Griffin, for example, coached North Auckland for an extraordinary 21 years. There were good years and bad for Ted, as you'd expect with a provincial side, but in the grudge matches against Auckland, the ones that really counted, his record was won 21, drew five, lost sixteen. He was a legend.

To me as a ball-boy at Okara park, it seemed as if Griffin had always been there. He seemed old, grizzled, with broad, hunched shoulders. At first I assumed that coaching North Auckland was a job you had for life, like being a teacher or a farmer, that sometime in the dim dark ages he had filled in an application form, got the job, and been there ever since. I would hang around the fringe of his panting players listening to his half-time team talks. No-one ever said not to, so knowing that adults had enormous lists of things you weren't allowed to do and never hesitated to announce them, I assumed that was a privilege that went with the job. But I never quite got the hang of his team talks. It was only later that I realised Griffin was simply honest. He said what was happening, what needed to happen to win, and...that was about it. He said what needed to be said and nothing else. It was an impressive economy.

But the fact is that Allen's name is inextricably tied to that of the '67 side and a great deal of credit for its success belongs to him. He was the centre of attention on tour, constantly sought out by a media that he played with considerable public relations skill. Allen was the crusading apostle of a new rugby world. If there was ego there was also a genuine desire to promote attacking rugby. His contribution to the tour was immense, not least because although he was a very different type of person and type of leader to the manager and the captain, his dedication to the team, like theirs, was total. For the few short months the tour lasted, that leadership triumvirate worked together as smoothly as the parts of an old Rolls-Royce, united in mutual respect.

***

If the 1967 tour was to be a happy and successful one – and the two usually go together – manager, coach, and captain needed to combine together harmoniously and form a management unit able to shape the character and progress of the tour. Saxton and Allen were perfectly cast for the first two roles. But a rugby team has a captain. The captain leads, on and off the field. The coach might pick the team and choose that captain, but at high noon, when the crowds roared and the whistle blew, it was the captain who ruled.

The position of All Black captain is revered. It is the highest accolade a player can receive, the only honour the game offers beyond the celestial reward of joining the elite club. Opinion polls usually indicate that something like 98.6 per cent of New Zealanders would rather be All Black captain than Prime Minister and most of the rest are assumed to have ticked the wrong box.

But even in the ranks of All Black captains, there are subtle distinctions in status. There are All Black captains and there are Great All Black captains. Those who are remembered as Great captains are inevitably winning captains. That is not totally unfair. Great leadership can win matches. The 1967 team had a Great All Black captain.

Allen inherited a winning side in 1966, but he needed a new leader following Whineray's retirement. Whineray cast a giant shadow. He'd been All Black captain for the best part of a decade and men of a certain age speak of *the Whineray years* just as Americans speak of *the Eisenhower years*. Before Whineray, the All Black captaincy had been a short-term appointment. The longest reigns had been those of Cliff Porter, who led them in seven tests long before the war and Fred Allen's six tests in 1946-49. Then came Whineray. After two debut tests in 1957 he became All Black captain aged just 23, and led the team in each of his next 30 tests. His were giant shoes to fill.

Most commentators favoured Kel Tremain or Colin Meads to succeed Whineray. Others pointed to the Wellington prop Ken Gray. Some – mostly those hoping for a little more excitement from the backline – favoured Otago halfback Chris Laidlaw, who'd captained New Zealand Colts on their 1964 Australian tour. They all captained their provinces. So too did Southland's Jack Hazlett, Whineray's replacement in the front row. He was also the South Island captain, which had to count for something. But there was another candidate too, Brian Lochore, the No.8 forward who was captain of Wairarapa.

Lochore was a farmer, a bony slab of country youth who made his provincial debut in 1959 aged just 18 and played against the visiting Lions that year. His then captain was the remarkable A.W. 'Kiwi' Blake, the last member of the Saxton's Kiwis still playing top rugby. Blake had captained the New Zealand Maoris – although he wasn't actually a Maori – and that disqualified him from selection for the 1949 tour. He made the All Blacks for the first test against the 1949 Wallabies, then had to withdraw from the second test after the tragic death of his child. Blake carried on, captaining Wairarapa to a legendary Shield capture in 1950. McCarthy wrote that he "played for Wairarapa for 20 years without ever playing a bad game." The former Kiwi became one of Lochore's early mentors. He was generous with his knowledge too; '67 lock Sam Strahan, as a newcomer to the Manawatu side, remembers getting tips from Blake after a game against Wairarapa.

The young Lochore was initially a lock-cum-flanker. He made his way in the game, with a little help from an anonymous fan when he made it to the national trials. To the young player's embarrassment, the fan kept yelling "C'mon Lochore." That alerted scribes like Morrie MacKenzie who "liked what we saw and wrote accordingly." A reserve at home against England in 1963, Lochore made Whineray's tour, where he played No.8 for the first time against Oxford University. Something clicked, as it may when a man finds his true calling, and with injury to Nathan creating a vacancy, Lochore made his test debut against England. He held his place for the Scottish test, but for the French test Nathan returned and Lochore was left out again. There was still something missing– confidence perhaps.

For all that Whineray was an acclaimed leader, there had been something of a division in his last touring side between the coterie of veterans around him and the younger players on the fringe. As Laidlaw later wrote, Whineray was, "Perhaps ... too much of a man's man and not enough of a boy's man." All Black rugby was a hard school. As with soldiers, newcomers were not necessarily welcomed. But those on the fringe felt there was a little more than necessary gap between those who were proven and those who were not. Lochore was not yet proven.

Over the previous decade, New Zealand had selected a variety of players at No.8 including Colin and Stan Meads, Tremain, and Canterbury's John Graham, who had captained the All Blacks in the 1964 home series against Australia when Whineray was unavailable. But for the first test against the Springboks in 1965, Graham was on the reserve bench with Lochore in at No.8. He held his place and after a definitive performance in the decisive fourth test his position in the side was entirely unquestioned. He had proved himself at the highest level.

But there was something more than playing ability about Lochore. There was a certain aura, a sense that there were hidden strengths to his character. He was country scrubbed and country honest, a clear-thinking straightforward man of intelligence, humour, and warmth, tinged by Scottish reserve. He had grown up in a good pioneering family, working long and hard on the land and he was secure in himself. There was no sign of a troubled soul in his demeanour, so there was no brashness or overconfidence; indeed there was an early shyness. He drank, of course, but he was never going to be drunk and disorderly; there was a touch of the gentleman and the authority in quiet speech of a man with that special quality, *mana*. Whineray himself quietly suggested Lochore as his ideal successor.

As chairman of selectors, Allen was the man who got to choose the new All Black captain, a choice traditionally rubber-stamped by the Rugby Union. Obviously the new man had to be certain of his place and to have a rapport with Allen. But there were other qualities the coach was looking for. Allen later wrote that he wanted:

> *...a man who is patient, observant, and a good student of men. A certain amount of abstraction is desirable. He must be able to hang off a little from his team, putting the slightest of gaps between them and him... Primarily, a captain must be aware.*

When Allen went through the candidates, he found that:

> *I could not go past Lochore. It was that integrity...the quiet dignity of the man... [his] strength of character, the quality of quiet leadership to which other men respond. There is in it the capacity to provide discipline by example and demand it as of right while still commanding total respect. There was resilience about Brian, the sort which creates the positive out of the negative. Brian would have been a leader of men in any field.*

So it was that Allen picked Lochore to lead his 1966 All Black side, a call that ranked with his best. Perhaps the greatest tribute to Lochore's promotion was that the senior men quickly offered their support, including those who might have wanted the captaincy. No-one could object to being passed over for this man. As soon as the choice was made, it seemed obvious. Lochore was entirely free of baggage and there was a straightforwardness and dignity about him that appealed to the wider rugby community. The All Blacks had a leader who represented the ideal of them all.

Lochore had never sought the leadership of the team, but he became arguably – and the arguments are of course eternal – New Zealand's greatest captain. And while there are different types of leadership it is worth reflecting on the qualities Lochore brought to the role. Many of them were innate, for leadership can only be taught to a certain degree. Not only did Lochore lead by example on and off the field, but his nature was such that the height of his own personal standards provided a model to emulate rather than a law to follow. Men chose to follow him, to do as he did in recognition of those innate qualities.

Allen considered that a captain's first duty was "to get to know his players". Lochore entirely agrees, stressing the need for a captain to be close to the individuals in the team, to be approachable and available to them. And – because he knew what it was like to feel "alone" on an All Black tour –he knew to seek them out and to "put your glass next to theirs." Lochore listened when they spoke of their problems in life and within the team, for there were always those disappointed by their non-selection. He answered sincerely and honestly. The many accounts of Lochore and the nature of his leadership invariably come down to that one outstanding characteristic: his straightforward honesty.

Meeting the man who is now Sir Brian Lochore for the first time felt like calling on cousins last seen a few decades past. The snow-capped mountains in the background, recent rain glistening on the verdant green pasture, the warmth of the country kitchen and Lady Pam's welcome, the man himself arriving from out on the farm. It was all part of some memory of childhood visits to neighbours and friends. There was coffee and fresh baked biscuits and then there was Lochore who, slightly to my surprise, turned out to be exactly as everyone had said he was. And he began by asking me who I was and what I was doing. That impressed me because I had known other great leaders, like the Dalai Lama, do just that when he met a fresh face. You have to be interested in people to do it.

In 1992, Stephen Ambrose wrote a book, *Band of Brothers* – later made into a TV series – about a wartime American parachute company. They dropped into Normandy on D-Day, fought on the road to Arnhem, held out at the Battle of the Bulge, and wound up capturing Hitler's mountain retreat in Bavaria. Through all manner of danger and hardships they were held together by good leadership, particularly that of an athletic but rather ascetic young officer named Richard Winters. Much of the character attributed to Winters seemed to match what I'd read of Lochore's, so never having lead anything more taxing than a tour group I used Winters' ideas about leadership as a basis for discussion.

Lochore immediately endorsed Winters' first point that a leader needed to treat people individually. "You can't treat them the same [or] you'll never be a leader," he stressed. His 1967 team contained an extraordinarily diverse range of personalities. There were certain sub-groups— some individuals who were close and some who were not—but overall they were 30 very different people. It was Lochore's ability to relate to each individual with integrity that enabled him to lead so many different types of personalities in the same direction. They understood that he was trying to bring out the best in them in order to best serve the team.

While the manager sets the tone for a tour and the coach sets the tactics, the captain, according to Allen, "Furnishes team pride." Lochore feels the importance of pride is often overlooked. A good team, one like the '67 side, had that pride in themselves; it showed in the way they trained. As he explained this I was tossing the word *pride* around in my head, for that quality has its downside. But Lochore used it in a sense that was entirely positive, pointing out that respect for each other helped at the crunch time of the game. Yes, pride as mutual respect. I liked that.

Lochore also emphasised the need for simplicity in command, communicating so that players knew clearly what was wanted and expected of them, both in the day-to-day matters and the wider tour. That included giving players responsibilities, without which there could be no accountability. He also acknowledged a quality he found within himself, that he was at his most decisive under pressure. As we shall see, that quality emerged most clearly in the final games of the '67 tour.

Ultimately Lochore concluded that leadership is a combination of two elements. Firstly, ensuring that "Everyone must know where the line in the sand is," and secondly, having a "psychological understanding of the individual." We had brought Winters' various points down to two baselines. But actually there was a third element. Winters wrote that a leader should constantly reflect on his own performance. That wasn't something Lochore did. "Honesty is paramount," he said after a pause. We'd come back to the word everyone uses about this Wairarapa farmer, the secret of his leadership.

***

—

# MANY ARE CALLED BUT FEW ARE CHOSEN

Choosing an All Black team is a process before it becomes an event. The national side is at the top of a pyramid, or more precisely a sand hill, each grain of which is constantly shifting; rising, falling, or being blown away. Players compete at club level for provincial selection and then greater recognition if they reach representative level. In the 1960s, good performances for their province in Shield games or against touring international sides were particularly important in bringing them to the attention of public, press, and selectors. Then came opportunities at national level with teams such as the Juniors and the Maori, University, North or South Island sides. Finally there were the All Black trials, the penultimate step on the ladder.

All Black selectors were appointed by the NZRFU Council, which in 1965 settled on three selectors as the ideal number, one of whom was the All Black coach. That position was never entrusted to anyone for very long. After all, there is never a shortage of candidates for a Kiwi's ideal job. The coach was convenor of the selection committee and took ultimate responsibility, at least in the public's eyes, for the chosen team. The other two committee members were effectively there to assist him in monitoring players' form, although one of them was usually his likely successor. That ensured a certain tension that at best guaranteed the future was kept in mind.

The selector's job was much sought after and selection ability could not really be measured. So becoming a national selector required some combination of proven coaching ability, wide experience of rugby and its players, and the personal and political skills necessary to be chosen by the Council, which retained the right of approval over the nominated teams.

In 1967, Allen's fellow-selectors were Wellington's Ivan Vodanovich and Southland's Les George. The trio seemed a well-balanced combination. There was regional balance with George, a South Island selector, and Vodanovich, a North Island selector, and there was a balance of positional expertise, for Allen had been a back while his two compatriots had been forwards. There was generational balance too, with George an All Black in the 30s, Allen in the 40s and Vodanovich in the 50s.

***

Ten players who were to tour in 1967 played in the convincing series victory over the 1965 Springboks. That victory meant that the first team selection after Allen succeeded McPhail as coach and chairman of selectors was understandably steady-as-she-goes. Allen used just sixteen players for the series against the 1966 Lions. Only two had not worn the black jersey before, neither was a surprise choice. The retired Whineray was replaced by Southland prop Hazlett, and Canterbury's Tony Steel, a former national sprint champion, debuted on the wing. They joined a side in which the veterans were Colin Meads, an All Black since 1957, and the great loose forward Tremain, there since 1959. Maori flanker Nathan joined early in 1962 and his school friend and Otahuhu club-mate Herewini came in at 1$^{st}$ 5-8 later that season.

Others made their test debut on Whineray's 1963-64 tour. Wellington prop Ken Gray and Auckland winger Malcolm Dick both established themselves in the test team on that tour. Lochore twice filled in for Nathan and halfback Laidlaw came into the side for the final test against France. Hooker Bruce McLeod then debuted against Australia in 1964 and by 1966 these players had all established themselves, though Dick was often injured.

There was one other test debutant in 1966: Ian MacRae, another brilliant pick by Allen. MacRae made his name at centre, scoring three tries as Hawke's Bay defeated England on their brief 1963 tour. He toured under Whineray later that year without playing a test but at 2$^{nd}$ 5-8 MacRae found his destiny. In addition to his vision and passing skills, he proved unsurpassed in the old Cavanagh-inspired role of ball-carrier, driving forward to set up the ruck.

Strangely, despite the Cavanagh model, no post-war player had managed to establish himself as All Black 2$^{nd}$ 5-8. In the 26 tests played between 1960 and 1965, they used eleven different players in that position. But by the end of the 1966 series, it was obvious that the hard-running MacRae fitted the team like a wetsuit. He was there to stay. So too it seemed were the other newcomers: Hazlett and Steel.

There were also four reserves in the squad, but they had no chance of an easy cap for a few minutes running around at the end of a game. In those days before injury replacements were allowed, being an All Black reserve was a thankless task. They trained with the chosen fifteen and got to wear the black jersey in the official team photograph. But unless there was a last-minute injury, the most they could do was create a good impression by their performance on the training field and their personality in the dressing room. The forwards who warmed the bench in 1966 were a prop, Peter Scott, who never made the final step up, and Taranaki hooker John Major, who had toured with Whineray's team but been supplanted in the pecking order by Counties rake McLeod. The back reserves were Canterbury half-back Lyn Davis and Gerald Kember, a young Wellington utility player who had the all-round skills Allen admired.

The 1966 side had then a good blend of youth and experience with a number of players at their peak. They looked likely to form the core of the 1967 team. Of course, there were always surprises. Stan Meads, who joined his brother in the team in 1961, called it a day at the age of just 28, and there was no obvious replacement for him in the second row. Then 1965-66 centre Ron Rangi fell foul of the Rugby Union and was banned for the season.

With the hapless Lions side losing all four tests to the All Blacks and a number of provincial games besides, New Zealand rugby seemed in good shape as it counted down to 1967, the 75th Jubilee of the New Zealand Rugby Football Union. The All Blacks were arguably the best team in the world and the transformation process was proceeding smoothly. Wellington's Mick Williment had inherited Don Clarke's position as a goal-kicking fullback, Lochore had succeeded Whineray as a winning captain, and one old hand from the Kiwis had given way to another as coach.

As Fred Allen contemplated his tasks for 1967, discussed them no doubt with Saxton and others, he faced two problems. One was the seemingly intractable South African issue. Allen had timed his run to All Black coach on the assumption that if he succeeded McPhail in 1966 he would take the side to South Africa in 1967. His desire to avenge 1949 burned deep. But no sooner had he become coach than the prospect of that tour vanished and its replacement by a northern hemisphere tour finalised. Allen's thoughts must then have gone back beyond 1949, to the '45-'46 Kiwis, his most enjoyable rugby days. A rerun of that tour would reboot rugby, reinvigorate and reorientate it into what it could be at its best. It also offered the perfect opportunity to develop a side whose attacking skills could beat the Springboks when next they met. If that was not until 1970, well, a three year term as coach was not set in stone.

Perhaps his own term, like Jack Sullivan's, could be prolonged until a South African tour.

The second problem was less simple. New Zealand rugby, the game Allen loved, indeed had devoted much of his life to, was static. The All Black forwards were awesome, perhaps the best pack they have ever fielded. They moved like a steel blanket across the field, dominating, even obliterating opposing packs. But such technical triumphs could never excite the soul of anyone but a technician. A man who had played the sublime fifteen-man rugby of the Kiwi side two decades earlier knew there were heights the All Blacks had not even begun to approach.

There was something else too. Allen's focus on rugby was total, but perhaps he sensed it, perhaps he feared it, for he had a young son who would in time fall under the spell of drugs. There was a new generation of Kiwis growing up who might not automatically love the New Zealand game.

That was a threat that attacking rugby could help Allen overcome. The dominant mindset of the New Zealand game still held that beating the Springboks required the most dour and physical of struggles, attrition by forward play; fifteen-man rugby was only for the festival games, the Barbarians versus the Harlequins, that was the gospel. But the threat to the national game posed by boring rugby was about to be resolved. Like most revolutions, this one was led by palace insiders.

\*\*\*

The choice of 30 players for the 1967 touring side was by no means straightforward. At the start of the season, thirteen players seemed certainties, and one of those was to miss out in the end. That certainties list comprised skipper Brian Lochore; Hazlett, McLeod, Grey, Colin Meads, Tremain, and Nathan from the 1966 forwards; and Laidlaw, Herewini, MacRae, Steel, Dick and Williment from the backline.

In retrospect, the 1967 season functioned as one long trial for the end-of-season tour. The successful candidates followed a variety of converging paths into the side. The first step was obviously to make the All Black team that would play the only home test that year, a one-off game against Australia on the 19th of August. That was to be the focus of the NZRFU 75th Jubilee celebrations. Selection for that team was complicated by injuries to Gray and Laidlaw, and McLeod's suspension after being ordered off in a club match. So with Stan Meads retired and Ron Rangi in disgrace, at least five new players were needed.

The Inter-Island game was then a major event, indeed the highlight of the season if no tests were scheduled. In 1967 it effectively served as a trial for the Jubilee Test. The North Island won 17-6, with North Auckland half-back Sid Going the player of the match while Major and young lock Sam Strahan stood out among the winning forwards. Injury-prone North Island winger Bill Birtwistle also drew accolades, side-stepping rival full-back Fergie McCormick on the way to one of his two tries.

So convincing was the Northerners' victory that losing skipper Hazlett was the only South Island player chosen for the Jubilee test. Steel, however, came in on the wing when the recalled Birtwistle dropped out injured after being selected.

Provincial form was important. Hawke's Bay held the Shield and along with Tremain and MacRae fielded several strong candidates for national selection. With a new centre needed, Bill Davis, who had toured with Whineray's side as a young winger and starred in the Bay's early Shield defences that year, got the nod. Davis was the kind of centre whose wingers scored tries and his performance in the Jubilee test made him a certainty for the tour.

To replace Stan Meads at lock, there were a number of older players in the running. But the selectors saw the need and the opportunity for younger blood in the forward pack. Manawatu's 22 year-old Strahan only made his provincial debut in 1965, but he impressed for Manawatu-Horowhenua and the New Zealand Juniors against the Lions the following year. The *Dominion* reported "unusual interest" in his performance in the inter-island match. Decoded, that meant the word was out that he had the inside running. Strahan got the nod for the Jubilee Test, virtually assuring that he would be one of the three locks accompanying Colin Meads on tour. They gave him the news as he trudged off the field after a losing game for his Fielding club, instantly elevating his mood. A letter of congratulations from the local council soon followed. Smaller unions didn't get too many men into the All Blacks.

Replacing the suspended McLeod at hooker, John Major finally won a cap after sitting on the bench fifteen times. His provincial teammate Brian 'Jazz' Muller joined him in the front row in place of Gray. At sixteen and a half stone (104kgs), Muller was the heaviest man in the team and like Strahan, his selection all but guaranteed he would make the touring team. The other vacancy in the side was at half-back, but Major's long-time companion on the reserve bench, Lyn Davis, was left there. The chosen half-back was another new cap, Sid Going.

Around that time, Choysa tea were proudly advertising that while Kiwis had drunk 23 and a half gallons of beer per head in the previous year, their intake of Choysa had been 24 gallons. But Sid Going hadn't drunk either, for he was Mormon and both a different type of person and a different type of player to Laidlaw, the man he replaced.

Going had been pretty much the typical Kiwi country boy growing up with his brothers at Maromaku, miles north of Whangarei among the dairy farms and the pukekos in the ditches and the old battle against the gorse. Strong faith of one sort or other has always gone with that land and that the Going family were Mormons made them only a little different from their neighbours.

After a brief debut as a replacement for North Auckland in 1962, Going volunteered to serve his church as a missionary. That brought what he later told biographer Bob Howitt were, "The two most memorable years I've had" in Alberta, Canada. When he returned home early in 1965, he didn't even know there was a Springbok tour that year. Within months he was starring for North Auckland as they hammered Auckland 32-12 at Eden Park and representing both his province and NZ Maori against the Springboks. The following year he played for the North Island, scored a try for the Maoris against the Lions, and while Lyn Davis was the All Blacks' reserve half-back, Going was the coming man.

Early in 1967, sports editor Gary Frew wrote an article in the *Northern Advocate*, championing Going for the All Blacks. Frew was a New Zealand table tennis champion, to whom I lost 21-0 at a time I was playing regularly and fancied I could take a few points off him. He was a decent young man and knew a good thing when he saw it. New Zealand didn't have a regular rugby magazine then; *Rugby News* only began in 1970. There was only *Sports Digest*, edited by the outspoken Brian O'Brian. As the title suggested, every sport was represented there. O'Brian was a fan of wrestling and that and other obscure sports had almost equal status with rugby. But O'Brian knew his audience – Colin Meads regularly figured on the cover because he always boosted sales. In the August 1967 *Digest*, Frew again blew Going's trumpet, this time for the nation to hear. Going, he proclaimed, was a "Bundle of barbed wire, rubber and cast iron, he runs like a slippery eel making for the river. He can explode without warning, like one of those 'jumping-jack' firecrackers."

Having a journalist on-side is a useful adjunct for an up-and-coming player. In Brian Turner's biography of him, Colin Meads remembers having been publicised early in his career by local journalist and former teammate Cedric Grey. But Frew, and no doubt Grey, were simply foreseeing the inevitable. Going made the All Black team, his debut coinciding with his 24th birthday. The next day he came down to earth. He and brother Ken, who had played in a Maori trial that been the curtain-raiser to the test, drove the 550 miles home to the family farm.

Their old car could never threaten the speed limit.

On the reserve bench for the Jubilee Test were four others who were clearly strong candidates for the end-of-season tour. Alongside perennial reserve Lyn Davis was Otago 1$^{st}$ 5-8 Earl Kirton, who toured with Whineray in '63-'64 without playing a test. He'd been a reserve for the defeated South Island side, and 1962-64 All Black Bruce Watt had played well for the southerners, so his selection was something of a surprise. Joining the halves were two young uncapped forwards, Wellington loosie Graham Williams and Marlborough's Alan Sutherland, who could play in the back or second rows. Neither had any experience in the frontrow but props didn't get injured in those days. Presumably the selectors felt that if Hazlett, Major or Muller overslept, there were plenty of former All Black front-rowers in the crowd to call on.

\*\*\*

## THE JUBILEE TEST

In 1942, the 50$^{th}$ anniversary of the founding of the NZ Rugby Football Union understandably passed almost unnoticed. But due celebration was planned for the 75$^{th}$ anniversary. 380 living All Blacks, along with life members, former national administrators and referees, as well as various notables, were invited to the celebrations. They came from as far away as Afghanistan, as well as more predictable places such as Britain, Australia, and South Africa. Conference hotels hadn't been invented, so the Union booked ten hotels and allocated them to various sub-groups. The All Blacks got to stay in the Grand Hotel, the visiting Australians in the St George, Maoris mostly found themselves in the Midland, referees were in the De-Brett, and so on. There was no sponsorship, no commemorative medallions, souvenir booklets, special jerseys, or even firework displays. This was 1967 and rugby union was an amateur game.

There was no sign of that changing, although New Zealand society was dealing with one massive financial change. On the 10th of July the country had dropped the British monetary system and adopted American-style decimal currency. Instead of a pound made up of 20 shillings each made up of twelve pence, there was now a dollar made up of 100 cents, with the old pounds worth $2. It confused a lot of old folks, but humans are pretty quick to reboot their thinking when it comes to what's in their pocket. For the All Blacks who would tour that year, it meant their daily allowance would be a dollar a day, instead of ten shillings (adjusted for inflation, that equates to around $17 a day in today's money).

There was a Parliamentary reception for the final total of 527 Jubilee guests; with 1905 legend Billy Wallace the unquestioned star of the show. The old and not-so-old timers had plenty to talk about. Being assembled in Wellington, they might have pondered the report that week by an American think-tank, which suggested exploding atomic bombs underground could release the stress that caused earthquakes.

More likely they discussed the Ron Rangi case. The Maori centre had recently been banned for the season. "Rangi in Tears" the headlines blazed. No reason had been given for the ban although it was rumoured to be in connection with a purloined bottle of whiskey. The following day, the Union regretted that the ban had produced "too much unhealthy speculation by the public", who were presumably only supposed to speculate in a healthy manner. NZRFU life member Tom Pearce had gone into bat for his Auckland man while the rumours swirled. Was it about his liberating a bottle of whiskey or was it, as one All Black told me, that Fred Allen had needled Rangi once too often and been dropped by a punch? The matter was resolved a week later after an acrimonious meeting. Pearce was not allowed to speak but Rangi's ban was lifted and he was selected for a North Island trial. Ironically, he was injured anyway and probably never seriously considered for the tour, particularly if the Allen story is true! The popular Aucklander never played for his country again and died an alcoholic.

The Jubilee Test was one of three official functions on August 19th, when Wellington turned on one of its justly celebrated fine and sunny days. The proceedings began with a wreath-laying ceremony at the Cenotaph in the morning. That seemed appropriate even without the power of the ex-soldiers at the helm of New Zealand rugby. Eighteen All Blacks had died in the two World Wars. Then after the schoolboys' curtain-raiser (which featured future All Blacks Karam, Hunter, Joseph, Green and Laurie Knight), the former All Blacks paraded around Athletic Park in front of the 50,000 crowd. At their helm were the three surviving veterans of the 1905 side: 89 year old Wallace, 88 year old George Nicholson, and 85 year old 'Bunny' Abbott. Their teammate and All Black coach Alex McDonald didn't quite make it; he had died in May.

There were some other All Blacks who missed the day as well. Since the advent of professional rugby league, some two dozen All Blacks had taken the money. In that amateur age this was the ultimate crime. They had, as Laidlaw put it, "committed social suicide." At the height of its power, the Rugby Union saw no need to forgive and forget. Those who had not taken advantage of a wartime amnesty were not invited to the Jubilee celebrations, although at least one quietly turned up and was warmly welcomed by his old teammates. The Union's critics duly expressed outrage at the league men's exclusion. They conjured up visions of heart-broken old men sobbing over their faded black jerseys, bitterly regretting their earlier prostitution, the choice they made only in desperation to feed their starving brood. But actually the big names like Bob Scott and George Nepia had all been forgiven their youthful folly and wry head-shaking was probably the strongest reaction among the handful of leaguers who missed out.

This game was the first 'one off' test match played in New Zealand since 1904. Tickets were for sale in Tom Morrison's menswear shop in Featherstone street. At the time, that seemed perfectly normal. The game was the first for which Saxton was at the managerial helm, although the position was something of a sinecure at home. Still, it did serve as a training run for tour management. 1970 tour manager Ron Burke, for example, had been manager for the 1966 home series.

After lunch that day the All Blacks left their hotel and wound around the hills in their hired coach. Young Strahan felt travel-sick. Allen as always was nervous, chain-smoking. The last game between the two Tasman rivals had unexpectedly ended in a comprehensive victory to Australia. Defeat in the Jubilee test was unthinkable! Strahan remembers Allen in the dressing room announcing, "No-one leaves the field unless it's on a stretcher". Now he knew– this was serious!

The Jubilee test kicked off at 3:15 in the afternoon after the teams had been introduced to the Governor-General. The All Blacks led 9-3 at half-time but they were in danger of spoiling the party. O'Brian wrote of their "Incredibly inept lineout work, mishandling, inaccurate kicking and bankruptcy of ideas." But with one injured Wallaby a passenger for much of the game and an attacking approach by the All Blacks that at the time seemed simply an appropriate celebratory style, matters greatly improved in the second half. The All Blacks ran in four tries and won 29-9.

O'Brian's report on the game mentioned that fullback Williment was not at his best. He reserved highest praise for 1st 5-8 Herewini, who had established himself in the side in 1965-66. Herewini, he wrote, "Was the man firmly at the controls...and one cannot recall an incorrect decision on his part [or] the boot being applied when an alternative course was open to him..." Herewini it turned out was following Allen's strict instructions to run the ball whenever possible.

The day ended with the grand Jubilee dinner at the not-so-romantically named Overseas Passenger Terminal in Wellington, apparently the only place with sufficient seating for the hundreds of attendees. The old stories were told long into the night, but overall the Jubilee celebrations were restrained. Elsewhere in the pages of that *Sports Digest*, O'Brian had deplored "kissing and hugging" by soccer players. "As if a good old-fashioned handshake or pat on the back wouldn't convey teammates' pleasure just as effectively – and in a manner considerably more masculine," he pronounced, no doubt to universal approval among rugby fans casually perusing the magazine. Even in its hour of celebration, New Zealand rugby would keep its emotions in check.

\*\*\*

The team for the '67 tour was taking shape. In addition to the players considered certainties at the start of the year, Major, Muller, Strahan, Going, Bill Davis and probably Birtwistle were now on the shortlist. But the rest of the places were still up for grabs.

An unusual number of trials were held to fill those final slots. They began in late August with two Under-23 games. In the early game, a young 1st 5-8 called T.L. Mehrtens, the son of a 1920s All Black, captained and scored two tries for the losing side. It didn't get him selected but two generations later his son Andrew made that position in the All Blacks his own. In the second game, Gerald Kember's team defeated a side led by his Wellington teammate Graham Williams. North Auckland's Denis Panther scored two tries and a young Aucklander named Grahame Thorne scored another. Kember's team included an unknown Canterbury loose forward, Ian Kirkpatrick.

There are always young guys who come through at a gallop, unknown one year, in the team the next. They don't always work out, but those that do have a certain aura. Kirkpatrick was one of them. He grew up in Poverty Bay and as a boy survived an attack of polio. Educated at King's College in Auckland, he returned to play for the Bay against the 1966 Lions but was now representing Canterbury during his military service. After his performance in this trial he was picked for New Zealand Juniors in a match against Taranaki, and having proved himself against their rugged forwards, he was fast-tracked into the final trials. 'Kirkie' was going places.

So too was Grahame Thorne. A star player for Auckland Grammar and now a law student, Thorne skipped rugby in 1965 and 1966, preferring to focus on cricket, where he was good enough to smash a double century for New Zealand universities against their New South Wales equivalents. But his early career had been noticed by Fred Allen. In 1967, after making his first-class rugby debut for the North Island University side, and playing one other game for N.Z. Universities against Auckland, Allen sent him straight into the Under-23 trials. From there he made the Under-23 team and then the North Island and final national trials. After six games for six different teams and a series of spectacular tries, Thorne had made himself a virtual certainty for the tour even before he played for his province

The two young men had played against each other as schoolboys and were very different personalities. Kirkpatrick was calm, mature, almost gentlemanly in his manner. Famously he had a resting pulse rate of just 48, the preserve of nature's fittest specimens. Thorne was precocious, restless, physically ill with nerves before a game and if not unconventional certainly extraordinarily self-confident for a young Kiwi. He publically celebrated his trial tries as "tickets to Britain" and spoke of his cricketing future as a double international. Rugby's old-hands frowned and reserved their judgement. Could the kid really deliver?

The next round of trials in early September were between South Island 'Possibles' and 'Probables' and their North Island counterparts. The human interest story turned out to be a Marlborough winger, Phil Clarke, who had not even been nominated by his provincial union. Clarke was an Air Force pilot who had played a few games for Canterbury but was best known as the brother of Adrian Clarke, a popular All Black in 1958-60. Coming into the side as a last-minute injury replacement, Clarke played himself into the next trials, the final hurdle after which the All Black team was announced. True, he was only in the early trial, which was usually the kiss of death for anyone's selection hopes, but at least he was there. As recent All Black reserves Gerald Kember and Alan Sutherland were probably a lot less pleased than he was to be in the early trial.

The final trial teams were effectively the 30 players the selectors considered most likely to make the All Black team. Everyone knew that only an outstanding performance in the early trial could make a difference. Realistically, the early game was most valuable to a young player wanting to put down a marker for the following season. But players in the final trial couldn't afford to relax. One player from the early trial might perform mighty deeds and earn selection, and then there was the matter of players unavailable for the final trial because of injury but who would be fit for selection.

Nonetheless, there were players picked for the final trial who were now in pole position for tour selection. The rugged Canterbury prop Alister Hopkinson was one of them and his teammate Wayne Cottrell, a promising inside back, was another. Graham Williams was there too, along with another speedy loose forward in Taranaki's Murray Wills. There were two new locks in Taranaki's Alan Smith and Arthur Jennings from the Bay of Plenty. Jennings got the publicity. He was to be the first Fijian All Black. (1960 All Black Steve Nesbit had Tongan ancestry, but Jennings was the first Pacifica to wear the black jersey.) Having played for Bay of Plenty since 1961, his experience along with his cheerful character made him a good bet to contribute well on a long tour. At the time his Pacifica background seemed just an exotic anomaly, not the beginning of a new trend.

Injuries were the wildcard. Ken Gray was a world class tighthead prop forward: smart, strong, experienced and an outstanding technician, one of the all-time greats. He was an automatic choice for the tour if he was fit. Gray, however, had injured a knee cartilage earlier in the season. What is now a routine keyhole surgery operation that sidelines a player for a few weeks was then an injury that could end a player's season, or even career.

Still, Gray had had an excellent surgeon, Dr Humphrey Gowland, and was optimistic he would recover in time for the tour. He was, however, unfit for the trial.

Legend has it that the day before the final trials, Gray just happened to run into Fred Allen, who promptly put him through a series of exercises to test the strength of Gray's repaired knee. A few squats, hops, and knee bends later, Gray was given the nod with the stipulation that he proved his match-fitness by playing in Wellington's game against Canterbury shortly before the team left. But the workout was in Morrison's menswear shop. Even in small town New Zealand it's hard to believe that Gray really just happened to wander in to peruse the racks of trousers when Allen just happened to be there as well.

There were other injured players who missed the trial. Auckland and North Island fullback Dave Laurie, tipped to tour as backup to Williment, was unfit. So too was Bill Davis, who dropped out at the last minute, whereupon the selectors moved Kember up from the early trial to fill his place. But if Davis was a certainty, the reserve full-back role was more open. Sid Going's brother Ken played well in the early trial, but his goal-kicking was not international standard. Canterbury's McCormick had played one test in 1965 when Williment was injured. But he'd missed most of his goal-kicks that day and although he was in the final trial most observers thought the selectors would choose a utility player to back up Williment. They had done that on the last two major tours and all but one tour of the northern hemisphere.

There were question marks over the back-up 1st 5-8 as well. Herewini was the man in possession, and Cottrell and Kember could play there. In the *Dominion*, the usually well-informed Veysey was tipping Wellington pivot John Dougan, while Bruce Watt was the South Island incumbent. Then there was *Almanack's* left-field tip. They had chosen King Country's Ian Ingham at 1st 5-8 in both their 1966 and 1967 editions, which had to count for something. Ingham, remembered by Colin Meads as being

**NEW ZEALAND RUGBY TOURING TEAM 1967**

Back Row—P. H. Clarke, W. D. Cottrell, W. M. Birtwistle, G. F. Kember, W. J. Nathan, G. C. Williams, M. C. Wills, B. E. McLeod, A. G. Steel.

Second Row—E. J. Hazlett, K. R. Tremain, I. A. Kirkpatrick, K. F. Gray, C. E. Meads, S. C. Strahan, A. E. Smith, A. E. Hopkinson, A. G. Jennings, B. L. Muller.

Sitting—W. L. Davis, M. J. Dick, S. M. Going, I. R. MacRae, C. K. Saxton, B. J. Lochore, F. R. Allen, G. S. Thorne, E. W. Kirton, J. Major, W. F. McCormick.
                                  (Vice Capt.)     (Manager)    (Captain)    (Asst. Manager)

In Front—C. R. Laidlaw, M. A. Herewini.

(Frank Thompson, Crown Studio, Cuba St., Photo Copyright)

Smiling giants: the official team photo of the 1967 All Black team. Copyright Crown Studios Ltd: Negatives and prints. Ref: 1/1-030662-F. Alexander Turnbull Library, Wellington, New Zealand. Courtesy NZRFU.

Sporting champions: former world-heavyweight Jack Dempsey at his New York restaurant with (from left) Murray Wills, Ian Kirkpatrick (obscured), Charlie Saxton, Brian Lochore and Fred Allen. Courtesy New Zealand Rugby Museum

Jubilee celebration: All Black captain Brian Lochore congratulated by NZ Governor-General Brigadier Sir Bernard Fergusson after the 29-9 victory over Australia in the NZRFU Jubilee test. Courtesy New Zealand Rugby Museum.

The ultimate test: McCormick on attack against France, with Lochore (centre) in support.

Northern hemisphere tours mean late nights.
Courtesy Alexander Turnbull Library & Lodge family:

"I'D SAY THEY ALL STAYED UP LISTENING TO THE RUGBY BROADCAST LAST NIGHT AND I'D SAY THE ALL BLACKS MUST HAVE HAD A GOOD WIN."

The game that never was: corner flag from the cancelled test against Ireland.
Courtesy Grahame Thorne.

(Above) Fingertips rule: Strahan and Lochore secure possession against England, Meads (5) waits to receive the ball. Courtesy Sam Strahan.

(Right) After the war was over: Lochore and French lock Benoit Dauga enjoy a drink together. Courtesy New Zealand Rugby Museum.

Sightseeing: (from left) Tony Steel, Murray Wills and Sam Strahan admire the view on
Carnaby street. Courtesy Sam Strahan.

And therein hangs a tale: Jack Hazlett meets the Queen. Other players from left are; McLeod,
Williams, Strahan, Lochore, Muller, Dick, Davis, and Laidlaw.
Courtesy New Zealand Rugby Museum.

An old All Black's best friend is probably his doctor: Arthur Jennings and 'Best Buddie Dr D'.
Courtesy Arthur Jennings.

New Zealand's modesty of fame: pinetree at Meads street, Te Kuiti.

"Very small, courageous, gutsy, a good kicker and all round sportsman, good enough to make it", suffered one handicap: there were already two King Country All Blacks. To add a third would have been unprecedented for a small union.

In the final trial, Earl Kirton was at 1st 5-8 opposing Herewini. As a dental student in Dunedin he had formed a distinguished partnership with half-back Laidlaw. They'd been together in 1963 when Otago beat the England team 14-9 and Kirton subsequently played a blinder in the inter-island game. Chosen for Whineray's tour, the 23-year old debuted for New Zealand in the third match against Newport. That was when it went all wrong. Newport won 3-0. Kirton, unfairly, got the blame. He was never seriously considered for Whineray's test side and while he made the final trial in 1965 he was generally considered to be on the outer. It seemed no matter how well Kirton played Newport would always be held against him. Now Allen gave him his chance of redemption outside the smooth-passing Laidlaw.

So it was that the players assembled in Wellington for the final trial. Hanging around the bar isn't a good look for an aspiring player at such times. So they filled in their spare time by playing cards, having a sports massage, or going to what the papers still called "the theatre" to watch the latest movies: the epics *Dr Zhivago* and *Cleopatra*, or the bleak 'New Wave' *Funeral in Berlin*. They thumbed through the papers, smiled at Nevile Lodge's cartoon, tried not to be seen lingering over McLean or Veysey's idea of the team-to-be, though the journalists usually got most of the selection right.

August's *Sports Digest*, with Williment on the cover, was still around, but September's issue was now out. A stone-cold certainty for the tour, popular Maori flanker Nathan was on the cover. He'd recently become a Public Relations officer for a brewery, an apparently unnecessary job. Still, the convivial Nathan was the ideal PR man. The job came with a decent salary and a company car and his new employers were happy to allow him time off to tour, unlike his previous employers in a freezing works. That was a reason to change jobs in that late amateur age. Still, the local newspaper headline "Panther changes diet from meat to beer" had embarrassed him and his school-teacher wife.

In theory at least, nothing about the team was set in stone; there was still all to play for in the trials. Even those who had played the Jubilee test had grounds to be nervous. In recent memory, Don McKay and Ian Uttley had both played for New Zealand at home in 1963, but missed Whineray's tour later that year. Yet all was not as it seemed. Players such as Davis knew they were almost certainly in, for they had received the "secret service call" to the Union's tailor to be measured up for their touring outfit. John Major was another who got the call so the likes of future brewery magnate Terry McCashin, a hooker in the early trial, didn't know it but they were going to have to wait to make the All Blacks.

Yet even the tailor's tape might not have been the ultimate reassurance. Various versions of a story later emerged that a few days earlier Morrison had contacted Allen and hinted that the Council would like several key players left out of the touring team. Those players were Gray, McLeod and particularly Meads. Their suggested exclusion was apparently on the grounds that their play was over-vigorous. But Allen was having none of it. His biography quotes him as saying, "I knew the people who were behind this move… It had nothing to do with them and I wasn't going to let the strength of an All Black team be undermined by Tom [Morrison] and his cronies… I was buggered if I was going to leave them at home."

It was not unknown for national rugby Unions to intervene in selection but – at least until the Rangi case – it had never been made public knowledge in New Zealand and the story is an odd one. A lack of social skills might conceivably have then been grounds for exclusion on a U.K. tour, but Meads and Gray at least were men who knew which way to pass the port. They had both toured the U.K. with Whineray's side without causing any embarrassment. Meads in particular, having toured Japan,

Ceylon, South Africa, Australia, and the U.K., France, and Canada, was widely considered an excellent tourist. He was the ideal team man and regarded as good honest company by those who encountered him socially.

Nor does the trio's exclusion on grounds of over-vigorous play ring entirely true. Meads did have a reputation for vigorous play. Much of the British press regarded him as a dirty player. The fiery McLeod also skated on thin ice in such matters, but Gray's transgressions were skilfully hidden in tight play. In any case, had Morrison really wanted to get rid of Gray he could surely have done so on fitness grounds the day he and Allen had met Gray in his menswear shop.

The whole thing might have been a card played in a long-forgotten piece of rugby politics, or perhaps the story really reflected a simmering conflict that exploded the following year. We don't know what Saxton knew of all this; if it was discussed in Council, he would have known. Were those really the men named? Was Morrison – "outgoing, comfortable with the players, a nice guy" – on one side? Was he just passing on a message that came from Council or even from Bernard Fergusson, the Anglophile with the Victorian-ideal of sport who presided as Union patron?

There is another possibility though. Fred Allen might have made up the whole story. It wouldn't have been the first time he'd done something like that and it would have been an effective means of ensuring those players thought about the consequences of a reputation for rough play.

\*\*\*

Trial rugby was traditionally an individual sport. The idea was to stand out and impress the selectors with your personal playing skills. This was New Zealand in the 60s, so tricks like dyeing your hair or wearing coloured boots to distinguish yourself were still in the future. But no-one with any ambition was going to pass the ball if they were within sniffing distance of the try-line. Even front-rowers long-hidden in the depths of scrums seized every chance to kick, run, and even side-step. Allen, however, was having none of it. He told the players exactly what was wanted. The selectors were looking for team-players who would run the ball. Lochore stressed to his side that a winning team was most likely to be picked more-or-less *en masse*. The result was that the players set out to win selection by playing attacking rugby as a team.

In the early trial, the Possibles scored seven tries and won 37-0, which effectively ended the hopes of those in the inaptly named Probables. Phil Clarke, the long-shot from Marlborough, scored three of the tries. In the second, or final trial– the one that really counted–Lochore's Probables beat Hazlett's Possibles 27-16 in what turned out to be a wonderful, flowing game. Laidlaw was judged the star and Thorne added another try to his tally. But perhaps the best thing about the game was its style. Winston McCarthy enthused that the two sides had "Treated the crowd to the finest trial it was possible to see, quite the best in my memory." Little did they know they were witnessing the future.

When the game was over, the players disappeared down the tunnel. They showered, changed and began the awful wait until the team was announced in the drab Athletic Park function rooms. Something about the setting made the waiting seem worse. Laidlaw remembered the rooms as a "cheerless cavern." Wallace Reyburn termed them "bleak catacombs". They were cold even in summer. In that harsh spotlight there was nothing to do but stand there and wait–there wasn't even a pool table in sight.

Something about that wait sears itself into their memory. The physical endeavour that precedes it may be forgotten, but the emotional strain of knowing their fate was at the whim of others was brutally memorable. At least Thorne was confident. Walking off the field he slapped Jennings on the back and said "Great game! You and I can't miss." Jennings wasn't so confident, "I knew he had played well, but me?" Jennings had played seven trials already, this was probably his last chance.

So along with several hundred officials, journalists, and various others with a taste for the macabre, 68 players and reserves, all damp hair and flushed cheeks, stood around in their suits and thin ties. They pecked at the sausage rolls and sipped from jugs of warm beer while trying to make time-filling conversation about anything but their sole concern – whether they were in the team or not. For the young blokes, there was the possibility of more chances in the years to come. For the rankers, there was only the lingering tension and for the older ones there was only hope.

In rugby terms, McCormick was growing old. He'd made his Canterbury debut back in 1959 alongside Tremain. Tremain scored two tries in that game and two more in the next against the touring Lions. He'd made the All Blacks that season and now ranked with the greats. McCormick was still just the Canterbury fullback. Like his father, who played a single match for New Zealand in Australia in 1925, (and that an oddity against E.J. Thorn's XV at Manly), Fergie had just that single 1965 test cap to his name. But while lacking confidence off the field, he was a tough, abrasive player on it and he'd become a Lancaster park hero for his total commitment on attack and defence. He was known around the traps. MacRae remembered as a young West-coaster taking him on, and McCormick flattening him. Still, his goal-kicking record wasn't great. It had let him down in that single test and now there were young men like Going and Laurie coming through and Ian Bishop was a quiet achiever with the Hawke's Bay shield team, the kind of player selectors just might pluck out of the hat. McCormick knew if he didn't make it now he never would.

The selectors, Allen, George, and Vodanovich, had headed to a private meeting room as soon as the trials ended. They had about 40 names to discuss, and perhaps a couple of 'what abouts?' For them time passed quickly. Outside there was another world where time dragged slow. Most of the team could be quickly inked in, but the last few names filled the hour and a half before they made their final tally. Was there pressure on Allen to allow Morrison's reported call for heads or did he rule unchallenged?

Were the discussions slow and rational or loud and passionate? Whatever was the case, it seems the three men couldn't count on their 30 fingers. The team list they submitted to Council chairman Morrison for formal approval contained 31 players.

Outside in the function rooms, stilted conversation among the players mostly gave way to anxious silence. Even the warm beer was still. It was no time for drinking. At least the smokers had something to occupy them and the air was greying. Some anonymous schoolgirls had just written to the *Evening Standard* questioning the propriety of their teacher smoking in class but nowhere short of a gelignite dump was a no-smoking zone in New Zealand then. Even All Blacks lit up in public without thought. While it was known to be bad for sportsmen and players like Meads spoke out against it, several of the '67 team were regular cigarette smokers. Some of the others, even the superbly fit Kirkpatrick, were then 'social smokers'; Clinton-like they didn't inhale.

The word came through that the team had been chosen and passed to the Council. There was a murmur of relief. A few minutes could now be used up in conversation and weak jests with fellow-players about how they'd probably have their selection vetoed on account of some sin against a Council member or his comely daughter. The players steeled themselves anew. Not long now.

Yet the minutes ticked by again. In the Council chambers, the careful mind of Cec Blazey had spotted the strange mistake and pointed out the chosen team had an extra player. They sent the list back to the selectors. Now, as Alex Veysey uncovered years later, Allen made the final call, against the advice of his fellow selectors. In a plain statement of intent, with characteristic decisiveness rather than forethought, he promptly cut a player who was in every amateur selector's team and every journalist's team, a player who had been a regular All Black since 1964. With that matter settled, he sent the team list back to Council. This time it was approved. Allen had picked his team and now Tom Morrison could read it out.

The opening door killed conversation. Council members took their place in the hall. McCormick was with his Canterbury teammates, largely oblivious to everything around him, making a poor effort to look nonchalant. As Morrison walked up to the microphone, Frank Kilby "Sidled up to him." As McCormick told biographer Veysey:

*Frank whispered, "You've made it Fergie." I was numb. I couldn't believe him... then Tom was speaking. My name was the first he read out. I was confused. I heard the name of Clarke follow it and it didn't mean a thing to me, a new fullback or something. Frankly I didn't care who else was in the team. I guess I was in some sort of state of shock... Then Tom read the team a second time and I was able to take it in. I was conscious of Mick Williment at my side, grasping my hand, saying "Congratulations, Fergie." It hit me firmly only then that Mick had missed out and I felt sorry for him... Then everyone was round and it was bedlam... Someone kept filling my glass and I kept emptying it. I was excited, so bloody elated....*

Mick Williment, who had debuted for Wellington as an eighteen- year old in 1958 and been first choice All Black fullback since Don Clarke retired, was the man Allen had cut at the last minute. He was out. The axe had fallen on a hometown player who had never let his side down, kicked his goals and even - in those days when fullbacks scoring tries were rare enough to warrant a page to themselves in the *Almanack* - scored a try against the Lions. And he'd been measured up by the tailor! Like making the cover of *Sports Digest*, that meant nothing in the real world. What did matter was what Allen wanted. That was to win by scoring tries, not kicking goals. Dropping Williment, when the other selectors reportedly favoured dropping McCormick, was a statement of intent. "This team," he assured the assembled press, "will run with the ball at every opportunity and it will win by scoring tries – not by kicking goals."

Dropping Williment caused an uproar. O'Brian called it "Suicidally irresponsible selection… one of the most inexplicable decisions in the entire history of rugby." In the *Evening Post*, Gabriel David, with journalistic license, described how, "When that axe fell, with stunning, almost unbelievable, impact, an astonished crowd waiting under the main stand at Athletic Park fell silent and brooding." It was, he concluded, "unforgiveable." Veysey and McLean's reports followed suit, echoing the astonishment at Williment's exclusion.

New Zealand traditionally insisted its fullback should be the goal-kicker. Only when the Welsh 1st 5-8 Barry John kicked the 1971 Lions to victory did New Zealand, slowly at first, turn to the best kicker in the team rather than exclusively the fullback. That he should most likely be the 1st 5-8 now seems obvious, but there are many things that are only obvious in hindsight.

That kicking with the instep rather than the toe gave much greater accuracy is another of those things obvious in hindsight. But 'round-the-corner' kicking was somehow considered effeminate in New Zealand rugby until Barry John proved otherwise. Goal-kicking was transformed by the new style. It seems remarkable now that Don Clarke, legendary as 'The Boot', only averaged around a 60% success rate and that a rate of 50% was considered international standard. For better or worse, the instep style has meant in the modern game a success rate of 80 or even 85% is expected. But McCormick only needed to hit 50% to be good enough for the time.

The 1968 *Almanack* gave its usual original take on Williment's exclusion. Writing after the '67 tour had ended, it pointed out that the Wellington fullback had been restricted by a groin injury in 1967 and that "it was no surprise" he was left out. But maintaining its independent line, the *Almanack* selected Auckland's Laurie at fullback in its team of the year, and commented that both Ken Going and Bay of Plenty's Bill

Potae rated above McCormick in that position!

Dropping Williment raised another issue. The selectors miscount seems to have stemmed from the selection of both Kember and Cottrell in the mid-field. Herewini had backed up as full-back on Whineray's tour, but Kember, whose original selection in the early trial suggests he was considered behind Cottrell as back-up to MacRae, became the de facto full-back reserve.

The Williment controversy bubbled on for weeks, largely obscuring the other controversial choices, but there were two players from the final trial who had missed out. With Gray fit, the Wellington prop John Finn was surplus to requirement and in a feel-good choice, Clarke's three tries in the early trial saw him included in the team at the expense of Bill Currie, a Taranaki winger who played a couple of games for the All Blacks in Australia the following year. The long-shot Clarke became the patron saint of early trialists, and prayers are probably still offered to him before All Black teams are picked.

In retrospect it was clear Allen had long admired McCormick and wanted him for the tour. But it wasn't McCormick's selection that was so controversial, that was something of a surprise but not totally unexpected. What shocked New Zealand and indeed the rest of the rugby world was that their team was now without a top-line goal-kicker. That threatened the whole basis of their successful approach since 1956. It took British journalist Peter Laker of the *Daily Mirror* to recognise that this really meant New Zealand rugby had had "a change of heart", one to make 1967-68 "the most vital season in the history of the game". The 1967 All Blacks really did plan to play attacking rugby. The revolution had begun.

***

Allen had one other choice to make: the team vice-captain. By tradition, if the captain was a forward, the vice-captain had to be a back and vice-versa. That was a gesture intended to indicate equality between the forces, although overwhelmingly forwards are favoured to lead. Laidlaw became vice-captain in 1965 and kept the job in Allen's first year in charge, 1966. But they had a complicated relationship. While admiring each other's qualities, they disdained what each saw in the other as faults. Laidlaw had a critical mind and was of a new generation. He was not going to accept the old ways for the sake of it. He loved playing rugby but hated the conservative mindset of its administration and was reluctant to fit himself totally into the short-back-and-sides model of the All Black. Not devoid of ambition, and a politically aware student, there was a touch of the amateur gentleman to his sporting life. Saxton admired him, but Allen struggled to empathise with him or fit him into his world. He thought the young man a little too outspoken and a reluctant trainer. Ultimately, the necessary rapport was simply not there and after missing the Jubilee test with injury, Laidlaw lost his stripes.

There was no obvious alternative to Laidlaw as vice-captain among the backs chosen for the tour; none of the others had any real captaincy experience. But there was one experienced player who was an automatic test selection. Christchurch-born and raised Ian MacRae began his representative career with West Coast in 1961 and he'd also had a season with Bay of Plenty before settling in Hawke's Bay. So he was experienced, and if captaincy was not on his resume, Allen recognised in him a keen trainer and good team man. MacRae got the job.

Truth to tell, while the All Black vice-captaincy was an honour, it was not overly taxing in a successful team and while Muller at least recalled him as active in the role, MacRae remembers being "pretty laid-back as vice-captain." He was on the selection panel for the tour games, but cheerfully admitted he was hardly likely to argue with Fred Allen! He roomed with Lochore occasionally and early on they discussed what they wanted to achieve, not least Lochore's desire for a more inclusive atmosphere that embraced the newer players. The two veterans of the fringes of Whineray's tour were in complete agreement about that.

MacRae was to captain the side just twice on tour, against Eastern Canada and Southeast France, with Meads captain in one game. That raises the question of who would have taken over as captain had Lochore been injured. At the outset, few would have considered that MacRae's promotion would have been automatic. Yet events on tour suggest Allen's choice as vice-captain was surprisingly prescient. Meads considers he was not ready for the national captaincy then and each of the other contenders, Tremain, Gray, Hazlett and Laidlaw, were sidelined for one reason or another at some point on the tour. MacRae was the only one of them who played in all the big games.

***

—

# "THEY'VE ALL GOT A BIT OF STEEL IN THEM"

The die was now cast. From the hundreds of representative players across the country and the dozens who played in various trials, thirty men had been selected to tour the northern hemisphere. The chosen ones floated into another room. Their wives were left to celebrate outside. Marilyn Wills remembers getting in a lift and in her excitement blurting out "My husband's just got in the All Blacks" to a very starchy lady who promptly leapt out at the next floor, convinced her fellow-passenger was insane.

The rest of the trialists were left to make their way sadly back to their hotel or, in the case of local men like Williment, to head home tired and empty. Except that Williment's bad day wasn't over. His car wouldn't start. He had to return to the grandstand and ask a couple of his former teammates to give him a push.

The empty feeling was worst for those like Currey and Finn who'd played in the final trial and knew how close they'd been. Early trialists like the two team captains Keith Nelson and Bruce Watt at least had All Black jerseys in their cupboard and memories of Whineray's tour. Some of their young players could be optimistic; they were obviously on their way up. Trialists like Sutherland, Alex Wylie and Tom Lister made the All Blacks in the next few years. Others had a long wait. A decade passed before Lyn Davis finally made it and Ken Going had to wait seven years. But Finn and others like Bishop and Panther would never make that final step up.

The team chosen was as follows:

| | | | |
|---|---|---|---|
| Fullback | W.F. McCormick | (Canterbury) | [Age] 28 |
| Three-quarters | W.M. Birtwistle | (Waikato) | 28 |
| | P.H. Clarke | (Malborough) | 25 |
| | W.L. Davis | (Hawkes Bay) | 24 |
| | M.J. Dick | (Auckland) | 26 |
| | A.G. Steel | (Canterbury) | 26 |
| | G.S. Thorne | (Auckland) | 21 |
| Five-Eighths | W.D. Cottrell | (Canterbury) | 23 |
| | M.A. Herewini | (Auckland) | 28 |
| | G.F. Kember | (Wellington) | 21 |
| | E.W. Kirton | (Otago) | 26 |
| | I.R. MacRae | (Hawkes Bay) [Vice-Captain] | 24 |
| Halfbacks | S.M. Going | (North Auckland) | 24 |
| | C.R. Laidlaw | (Otago) | 23 |
| Backrowers | I.A. Kirkpatrick | (Canterbury) | 21 |
| | B.J. Lochore | (Wairarapa) [*Captain*] | 27 |
| | W.J. Nathan | (Auckland) | 27 |
| | K.R. Tremain | (Hawkes Bay) | 29 |
| | G.C. Williams | (Wellington) | 22 |
| | M.C. Wills | (Taranaki) | 25 |
| Locks | A.G. Jennings | (Bay of Plenty) | 27 |
| | C.E. Meads | (King Country) | 31 |
| | A.E. Smith | (Taranaki) | 24 |

| | S.C. Strahan | (Manawatu) | 22 |
| Props | K.F. Gray | (Wellington) | 29 |
| | E.J. Hazlett | (Southland) | 28 |
| | A.E. Hopkinson | (Canterbury) | 26 |
| | B.L. Muller | (Taranaki) | 25 |
| Hookers | B.E. McLeod | (Counties) | 27 |
| | J. Major | (Taranaki) | 27 |

What sort of men were these chosen thirty? Certainly they represented all of New Zealand to a degree rarely seen. There were players from Southland and North Auckland and thirteen other provinces in between. Fourteen were from the metropolitan centres – five from Canterbury, four from Auckland, three from Wellington and two from Otago – while there were four Taranaki forwards and three players from Ranfurly Shield-holders Hawke's Bay. The team was truly representative of all New Zealand, which must have helped it remain entirely free of provincial cliques.

For many of those selected, rugby was in their blood. Meads, Clarke and Going had brothers who wore the black jersey. McCormick and Dick were sons of All Blacks. Hazlett and Smith both had uncles who'd been All Blacks (with Smith uniquely to later be uncle to an All Black when Conrad Smith was selected in 2004). Several other players had fathers who played provincial rugby, with Smith and Wills seniors playing together on either side of the Taranaki scrum in the late 30s. There were other sporting talents among them as well. Aside from Steel's sprinting performances, Davis later represented New Zealand at softball, while others such as Thorne, Kember, and Smith played cricket to a good standard.

Six of the ten newcomers had progressed steadily up New Zealand rugby's ladder to the point where their selection was a logical progression. Two had toured with national sides in the past. Smith toured Australia with the 1964 Colts side coached and managed by Council members and '45-'46 Kiwi's Finlay and Ingpen. Kember toured Hong Kong and Japan with a NZ University team in 1966, the year he been an All Black reserve. Williams spent three seasons in the Juniors, and captained them the week after he sat on the bench for the Jubilee test. His Junior team that day included Kember, along with Kirkpatrick and Thorne, while Cottrell played for the Juniors in 1966.

There were therefore just four players whose potential had not been obvious. Clarke had played for Combined Services and toured with them to Fiji in 1964, but he was a 100-1 shot before he was called into the trials as a replacement. Of the others, Hopkinson came to the fore in the trials, Wills was in the 1964-65 Taranaki Ranfurly Shield side, and Jennings was an experienced provincial performer picked to do the hard yards in the mid-week games.

The team was a blend of youth and experience. Their average age was 25. Ten were new All Blacks (two of whom had been test reserves), while twelve had been members of Whineray's side in 1963-64. That had its benefits. Hooker John Major, for example, is remembered for quietly steering some of his younger teammates through the protocols and personalities of British rugby.

The players were versatile athletes. Even ignoring the distinctions between tighthead and loosehead prop, at least fourteen of them played provincial rugby in more than one position. Seven of them would play tests in more than one position, including Meads who was tried at both No.8 and flanker during his long test career. Rather oddly, three of the props originally came into provincial rugby as locks and Muller had usually played there in his youth.

Famously – in those days when a player's occupation was listed after their names – ten of the side were farmers, including nine of the forwards. Today, when oldtimers yearn for the days when the All Black pack had man-of-the-land hardness and fitness, it is that '67 team they yearn for. Neither before nor since have so many farmers made the side. Adding to that agrarian aura was the fact that two of the pack were stock agents while McCormick and Muller were working in the freezing works.

Nathan had just left that line of work, which meant that half the team had worked in the farming industry.

There was a reason for the dominance of farming among the players' occupations. No-one would expect many All Black candidates to appear in a New Zealand Librarians XV. Farming was a tough physical occupation providing the basic rugby requirement of muscular strength. In those times, All Blacks as Strahan put it "never darkened the doors of a gym." Prop forwards might lift barbells on occasion, and there were press-ups and sit-ups for variety, but it was felt that weights work hindered flexibility and restricted speed. This meant that not only were the All Blacks' body-shapes recognisably human then, but that the fitness and strength the forwards required developed not from an exercise plan but from their day-to-day life. Tractors and other mechanical aids were by no means standard on farms in the early 60s. Farmers still walked or rode their horses and lifted or chopped up whatever needed lifting or chopping, be it sheep or tree trunk. But that had been the case since rugby began in New Zealand and the number of farmers had never been that high before.

Probably the difference was that farming in the 1950s and 60s was a profitable occupation, not the subsistence one it had been in the pioneering and Depression days. Protein rich diets reflected that. In addition, the comparative prosperity of rural life at that time allowed men more time to focus on rugby and even to employ labour when they went off on tour. Many a rugby-playing farmer in harder times was forced to focus entirely on working and give up developing his rugby talents.

If the gym was still foreign ground, the farmers did add endurance gained through running to the basic power their lifestyle gave them. Their cross-country miles were usually on the Arthur Lydiard principle of 'run till you drop', which became particularly closely associated with Colin Meads. For variety on country roads, there were sprints to the next telegraph pole and perhaps the odd side-step if cows had recently been there, but it was the miles that counted. Lochore ran to and from club training. He wasn't the only one determined to simply run more miles more often than any of those competing for his place. In the tour to come, that would pay off.

There were those who were not so keen on training. Hopkinson famously hid behind the goalposts in order to sit out a lap of one of Allen's training sessions while Laidlaw described himself as "one of the least avid pre-season trainers." Nonetheless, these were men who were determined not to be bested by any opponent or contender for their All Black jersey. They were out to win.

That most of the chosen All Blacks should be highly competitive is hardly surprising. The desire to wear the jersey burned quietly in most of them, but it burned deep. Their hearts were set on making the grade. Of course, so were the hearts of many who didn't make it. Alan Smith recalls players who had missed selection stumbling from the Athletic Park club rooms in tears. But those picked were often the most determined and those who kept getting picked could be the most determined of all. Men like Meads weren't going to surrender their place easily.

A psychologist would doubtless note the high percentage of the 1967 squad who grew up without a father, or at least a father absent for reasons better or worse. They include Saxton and Allen, Clarke, Major, Birtwistle, and Smith. Thorne discovered later in life that he had been adopted. But if a troubled background is often an excuse for failure in life it can also drive success. As Smith reflected, without a parent, "You get stronger in the mind."

It is notable that Allen, Meads, McCormick (and writer Terry McLean), are all revealed by their biographers to have lacked confidence after a tough early life. The constant reinforcement of self-worth by team victory brought the confidence they eventually gained. Discussing the '67 All Blacks' character in the British *Daily Express*, Pat Marshall wrote, "Every player I quizzed about his purpose in striving to get to the top at

Rugby admitted that somewhere he found a need to prove himself."

As Director of the NZ Rugby Museum in Palmerston North today, Stephen Berg has met a lot of All Blacks. As I talked to him about how different I found their individual characters, I idly wondered what united them? "They've all got a bit of steel in them," he promptly replied. In one way or another, that does describe them. They had that quality, and they were determined to prove themselves to the world.

That level of determination in a man comes at a cost. As they now recognise, wives and families paid much of the bill. They reflect on parents who took them to games when they were barefoot kids, brothers who'd covered their absence from the farm, and wives who cared for home and children during their husband's absence.

In those days, men tended to marry young. More than half of the '67 team were married, many with young children. While being an All Blacks' wife had its compensations, they paid a price. When their men went off on tour they were expected to just "get on with it", and player's careers sometimes ended because their wives couldn't fill that role. Without that support network of family and friends, going on tour would have been much tougher, if not impossible. The players' clubs helped out as well, sometimes with labour and usually by passing the hat around when a player was going off on tour.

In those days of strict amateurism, there was no question of players being paid for representing their country. They got their travel expenses and on tour they got their laughably small allowance of a dollar a day. But there was nothing in the regulations stopping a player's club from passing the hat around for its off-on-tour All Black. In a free country you can *give* your money to whoever you like and the person accepting it can hardly be held to account. So the NZRFU turned a blind eye and without that perk many players simply couldn't have afforded the trip away.

When a player was picked for a tour, his club would hold a dinner in their honour, and at some point there would be an envelope passed his way. It wasn't always that unsubtle. Some clubs preferred to buy their man a suitcase, an alarm clock, or some other such item that the traveller might need. But in Otahuhu, where the community was proud of its two All Blacks, they simply shook the hat outside the biggest supermarket and presented Nathan and Herewini with the proceeds.

Muller was one of the few who had a retainer from their employers. With his ultimate company bosses involved in the upper echelons of British rugby, there was even an envelope passed to him in the august surrounds of the British Sportsmen's Club, a bastion of amateurism. But it wasn't that simple for all of them. There had been All Blacks in the past who declined tours for financial reasons, and some never got asked again. Many of the '67 side had to carefully consider the cost of touring, notably Birtwistle whose employer promised to keep him on if he made the team, then laid him off after he'd been selected. For the newly-married winger, financial concerns were a heavy burden to carry on tour.

Easily forgotten with all the talk of the team's domination by farmers is that the players were, individually and collectively, intelligent. Thorne, Kember, Laidlaw and Kirton were university students, Tremain and Steel had been, Dick was a qualified accountant and others like MacRae and Davis were what we might call white-collar professionals. But intelligence was also manifest in the farmers, who demonstrated that in their working lives with successful farming operations in a harsh, competitive market. On the playing field they applied that intelligence to the task at hand.

Other great teams – Otago in the 40s, the 1971 British Lions – similarly included a good percentage of highly intelligent men. Time and time again the All Blacks individually and as a team made the right decisions, in selection, in tactical planning and in execution of those plans under pressure on the field. That they did so was testament not just to fitness, talent or desire, but also to their intelligence.

With one or two exceptions, the chosen players were probably more mature than their non-All Black counterparts. Old hands like Meads, Tremain and Nathan had toured widely, learned to get on with their fellows as well as with highland Scots, urbane Parisians, titled Englishmen, and Japanese enthusiasts. Strahan had headed off to Europe on O.E., something which teaches independence and self-reliance as well as how to sleep in the front seat of a VW van. Several of the players had been in the armed services. Clarke had joined the RNZAF, others like Kirkpatrick and Meads did national service, and whatever else it might or might not do, military service does bring a certain maturity. So too do did marriage and children. But maturity also came with the selection; 75 years of tradition imposed a responsibility and a standard. Selection meant, 'It's time to step up. This is serious.'

Both intelligence and maturity are elements in the make-up of a leader, and another defining characteristic of this team was the number of its players with leadership qualities. Aside from Lochore and vice-captain MacRae, it included New Zealand Junior captain Williams along with five players who were then captains of their provincial team and four who would later captain the All Blacks in at least one test. That abundance of leaders, fully united behind Lochore, undoubtedly helped him on and off the field. Only the England team that won the World Cup in 2003 with an extraordinary ten players who would captain the Red rose nation could match that breadth of leadership within an international side.

***

The chosen 30 were now ennobled young men charged with representing their country and their traditions on the northern fields. Whatever lay ahead would stay with them for the rest of their lives, and change it in ways they could not predict. They would need all of their personal and playing qualities to prosper. But if it was a challenge and a responsibility, then it was also an adventure, a free holiday. Travel to far-off lands was not common then. Today, when any Kiwi with any get up and go gets up and goes, no corner of the world remains unvisited. Young Kiwis wander through Korea and Kyrygzstan almost as easily as they wander through Dargaville and Danniverke. But in 1967 Britain, "home", seemed a long way away.

***

—

# CHAPTER FIVE

# "FROM A FARM IN MANUTAHI TO CARNABY STREET"

After the final trial on September 9th, the chosen 30 had to pass testing at the Army medical board. Then it was off to the official All Black tailor, Bob Kidd in Adelaide road, where those who had not been measured up in advance now braced themselves against the tailor's tape. The players filled out a few forms of the kind useful in case of affliction, nominating family doctor, identifying marks, and next-of-kin, and then assembled for the team photo. This was one where the smiles couldn't help but shine through. Even for the veterans it was a moment when they could reflect on their achievement and allow themselves a little pride as they pulled on the black stretch cotton jersey with the silver fern. For the guys wearing it for the first time, this was a special moment, yet tinged with an anxiety that would only disappear when they actually ran onto the field in that jersey and the referee blew his whistle. You weren't really an All Black until that happened, and there had been those who'd stumbled at the final furlong.

There is nothing sombre about the men in this official photo; they are smiling giants. The photo was a cheerful image to put out. Saxton's men are not going off to war; they're amateur sportsmen off on a fine adventure. They know it's going to be fun. For a moment, the burden of the All Blacks' great history – which they must live up to – is forgotten.

Perhaps there is a certain symbolism about the photo, especially in the way the players are arranged around the three leaders seated in the centre. Aside from Major, the eternal reserve, it is not the team's old sweats who take up the other seats but the backs. Vice-captain MacRae of course, but also the come-back men McCormick and Kirton, with Thorne confidently seated on Allen's left, along with Davis, Dick, and Going. The experienced forwards form a solid phalanx on the row standing behind them. It suggests a team that will put its backs at the centre of the attack, and rely on the Old Brigade to hold the line.

Now they were part of the national team, the players were absolved of any personal responsibility for the tour organisation. That was a mark of their distinction. Their contemporaries with backpacks took a certain pleasure in getting their inoculations, insurance, visas, and all the other requirements of travel, ticking off each one as a step closer to the great adventure. But the All Blacks' travels were arranged for them, leaving them free to focus on the home front. They needed to hire managers or sort out family rosters to maintain the farms, arrange leave-of-absence from jobs, try to sort out funds to feed their families and pay bills in their absence.

With the formalities done, the players returned home. They were not due to fly out for another month and in the meantime there were important games to play – and injuries to avoid. Most importantly, Ken Gray proved his fitness by playing for Wellington against Canterbury on September 23rd, the same day that Thorne made his Auckland debut at 2nd 5-8 against North Auckland. A week later the Tremain-led Hawke's Bay side snatched a last-minute draw in the final Ranfurly Shield game to bring the domestic season to a close. The chosen 30 players had all come through unscathed, and they were ready to go.

They reassembled at the Grand hotel in Wellington on Thursday October the 5th. Each player was given a tour number so that in military fashion their presence on buses and trains could be quickly confirmed by 'numbering off'. The next morning they got their official kit: a dinner suit with small silver fern embroidered on the pocket, a pullover and a scarf, two white shirts, two pairs of grey slacks and socks, an ordinary blazer, a dress blazer, and six ties, the latter number in recognition of their prized status as souvenirs. In addition, Charlie Saxton received a supply of silver fern lapel badges that were issued to players to give to well-wishers. They also got two towels and a tracksuit, along with a gear bag to stow it all in. They were expected to provide their own shoes in regulation black.

Neither the menswear professionals Saxton and Allen or the more fashionable members of the team were overly impressed with either the quality of the gear or the overall appearance of the uniform. Laidlaw later wrote that:

> *It is as grim an outfit as one could imagine. One could be forgiven, when seeing the full touring party together for gaining the mistaken impression that one had stumbled upon a pallbearer's convention.*

The players provided their own boots and training jerseys so their practice sessions always featured a colourful array of outfits. Most players favoured an old club jersey, although Allen sometimes stood out in a bright red British Lions jersey.

The team's first practice came on the Saturday morning at the Wellington College grounds. Rugby Union patron Sir Bernard Fergusson, in his last days as Governor-General, stopped by to wish them luck. That night there was an official dinner in the hotel at which the Rugby Union President stated with undue-but-characteristic Kiwi modesty that the All Blacks "do not want and do not deserve" the title of 'World Champions'.

Sunday the team had a day off. On Monday morning before they flew to Auckland for a special lunch, they were farewelled at the airport by some of their families and Wellington players including tour discard Mick Williment. He sportingly wished them all the best, for that was the right thing to do. At some point there was also, Laidlaw wrote, "A lecture from a doctor about the dangers of women and whiskey". That was as effective as such lectures to young men usually are.

After a night in Auckland's Central hotel there was a brief training run at Cornwell Park and an official farewell lunch. There Saxton reiterated to the press that the team would play fifteen-man rugby and, what's more, that the tour offered an opportunity for New Zealand rugby to rid itself of the stigma of rough play. That comment was certainly aimed at the British press, whose complaints about violence inflicted on the '66 Lions had been long and bitter. But perhaps it also acknowledged the idea of omitting Meads, Gray, and McLeod.

In the evening the team headed to the airport, where a crowd of 400 people – including the discarded Ron Rangi – farewelled them with the old songs, Now is the Hour and For they are Jolly Good Fellows. At 9:30 that night, their Air New Zealand DC8 left for Nandi, where they changed to a British Airways flight on the long haul to Honolulu and San Francisco.

New Zealand's daily newspapers dutifully reported this official programme of the All Blacks in the last days before their departure. What they didn't mention was that the team were actually enjoying a week of what they now call 'bonding'. Sid Going duly accepted, the rest of the squad were mostly occupied in doing some serious drinking. McCormick recalls "A week locked in the bar getting to know each other", with the so-called training run in Wellington not even rating as a warm-up. Of course, there was a serious purpose to it. They learned to look after each other in the confines of the hotel, to know when to tell a teammate he was too far gone and it was time for bed. It was the old military way, and

Major Saxton and Lieutenant Allen were in charge.

There was something special about Monday night's drinking session: it was being replicated all over the country. The new law permitting bars to stay open until 10 o'clock came into force that day. It is doubtful that anyone on the streets of New Zealand at 10:30 that night was sober.

On the other side of the world, however, where the All Blacks would soon arrive, a savage blow to the drinkers' lifestyle was about to be struck. On the day the All Blacks left home, random breath-testing was introduced in the U.K. Within a week, kits would be ordered for testing in New Zealand and the idea of 'one for the road' would be doomed. So too was the murderer sentenced to hang by Wellington Crown Court, for the death penalty was still in force in New Zealand. Another death, that of the revolutionary icon Che Guevara, also made the papers. But there was a bigger story on the middle pages of the Dominion. It was about a computer flown in from the U.K. for the New Zealand Post Office. The story was illustrated by a photo of an enormous crate containing the giant beast as it was unloaded at Auckland airport.

In his book on the 1953-54 All Black tour, Terry McLean had devoted a page to describing the glories of air travel and its splendid views. Air travel still carried a certain air glamour in 1967, at a time when the majority of New Zealanders had never flown. But it was a hungover team that endured the long haul across the Pacific. Those '53-54 All Blacks had stayed in fraternity houses when they stopped over in San Francisco, but this side had a decent hotel awaiting them: the famous Drake Wiltshire.

San Francisco provided its own reminder that the players were a long way from home. Allen, Going, Tremain and a few others witnessed an argument about the Vietnam war between three bar patrons, at least one a uniformed veteran of that conflict. No sooner had the All Blacks left the bar than the argument spilled out onto the street behind them, with the three men pulling guns and shooting each other. In what the papers headlined as an "Eye-Opener for All Blacks" one of the gunmen died on the spot, the other two lay wounded. That sort of thing didn't happen in Hamilton. Most of the players watched in disbelief. Smith walked away, determined not to allow the images of death to affect his focus on the tour. Allen, no stranger to gunshot wounds, ran in to help the wounded, but with armed police swarming into the area the All Blacks quickly pulled their coach away before he attracted undue attention.

Other All Blacks saw another side of 60s San Francisco. Walking home through Golden Gate park, they stopped to chat for a while with the hippies sleeping out there. Young men together, relaxed as young men are wont to be at that hour after their chosen intoxicants, they communicated from opposite ends of a cultural spectrum. As Phil Clarke remembers, "They were way out, but the players were interested, they were what was happening." So the All Blacks learned what a peace sign was and thought anew about flowers. As for the hippies, it was the 60s and they were there, so they have presumably entirely forgotten the encounter.

After that night there was plenty to talk about over breakfast at the hotel before the team flew to Vancouver, where the real business would start. Canada, then as now, was one of international rugby's poor relations. But British Columbia had beaten the 1966 Lions and their Under-25 side had held Whineray's All Blacks to a 3-6 scoreline, so they were no push-overs. While tactically naive, they had some hard-tackling ex-gridiron players and big tough forwards. Against the new breed of All Blacks, however, they came up short.

Both games in Canada were played at night, a new experience for players accustomed to afternoon rugby. The tour opened against British Columbia, the province that supplied most of the Canadian national side. 5,500 people turned out at Vancouver's Empire stadium, the kind of numbers Southland would expect for a game against Otago. Southland had regular rugby posts too, while the Empire stadium had gridiron-style tuning fork goalposts. The ground was wet, with the city recovering from one of the worst storms in its history. Herewini had played that up for the photographers, kicking goals at practice while a spectator held an umbrella over him.

Thorne, Cottrell, Jennings, and Wills made their debut for the All Blacks in this game, and McCormick was at fullback. He had a point to prove after all the controversy over Williment's exclusion. Within half an hour he scored three tries. Point made, or very largely because his goal-kicking wasn't great and that had been the main criticism of his selection. But three tries! That was a statement.

Oddly enough in those days when most full-backs stayed back on defence, he wasn't the first full-back to score three tries in the opening game of a major tour. Ken Scotland, who'd become a friend of McCormick's, had done the same for the 1959 Lions and the beauty of their running rugby was a legend in the game. It was a good omen.

The All Blacks ended with nine tries in a 36-3 win, and local supporters went home with some solace after their experienced 2nd 5-8 Gerry Lorenz had scored one for them. The British Columbia forwards left the All Blacks with their share of bruises and worse. Up-front Ken Gray broke a bone in his hand when, as they say, his fist was head-butted by his troublesome opponent.

The second game was in Montreal four days later. Just 2,500 people showed up at the University of Montreal stadium in this rugby outpost, but there was a public transport strike on and it was freezing cold and pouring with rain. The All Blacks had already had their strike adventure when the bus sent to take them to their reception at the New Zealand High Commission turned out to be a yellow school bus. Given the sudden passenger weight increase, it promptly broke down and a replacement had to be found.

Just one of the Eastern Canada side was actually born in Canada. Their captain George Wyman had even played alongside Herewini and Nathan in the Otahuhu College side in a curtain-raiser to the legendary 1956 Eden Park test against South Africa. Six All Blacks made their debut, including Gerald Kember whose selection at full-back was a pretty clear indication that Allen saw him as the reserve full-back to McCormick. Accustomed to playing at 1st or 2nd 5-8 in the Wellington team for which Williment was full-back, and out of practice as a goal-kicker, Kember's pleasure at an All Black debut was tempered by doubt as to the wisdom of the selection.

The game was played on a narrow field and again there were tuning-fork goal-posts. But the rain was the biggest problem, a downpour covering the ground in a sheet of water that meant the halfback had to float the ball into the scrum. Despite that hindrance and a referee who awarded 37 penalties in the course of the match, the All Blacks tried their best to run the ball. Williams and Kirkpatrick both celebrated their debuts with a brace of tries in the 40-3 victory. Kember turned out to be one of the best players, and kicked sixteen points out of the mud. Allen's ideas about full-backs were starting to look inspired.

The days in Canada got the team off to a good start, despite Gray's injury. They had several training runs and fun off the field, with time to visit Montreal Expo and search out its unofficial New Zealand exhibition, situated in a tent next to the Australian pavilion. While Sam Strahan, sending flowers to his wife Rosemary for her 21st birthday, discovered the player's daily allowance wasn't designed for such gestures, the Canadians had been great hosts. Even the receptions were enjoyable. There wasn't much of a gap separating the culture of New Zealanders and Canadians, the formalities were at a minimum.

Canada was, as Smith put it, "fabulous". The new men made their debuts and enjoyed the experience. Those who had been there with Whineray enjoyed the chance to come back and Going, whose missionary term there had been a totally separate part of his life, was another fan. They were all ready for the U.K. If there was a sore point about this section of the tour it was only that which other rugby tourists had felt – that more should have been done to encourage Canada's participation in world rugby. Their neglect was a little embarrassing.

\*\*\*

From Montreal, the All Blacks flew to New York. They had an evening in the sportsman's bar of choice: former World Heavyweight champion Jack Dempsey's famous night club. The next morning they saw the Statue of Liberty and took in the view from the Empire State building, then the world's highest. They stopped in at the United Nations building and also helped out the local rugby fraternity, with Thorne seconded to cover a request for an All Black to give a coaching session to the New York (University) Old Blues. Given that Thorne was the least experienced player in the team it was a short straw call, but a welcome one to the local side in a city where rugby ranked way below the radar.

On the Friday night, while 100,000 protestors gathered in Washington for an anti-Vietnam war demonstration, the team boarded a British Overseas Airways Corporation VC-10 for an overnight flight to London. With twin Rolls-Royce engines on the tail section of the plane, the VC-10 was the latest passenger jet, one of the last brilliant innovations of British commercial aircraft design. While the team were travelling in economy it was as good a service as any in the world at the time. But it did run three hours late.

On the morning they arrived in the U.K., in order to loosen up and get over jet-lag, the team headed straight to a training run at Aorangi Park, home of the London New Zealand Sports club. That exercise after hours of confinement mightn't have been a good idea for Phil Clarke, or perhaps he didn't warm up sufficiently.

Clarke had had grown up without parental support. His absent father was Vernon Clarke, the official All Black photographer. His mother returned to her Australian homeland when Phil was just nine years old. The children looked after themselves with brother Adrian, the 1958-60 All Black and Phil's 'guiding light', acting as their father. Phil did the cooking and attended school in Henderson. Two weeks before his seventeenth birthday, he joined the Air Force as a boy cadet and threw himself into rugby and athletics. Clarke was not unknown in rugby circles; he'd played for Auckland 'B' with Herewini, and for Canterbury in 1963 with Birtwistle, Hopkinson, and McCormick. Now the fortunes of trial rugby had given him his chance with the All Blacks. He knew he was lucky yet he felt he might have the attributes and wasn't overawed. He was prepared to give it everything.

But Clarke had a problem, by 1967 his body was starting to rebel and he went on tour knowing his leg muscles might not survive. They'd got through the Montreal game but in the mud and rain Clarke hardly saw the ball. He'd been picked again for the first match in England but in that first training run he pulled a muscle in his leg. "Do you want to play or not?" said Allen when he reported the strain. Clarke stepped down. It was the beginning of a frustrating tour for the Marlborough winger.

The All Blacks checked into their London home, the luxurious Park Lane hotel, and discovered the little pub behind it that would be their watering hole. Sunday was always a day off on tour with the mornings given over to the team's court sessions. Judge Laidlaw presided and they had a beer or three to lubricate proceedings. Those who had slept in, forgotten their ties, or otherwise breached tour rules known or even previously unheard of were duly punished, usually with a fine that went into the team funds. Saxton and Allen were in attendance and the courts served a purpose in that they were "quasi-disciplinary." It was generally good-humoured, a time for the players to unwind and to let off a little steam. They didn't necessarily enjoy it but in the confines of the group, rough edges could be smoothed and grievances could emerge safely. At times such sessions could walk a tightrope between laughter and umbrage, but it was in-house and there it stayed. Giving and taking were a part of team-building.

Sunday was also pay day. As amateur sportsmen, the touring All Blacks were restricted by International Board regulations to their allowance of a dollar a day. A packet of cigarettes cost 50 cents, a pint of beer 45. The remaining coins would have bought a newspaper. In other words, it was a pittance. Yet no-one seriously questioned it. That was the way things were. They accepted that as amateurs playing their chosen sport, even for their country, it was going to cost them money. Even with the whip-rounds from their clubs and any other loose change they might make along the way, the most they could hope for was to break even.

Of course they had an option. They could have taken the rugby league shilling. Sydney's rugby league clubs would certainly have come up with a decent sum for anyone with an All Black jersey and for star players there were tempting offers, far, far more inviting than a dollar a day. McCormick had recently turned down a league offer to make one more shot at the All Blacks. But actually none of them were seriously tempted, even when the dole queue beckoned. In the world in which they were young, you couldn't put a price on a black jersey. Money was not then the highest god; there were values that ranked above it, things like loyalty, respect, and friendship. Even five decades later none of the players regretted they had played in the amateur years. While accepting the inevitability of professionalism and acknowledging its benefits, they were adamant that money couldn't buy the spirit of the amateur game and the friendships it generated.

While a dollar didn't go far, host nations were generous to the players, just as New Zealanders were generous to their visiting rugby sides. Tickets to shows at places like the London Palladium came free and there was no shortage of people willing to buy an All Black a drink. There was also a team fund for incidentals like shared taxis to shows. Saxton controlled that, and Fred Allen was probably its main contributor when he enjoyed a successful night at Biarritz casino and turned his winnings over to the team.

Just how meagre a sum a dollar was soon became clear. The All Blacks were now mixing in entirely new social circles to those they had grown up in. For those who had been with Whineray it was easier to deal with the upper end of the British class system, but the new men discovered a new world. They were thrown in at the deep end on the Monday after their arrival when they attended the great social event of the tour: the British Sportsman's Club welcoming lunch at the Savoy hotel. There was nothing less than a Bentley in the car park and the cheapest glass of wine cost more than the players' daily allowance.

There were 48 tables laid out for the lunch, each seating eleven or twelve people, with one member of the touring party per main table. Other guests – almost entirely male – included the hierarchs of British rugby and a smattering of great players from the past. Then there were media stars like television's David Frost and a selection of the upper echelons of British civil and military society. Lords, Bishops, Generals, even Field-Marshalls were scattered around the room, together with a sprinkling of ambassadors and a few Directors of companies with ties to New Zealand. It was an insight into how much money was available to British rugby with its upper-crust supporters.

Although the players "weren't expected to carry the conversation", they were naturally the centre of attention at their table. As Malcolm Dick remembered, that could be tough for those brought up not to talk much about themselves. Old hands like Meads and Tremain could keep a conversation going. They knew what to say and what not to say, as did those like Clarke and Laidlaw who were accustomed to an Air Force mess or a college dinner. Strahan had actually attended the corresponding function on Whineray's tour as a guest of farm suppliers Dalgettys and so had an idea of what to expect. Then there a few social types like Williams, Thorne and Davis – even if he was "blown away" by the setting – who enjoyed the opportunity to meet the guests. But it wasn't easy for those like Wills, who were "petrified" by the formality, or Going as a quiet non-drinker who grew frustrated by the lack of anything non-alcoholic except water. And if Muller's natural humour got him through, it was still "a big eye-opener for a boy from Eltham."

One or two of the players might have had some advice on social matters from Saxton or guidance from old hands like Major and Tremain. A couple of others were reasonably sure of what they were ordering from a menu in French. But in general the players were left to mix as best they could; only on Saxton and Lochore's visit to Buckingham Palace later that day was there a lecture on protocol. Somehow they managed. Kember recalled the All Blacks were "Still a bit of a novelty, so you got away with being a bit different", and in any case as McCormick pointed out, "We had good manners."

The formalities were toughest for the captain who, with Saxton's help, had to get the protocol right in such matters as rank and who to thank first. The British officials, Kember noted, tended to be very good public speakers, amusing and understated, the epitome of the talented amateur whose ethos dominated British rugby at the time. Saxton had a standard self-depreciating joke about not being tall enough to reach up to the microphone but he and Lochore had a very different style of speaking. Yet their straight-talking unadorned speeches proved popular.

Sandwiched between the Very Reverend Bishop of somewhere and Lord Randolph Huffington-Smythe ("Call me Huffy") of somewhere else, it was easy to lose track of who you were talking to. Smith was seated at a table dominated by Air Force officers, none of lesser rank than Air Commodore. But he found himself talking to a grey-haired chap who said his name was Norfolk and that he like Smith was a farmer. So Smith, calling him Mr Norfolk, enjoyed an agreeable conversation about farming. Only later did he realise that his dinner companion was England's largest landowner, His Grace the Duke of Norfolk. It was the same for Davis. Conversation at his table turned to the matter of chocolate, and he was asked if he liked British chocolate. Luckily he said he loved it, for the man asking was Lord Cadbury.

There were plenty more formal events to come. But the first match against the North of England was coming up that Wednesday. British rugby was then in the middle of a bout of soul-searching. The '66 Lions had lost all four tests in New Zealand and with the Lions touring South Africa in 1968, the British game was coming to terms with the need for better preparation to succeed in the modern era. That included coaching– a controversial step because it was associated with professionalism in their ethos of the time. England had undertaken a short tour of Canada to prepare for the 1967-68 season and the All Blacks offered them a chance to measure their progress.

Better prepared opponents were not the only new challenge. This tour was much shorter than previous visits to the northern hemisphere. Whineray's men had played 36 matches in four months, but club sides that had played the All Blacks in the past were now combined into regional combinations. The result was tougher games and a tour that would be over in time for the players to get home before Christmas.

At the time, it seemed like an aberration, something to do with the tour being a short-notice replacement for the cancelled tour of South Africa. But it established a precedent, paving the way for tours where only tests were played. Something was lost along the way. Newport's victory over Whineray's All Blacks will be celebrated as long as there is a Newport club. There is now a painting above the club bar of Uzzel's winning drop kick soaring high above the sun-dappled posts, ascending for all eternity into the blue sky above. Actually, the kick scraped over in the driving rain, but triumphant art is about myth and vision, not prosaic fact. And where would they honour such a victory if Monmouthshire should triumph over Lochore's men? The game might be played at Newport, but there were just three Newport players in the side. Shorter tours meant games becoming increasingly less significant, less emotionally engaging, less legendary in the long term.

The All Blacks were scheduled to travel by train to their next destination, Wilmslow, some eighteen kilometres outside Manchester where the North of England game was played. But there were rumours of a train strike and they switched to coaches. The All Blacks couldn't help but notice that strikes were becoming a fact of life in Britain. Some of their gear had been held up in the Liverpool docks by industrial action and in Leicester the hotel kitchen staff were on strike. Politics in sport indeed!

The comparative isolation of the Stanneylands hotel was ideally suited to intensify the team's focus. There was the usual air of expectation around what was, in many senses, the real opening game of the tour. The weight of tradition, the years of training and trialling, the days of travel, the whole life in the spotlight– they all came together here; this was what they meant.

Yet the location was uninspiring. To accommodate a good crowd, they played at White City Stadium, a greyhound racing track in Manchester's industrial suburbs with a rugby pitch barely fitted in the middle. It was narrower than normal and the in-goal area was short. It was also raining. The North of England side was full of internationals and highly rated, but in the event their combinations didn't work and they put up a lack-lustre performance. The All Blacks set out to run the ball from the first. In the usual tour opening blues their timing and handling were off. Then it all changed. In the second half, the passes started to stick. Lochore led from the front and his team ran away with the game, scoring six tries in a 33-3 victory. The 1967 All Blacks and their new style of play were up and running.

Next up was a Midlands and Home Counties side at the Leicester Club ground. As the coach passed through England's farming heartlands, there was plenty for the farmers to notice – not least their English counterparts wearing ties as they worked! The farmers had something else to discuss as well. From a butcher in Manchester, they discovered that while the price they were getting for lamb in New Zealand had dropped in half, the price it was selling for in England had remained the same. That got them thinking.

Leicester has always been a keen rugby town and for those who weren't playing, it had welcome diversions. The All Blacks had been in London at the weekend, when the shops were all closed because weekends were holidays then, not working or shopping days. Thorne had gone for a net at Alf Gover's cricket academy and guys like Williams and Birtwistle had found a bowling alley, but most of the capital's attractions were closed. Even the pubs shut on Sunday afternoon. Then the team had been at a country-house hotel, out of town. Now they were in an English city and they discovered Marks and Spencers. Baggage straps were soon strained.

The Midlands game might be remembered for a hard fought contest in which each side scored a single try and the All Blacks ran out 15-3 winners thanks to penalties and a Herewini dropped goal. It might be remembered for Bob Lyold who scored the Midland's try, for he was to score a third of the tries scored against the '67 side. Or it might be remembered for the injury suffered by Nathan, whose jaw was broken by a punch from the Midlands and England flanker Budge Rogers. Instead, it is remembered for a far more serious injury.

The day started brightly. The Royal Leicestershire Regiment band even played Puppet on a String, the infuriatingly catchy tune of Sandie Shaw's hit. Not only was it one of the tourists' favourite songs but it was also just about the only song any pre-match band played that wasn't either martial or classical. And it didn't rain.

Very serious injuries are rare occurrences in top-class rugby—mostly they occur to players in the lower ranks of the game. Only once had they involved an All Black side. The histories record that back in 1913 in a match against Victoria (British Columbia), the local full-back, one Peter Ogden, returned to play after a second concussion. He collapsed on the field and died en route to hospital. Four minutes into the game against the Midlands came an incident almost as serious.

Danny Hearn was partnering Lyold in the centres. A doctor's son, Hearn had a blue-blood education at Cheltenham College, Trinity

College Dublin where he was university boxing champion in 1963, and then Oxford, where he won his blue. Now he was an economics teacher at Haileybury, a distinguished public school that had trained generations of men to administer the British Empire. On the rugby field, Hearn was a renowned tackler. He already had six caps. Now he ran out to face the All Blacks, determined to show the selectors he deserved another in the following weekend's test match. As he ran onto the field, he heard an official say, "Keep the stretchers close the touchline," and thought it, "A slightly macabre note...This is sport, not war – or a student demonstration!"

Four minutes into the game, Hearn got the chance to show his opposite number, Ian MacRae, just how hard he tackled. Slow ball from the inside meant that Hearn was able to crash-tackle MacRae with full force just as the All Black 2nd 5-8 passed the ball on to centre Thorne – who dropped it. Such was the force of Hearn's tackle that MacRae's first thought was that it had injured him. But as he picked himself up he realised it was Hearn that was hurt – and badly. The English centre lay motionless on the ground.

A year later in an article in the Daily Express, Hearn recalled that:

> *Everything went black then – ALL BLACK, to salvage whatever humour...can be found in this bleak situation.*
>
> *Lights flickered before my eyes like a pin-ball machine gone crazy and I could taste the grass as I lay face down on the ground. From the bottom of my mind or from some elementary sense of self-preservation present in the human animal I tried to cry out: "Don't move me, don't move me."*

They heard Hearn's plea. Lochore ensured Hearn was not moved until he was eased onto a stretcher in the proper manner and taken to the ambulance. It was clear the injury was a serious one. At first there were hopes that Hearn would recover, but in the days that followed it was confirmed that his neck was broken. He would spend the rest of his life in a wheelchair. Hearn had mistimed his tackle and his head had hit MacRae's hip, leaving the All Black with a massive multi-coloured bruise just above his hip bone. It lasted for weeks.

MacRae was in no sense responsible for the injury, and with his friend Davis and a number of other All Blacks, wanted to visit Hearn in hospital the next day. But Saxton decided it was best if Lochore went as team representative. The skipper presented Hearn with an All Black kit and it was only at the end of the tour that MacRae and the others met up with the injured warrior. "Their visits," Hearn remembered, "cheered me hugely. We all hoped that my accident would not put anybody off rugby."

Hearn was transferred to the National Spinal Injuries Centre at Stoke Manderville Hospital outside London. There he would try to "Live and salvage whatever could be snatched from nature's wreckage". His life was reduced to a long primal struggle to recover some semblance of control over his broken body. No longer did he care "How many shopping days there were to Christmas." Gradually he regained some basic muscle control and by February he was allowed a weekend at home. Rugby didn't forget him. He was inundated by letters of sympathy, including many from New Zealand. There was no insurance scheme for injured players then and ironically he had taken out private insurance only a few days before the accident and had not fulfilled the qualifying period. But the English Rugby Union paid for him to holiday in Spain as soon as he was able and by the end of 1968 he was back teaching at Haileybury and coaching the school's first XV from his wheelchair.

Danny Hearn remained wheelchair bound, but he is still alive today, retired and living in Ireland. He has enjoyed a full life, one he shares with a lady he met at Stoke Manderville. In a strangely heart-warming postscript to the tragedy, MacRae is one his greatest friends. The two men have stayed close ever since those days. Hearn was able to visit New Zealand in 1969 and stayed with MacRae and his wife and the MacRae's stayed with Hearn in Ireland in 2005.

The tragic injury to Hearn overshadowed Nathan's broken jaw. But that injury was a sad one. When fit, Nathan was an automatic choice in the test team. He had been at the heart of Auckland's Ranfurly Shield side and a star of NZ Maori teams; a player, as Allen put it, with a "Cool head, good hands and the eye of a hawk." A cheerful, easy-going personality, Nathan was popular within the team and with the public. But he was unlucky with injuries in the Northern hemisphere. On Whineray's tour, a broken finger had kept him out of six games including the Irish test. Then his jaw was broken in the Llanelli game and he missed eight more matches including the English and Scottish tests. Now his jaw was broken for a second time and his chances of recovering in time to play again on this shorter tour looked poor.

Nathan's first thought was to go home. But with Allen's encouragement he resigned himself to a diet of eggs and vowed to recover in time to play again before the tour ended. To make himself useful in the meantime, he volunteered for the full-time role of duty boy, a job usually assigned by the manager on a daily basis. His task was to knock on doors and get players to the bus on time, clean up, run errands, and generally make himself useful. It wasn't the most popular job in the world and Nathan's application for the position was greeted with considerable enthusiasm by his teammates.

There was an odd point about Nathan's broken jaw though. While inflicted by a punch in clear view of the crowd, it seemed to entirely escape the notice of the British press, which was never loath to point out transgressions by the All Blacks. In his tour book, David Frost (no relation to the television host of the same name), for example, briefly mentioned a "scuffle" between Nathan and Rogers. Several pages later he simply stated that, "Nathan was found to have broken his jaw."

Rogers was duly picked to play for England the following week. It was the kind of thing that made the team wonder about the British commitment to fair play, and there would be further cause to ponder that question before the tour was over.

Nathan's old mate Herewini was another whose luck didn't extend to northern hemisphere tours. Herewini had debuted for Auckland in 1958 while still at school and made his name with the Shield team. By 1962, he was an All Black and he played three tests on Whineray's tour. Not until the 4th test against South Africa in 1965 had he been called on again, but he had played through the whitewash of the Lions in 1966 and in the Jubilee test.

The critics said Herewini was a gifted player but not a great tourist. He got homesick. But there good reasons for that. His sister had died shortly before he left on Whineray's tour and they'd had to persuade him to go. Then in the hours after playing in the French test, he heard that his brother had died in an accident. Now it seemed to be happening again. He'd arrived in Vancouver to find that his son had been taken to hospital. If he never found his best form on Lochore's tour then apprehension as to what bad news might come next has to have been a factor.

Nathan and Herewini were at the heart of the All Blacks' off-duty music making. Nathan travelled with a guitar, a combination that proved irresistible to press photographers and there were times when he gave it to someone else to escape their attention. Herewini had a ukulele, which had the advantage of being less prominent baggage. Puppet on a String was the tour's jukebox hit but the sing-along number was Ten Guitars, with Green Green Grass of Home another favourite along with Po Kare Kare Ana. Jack Hazlett was probably the best of the singers and Hopkinson was an enthusiastic part of the choir too, while somewhere there is a recording of Laidlaw and Nathan singing Blueberry Hill. When the tourists got to Wales there were even attempts to respond decently to the Welsh after-match singing, but no-one claimed a New Zealand victory in that contest.

Graham Williams had no great claims to musical talent but he was one who took advantage of Radio New Zealand's offer to the players to dedicate a song to their wives back home, with the record played on an evening programme. Williams' wife Sharon remembers Graham choosing the theme to Dr Zhivago, Somewhere My Love, and crying when she heard it.

Mostly the players made do with weekly letters to communicate with their spouses – usually aerogrammes and post-cards because they were cheaper. For wives at home coping without their husbands, life carried on. Family and rugby club mucked in, but there was a special air of expectancy when they saw the mail man coming.

Phone calls were expensive then. You had to go through the operator and the connection was often so poor that calls were a frustrating round of stop-start conversations, with "sorry" and "what was that?" the most common phrases. Jan Nathan remembers booking a Christmas call a month in advance during the Whineray tour and as McCormick put it, you were "Lucky to get a phone call to your wife when she was having a baby." Most of the players called home once, if at all. Clarke saved his call to wife Shirley until he stepped out during the final function of the tour, for that was their wedding anniversary.

Sometimes there were explanations to be made, notably about photos that appeared in New Zealand papers before the letters explaining them arrived. The player "drinking" a yard of beer photo is always a trap for newcomers but three young All Blacks, Strahan, Wills, and Clarke, were caught on a visit to Swinging London's Carnaby street. A photographer wanted a shot of them admiring one of the mini-skirted damsels for which the fashionable quarter was famed. They agreed on condition he didn't use the photo for a week or so. Two passing beauties in mini-skirts were promptly called on by the photographer with All Blacks dutifully admiring (it can be tough being an All Black). But there were embarrassed explanations hurried across the miles after the photo appeared in New Zealand papers the next day!

The press were a constant presence, part of a group that travelled with the team. That group included Ralph Love, the Maori member of the NZRFU Council. He accompanied the team in an unofficial capacity but Saxton made him an official member of the side as team number 33. Love was Mayor of Petone and as a modest and social man he gave considerable help to the team in any area he was needed, not least in meeting its social obligations. Then there was Derek Lever, an Englishman they christened "Laurie" ("Because it rhymes with Lever!"). He served more than satisfactorily as Saxton's secretary. The year before he had answered a newspaper advertisement for a secretary for the Wallaby side that had toured the northern hemisphere in 1966-67. The Wallabies liked him and recommended him to the All Blacks as they did Richard Walker, a young cricket professional with Glamorgan. Needing a winter job, Walker took on the generally thankless task of laundryman and baggage master. He ensured the team's 83 bags were transferred from place to place – and for this he was duly thanked by an All Black team that was always smartly turned out and close to their gear.

In addition to these three insiders, each of the countries they visited allocated them a liaison officer. An Englishman called Peter Horn filled that role for the Canadians, 1938 British Lion forward Stanley Couchman for the (English) Rugby Union, 1959 Lions manager Alf Wilson for Scotland, and Handel Rogers for the Welsh. They were generous hosts and in France a Maurice Delbos, despite the minor handicap of being non-English speaking, managed the job as well as any of them. With the national liaison officer, there was a touring party of 36 men.

The press paid their own way, or at least had their way paid, which is not quite the same thing. Bob Irvine, son of an All Black and a product of Whangarei Boys High School, had succeeded Winston McCarthy as the voice of New Zealand rugby. He called the tour for the New Zealand

Broadcasting Corporation. It was Irvine's voice that you heard on the crackling air-waves in the early hours of a cold New Zealand morning, his voice that painted the mind-pictures of those games. Those images came before the real ones because the spectator's dollars were still important to rugby then so there was no live television coverage. Black-and-white film of the tests taken by the BBC was flown to New Zealand and broadcast some days later. That gave New Zealanders their first experience of Bill McLaren, the master of television rugby commentary who was then beginning his career. Only scraps of the footage survives.

In record shops you can still sometimes find the L.P. of Bob Irvine's commentary on the England, Wales, and Scotland tests and the Barbarian's game. It was one of a series of Irvine's rugby commentaries released in the mid-60s, on Polydor, in mono, "By arrangement with B.B.C. Radio Enterprises". So while people couldn't watch recordings of these games (until Youtube came along), they could listen to the record and see again in their mind's eye the tour triumphs and hear the horror in Irvine's voice at Murrayfield.

Irvine was accompanied by several New Zealand journalists. Graeme Jenkins was the official correspondent for the NZ Press Association, whose reports were disseminated to both international media and provincial papers. The *Christchurch Star* sent Larry Saunders on the tour. For some reason his status was considered unofficial, which probably had something to do with his lack of an expense account. For the *NZ Herald* and another feeder organisation for provincial papers, the NZ Associated Press, there was Terry McLean.

McLean, then aged in his late 50s, was New Zealand's foremost rugby journalist and on his third northern hemisphere tour with the All Blacks. He had started with the Herald after he left the army, and was soon Sports Editor. He was very much an Anglophile. His polished brogues, tweed jackets and Barbarians' tie gave him, as his biographer put it, "something of the air of an English gent." It was appropriate, therefore, that McLean championed running rugby as embodied in the Barbarians – and Saxton's Kiwis. Having often been a lonely voice in the wilderness crying for the Kiwis' brand of attacking rugby during the grim 50s and early 60s, the rugby played on Lochore's tour delighted him. As he put it in All Black Magic: "They played attacking rugby, all the way. Ain't that magic?"

Sports journalism comes in different forms. There are the hard-bitten down-among-the-punches boxing writers like George Plimpton and Norman Mailer, the elegant and socially engaged Cambridge men like cricket's Peter Roebuck, Neville Cardus's "wonderful story, never-mind-the-facts" school, and the racy "one book a tour" types, cutting and pasting their daily journalism. There are even the bizarre ones like the inventor of Gonzo journalism, Hunter S. Thompson. He secured the last interview of Richard Nixon's presidency by agreeing that they would only talk about (American) football.

McLean ranked with the best of them. He was a hard-working journalist and a prolific writer who developed his own unique style, weaving both classical references and colloquialisms through his articles and confidently and often elegantly deploying his opinions as facts. Like the erudite Cardus, the only other sports journalist to be knighted, he wrote while others reported.

McLean had shared the war-time experiences undergone by Saxton, Allen and so many others of his generation. Through the post-war years he was in tune with players and readers, accepted – sometimes reluctantly – as an authority on the game. While Jack Sullivan famously asked him "Whose side are you on?", he was close to mid-60s coach McPhail and particularly to Whineray. As his stature grew, McLean became something of an All Black insider, part of Whineray's card school. But when Whineray's era passed, his closeness to the centre of the team lessened subtly. Lochore was more cautious in widening the circle, and while McLean admired Allen as a coach, they were never friends. Players too were becoming less fond of journalists as the general press became increasingly concerned with their off-the-field activities.

By 1967, some of the team hadn't been born when McLean returned from the war. When he compared their tactics with those of (Generals) Montgomery and Patton, he was speaking to his own generation. While such references remained common currency among the wartime generation, they could baffle younger readers. Bill Davis remembers Vodanovich equating a coming game with Passchendaele and some of the younger players looking askance at talk of a battle they had never heard of. If McLean's performance reached its peak with this tour like so many of the players, perhaps that slightly greater distance from the team, as well as reporting on the style of rugby he most loved, brought out the best in him. There were no less than four books written about the 1967 tour, and while Wallace Reyburn's account has its merits, McLean's reigns supreme.

In his book on the 1966 Lions, McLean had noted a good speech given by my father at an after-match function. "Gee Dad, you're mentioned in Terry McLean's book," I said with some excitement, for I had never considered that my father could be so ennobled. Dad greeted the news with a notable lack of enthusiasm, glancing briefly at the book before returning to his task at hand. "What's he like?" I asked with childish insensitivity. "Bit full of himself," said my father in conversation-ending tone. That was the severest of critiques for a Scots Kiwi not given to swearing in front of children, except perhaps in Arabic honed in wartime Cairo.

There the matter rested until decades later when both men were dead and McLean's life found its biographer. Paul Lewis recounted how Major T.P. McLean had been a journalist on Napier's Herald Tribune in the 1930s, an Intelligence officer who served at Cassino and Trieste, and was later attached to J-Force. He was a man sure of his opinions and perhaps not given to suffering fools gladly. So to was Corporal, and sometime Sergeant C.J. McKay, who having been dux at Wellington College in 1939, had also been an Intelligencer in 22 Battalion, serving at Cassino, as a translator with Italian partisans in Trieste, and later with J-Force.

Back in New Zealand he'd become a journalist, including five years at the Herald Tribune.

They'd both been in the NZ Intelligence Services as well and I realised that there was a story there somewhere. Back in the war they must have known each other, and the officer and the NCO had fallen out. My father's military records revealed nothing of this. Even with the best of records the truth is never entirely there for the historian. Death erases some of the best stories, the facts that were never written. So in the end I can only imagine how these clones fell out. But the important point is not only that everyone in the close-knit world of New Zealand at that time had such stories linking them to others, but that there must have been many such hidden memories among that war-time generation, silently shaping opinion and opportunity.

Religion was a factor for that generation as well. Whether you were Protestant or Catholic mattered to people. Sid Going aside, however, it mattered little to Lochore's generation. The days when a good percentage of the All Blacks went to church on Sunday passed as New Zealand became a society where religion was a private matter.

A mixed band of British journalists also accompanied the team. Some were distinguished ex-players, others products of the public schools and Oxbridge. The players treated New Zealand journalists with a certain caution, or even a whispered "give them nothing". But the British journalists were regarded with much greater suspicion, not least by the New Zealand journalists. Reyburn, a skilled and often original writer, was born in New Zealand and began his journalistic career with the Herald. He even covered the 1935-36 All Black tour of the northern hemisphere for them before becoming a war correspondent with the Canadian forces and winning an OBE at Dieppe. But he had settled in England and was thus, as he put it, "Neither fish nor fowl". The title of his book on the tour, The Unsmiling Giants, was untrue as well as unkind but perhaps his publisher chose it, for there is much there that is fair as well as attractive.

But his comments on Bob Irvine and the New Zealand journalists are scathing. Accusing them of trying to run "A closed shop," he concludes that, "they were found to be not very rewarding company"! Reyburn had chosen his side.

By the standards of the 21st century, when a meaningless late-night scuffle becomes the centre of a media storm if a footballer is involved, the '67 All Blacks had an easy ride in the local press. In general the press still left their nocturnal activities unexplored, but by the standards of the time their off-the-field activities were nonetheless the focus of unprecedented media interest. There was a growing demand for human interest stories about the All Blacks, as well as for an explanation for the all-conquering nature of their rugby that might be found in their personalities and team culture. But for the players there was a big question mark over the emphasis the local press placed on rough play by the All Blacks as against rough play by their own sides. They considered that balance unfair. They could simply state "Budge Rogers" and rest their case. That case for the defence was to be brought forth anew a few weeks later.

One reason for the mixed press coverage was that New Zealand – and indeed world rugby generally – had not moved with the changing nature of the media. There was no real understanding of the need for public relations, no effort to influence or control the public debate over issues or to fill the growing demand for rugby-related 'news' with positive stories. Rugby officials were generally suspicious of the press. Instead of trying to get them onside with official views through background briefings and the time-honoured method of free drinks, they tended to treat them as a barely necessary evil and tell them as little as possible.

There were no regular press conferences on the '67 tour; journalists simply asked Saxton for news and comment whenever they had the chance to grab a minute with him. Saxton was certainly cooperative with the Press. He gave them access to coach and players and when they asked him a question he gave them a straight answer. That honesty was much appreciated. But the ad hoc release of information meant the journalists were constantly trying to grab a moment with the manager, desperate to prevent a rival from getting a story before they did. Regular press briefings were sorely needed, as was skill in media management. Those developments, however, came years later.

One example of the new journalism came in the Observer magazine, a weekend newspaper supplement popular with liberal and progressive readers including educated women. The Observer sent a woman, Mary Holland, who talked to a number of the All Blacks for an article oddly entitled "We are the Children of the Sun" – which suggests she had never spent a winter in Greymouth. The article was illustrated with several photos including a rear view of two naked All Blacks heading for the showers and a shot of Meads straightening his tie at a formal dinner. That was captioned with a description of him as having "The husky good looks of a Hollywood he-man". His teammates doubtless debated the definition of husky with him in their dressing-room banter, but it was a fair comparison. Holland was clearly aware that sex sells, and she contrived an ending with the implication that an All Black victory over Wales would give them the "traditional spoils" – a match with the "beautiful and ardent" Welsh women.

Her article was almost entirely positive about the All Blacks, if not the violent nature of the rugby game. Much of her attention was given to trying "To reconcile the bruising battering-rams on the pitch with the strong, sweet guys one meets off it...drinking sensible half-pints of bitter...diffident, courteous...fresh faced boys." It was an article that recommended the All Blacks to a new audience, introduced them as admirable guests and dedicated sportsmen from a slightly old-fashioned colony. Still there were limits. When the writer had asked Saxton for a lift back to the hotel on the team coach as the rain poured down in Leicester, Saxton explained that outsiders were never permitted on the coach. "I'm sorry, Mary," he told her, "the boys would revolt."

***

From Leicester, the team moved to Bristol for the match against the South of England. They went by train, a means of travel then slowly fading from rugby itineraries. Train travel meant card games– cards being how young men passed the time before Playstations and iPods. Mostly the game was euchre, with Meads, Tremain, Herewini and Nathan a regular foursome. But it varied. Allen preferred his old army game crib and 500 was starting its later rise to pre-eminence. Some of the players might have had a drink along the way. The Wednesday team was announced on the Saturday night or Sunday morning and those chosen had their last drink on the Saturday night, but there no restrictions on those not playing the next game. Players in the next game roomed together. Otherwise rooms were allocated according to certain aims – a young player with an old hand, forward with back, combinations on the field sharing off it, and so on. Just occasionally they might even get a single room if the hotel was short of doubles.

The All Blacks' performance against the Midlands had been disappointing. With no replacements allowed, the local side had only fourteen men after Hearns' injury in the fourth minute. Yet the All Blacks managed just one try against their weakened opponents, and had conceded one as well. There was an unusually long discussion before the next training session. One problem was the need to replace the injured Nathan in the tests. Williams and Kirkpatrick were given their chances to shine. Tremain had one flank locked down and the remaining contender, Wills, was hampered by injury and yet to play on the British section of the tour.

After an official welcoming party when they arrived in Bristol on October 30th, the team moved to the Grand Hotel where another formal evening awaited them. The following morning, bad weather forced their training run into the Bristol university gym. The playing fifteen had match training and the remaining players – the so-called 'dirt trackers' – played a vigorous game of basketball. Bristol's Lord Mayor stopped by, autograph hunters hung around, and later there was a session in the university pool. Saxton was happy that the players could at least "throw off some of that lethargy that hotel living sometimes brings." He added a quote he used more than once with journalists:"I like my men to be like sheepdogs – lean and hungry… and working!"

Except on match or travel days, players were generally free to amuse themselves after morning training, and with the crowded itinerary Lochore's men followed, there were fewer opportunities for sight-seeing compared to earlier U.K. tours. In Bristol, however, there was the chance to see the second prototype of the supersonic passenger jet Concorde at the British Airways Corporation factory, where there were still bomb craters left over from the war.

Otherwise players filled spare time with golf or bowls, or some task of their own – looking up a relative, a work contact, or perhaps a lady, writing letters, studying for exams, or doing some extra training. Then were those who simply relaxed, or enjoyed an afternoon drink and a game of cards. Indeed after Allen's training sessions, some players had an afternoon nap. Saxton trusted his men to know what was best for themselves.

For some players, off-duty time was an almost unwelcome distraction; they wanted to stay focused on rugby. Ian Kirkpatrick was one of them. Although a keen rugby fan who knew his rugby history back to the 'Originals', he'd only been playing senior rugby for two years and in April 1967 he was drafted into the army. That meant he could only play the "pretty average" standard of rugby at Burnham military camp, where he trained alongside Vietnam-bound regular soldiers. If the 1967 tour had been to South Africa and so left early in the year, he wouldn't have been considered. But in the course of the 1967 season, Kirkpatrick grew in stature and the trials confirmed he was ready to step up. It had, he said,

"Happened so quickly I was in dreamland – it was more than a dream come true."

For Kirkpatrick, knowing his rugby history meant that:

*You knew what you had to do, what it all meant – self-responsibility – and if you were given that opportunity then you'd think, "Well I won't be going out for a few [drinks]." It doesn't come to too many guys, so I was going to give it 100%...It was a great way of life, it suited me. I didn't have any doubt about what my attitude should be, it was pretty obvious.*

So while many players needed a break from the focus on rugby, Kirkpatrick avoided the social distractions and concentrated on soaking up rugby skills from the teachers around him. He was interested in history but tourism could wait. He was still raw, a player picked on potential as Lochore's understudy at the back of the scrum, but he could play on the flank as well. With the tour only a fortnight old, he was already building up muscle and impressing good judges with his performance on and off the field.

It wasn't that easy for everyone. Laidlaw later wrote that:

*An international tour is a most demanding experience, both emotionally and physically... Players have been known to wilt dramatically under the stress, and several personalities in my experience have been partly warped by the harrowing social pressures placed upon them.*

Yet others thrived on the touring life. Compared to working in the freezing works, McCormick found, "Being on tour was like a holiday for me", and Laidlaw's first book noted how:

*Of recent All Blacks Kel Tremain has probably been the best example of a personality temperamentally suited to the sort of social pressures which one must face [on tour]. The one and only Tremain seemed to thrive on constant recognition without any apparent signs of annoyance or frustration. His was the ideal image, the happy wisecracking popular figure epitomising the modest down-to-earth Kiwi who takes success in his stride without ever changing.*

Tremain was one of the great names of New Zealand rugby, famed for his try-scoring ability. Auckland born and schooled at Auckland Grammar, Tremain had studied agriculture at Massey and Lincoln. Originally a lock forward, he debuted for Southland in 1957 and won a place alongside Colin Meads in the 1958 NZ Junior side that toured Japan. After a season with Manawatu, he moved to Canterbury and made his All Black debut in 1959 in the second test against the Lions, playing on one flank with Meads on the other. Returning from the 1960 tour of South Africa, he was briefly in Auckland, where Allen picked him for three Ranfurly Shield matches before he returned to Canterbury. In 1961, he captained a NZ Universities side to California and British Columbia, then in 1962 he settled in Hawke's Bay. By 1967 he was at the core of the Bay's great Shield team, a dynamic and popular captain and automatic choice in the All Black test side.

Tremain occupied by right one of the jealously guarded places at the back of the bus, alongside Meads. He was liked, respected, experienced, and naturally situated at the core of the team, one of a small group of senior players who provided the key structure supporting Lochore's leadership. One other player, however, was of supreme stature.

'Pinetree', the other players called him, or sometimes just 'Piney'. He was Colin Earl Meads of King Country and New Zealand, and he had locked the All Black scrum for a decade. His stature as an All Black, which would grow to legendary proportions in the years to come, was already verging on the iconic. Other countries had star wingers, or 5-8ths. The All Blacks had a star lock forward. The epitome of the 80 minute player, Meads' strength and ruthless determination were at the heart of the forward's effort and his bulldozing running brought the crowd to its feet. When Meads was on the ball, the country was secure– all was as it should be. He was everything New Zealanders admired in a rugby player and a man.

For all his stature, there was never any doubt that Lochore was the captain and Meads a player. They had a friendship based on mutual respect. Neither had the ego to do anything but try to ensure the other was at their best. That relationship added immeasurably to the strength of the team.

Meads was the ideal rugby tourist, the perfect model for a young player. He "loved training" and enjoyed the opportunity that tours provided to train even harder than normal – for aside from match days and some travel days, the '67 team devoted most mornings to training. Meads went for an early morning run anyway. His off-the-field contribution to the tour was similarly immense. His biographer Alex Veysey quoted former All Black captain John Graham praising:

*The contribution he [Meads] makes to the side's corporate welfare... always the unofficial adviser, guide, assistant, leader of any All Black party outside the official leaders of the side. Meads does not seek this position, the rest of the players simply place him in it.*

Major remembered Meads as, "Quite unique in his ability to be one of the boys and not a star." The King Country man was, within himself, immensely proud of being an All Black. But he was humbled by that status and his pride was most manifest in a sense of duty, a belief that representing New Zealand meant upholding the highest standards of the game – respect for opponents and hosts among them. His legendary toughness on the field never manifested as arrogant or boorish behaviour off it. It was impossible to imagine Meads being involved in some sordid late night incident that turned into morning headlines. He stands as a definition of *mana*.

Of course, you had to be very foolish indeed to even think of provoking Meads, but there are very foolish people around. Meads off the field, however, had a way of disarming them, treating people and their opinions with respect and never forgetting he was representing his country. And when they got too foolish, or simply too boring, he could always use the team code, just scratch his ear and know that a teammate would see the secret sign and step in to confidently announce that Meads was wanted on the phone or in the team room.

Meads was in considerable public demand on the '67 tour, a demand he did his best to satisfy. Reyburn recorded that he "Signed an average of 100 autographs a day" and that Meads "never refused. 'You must do it for them', he said". Reyburn was clearly impressed with the King Country forward, careful to distinguish him from his criticisms of many others. "There were," he wrote, "surly ones among the 1967 All Blacks, ones you would call mean in the Western idiom, on the field and off. But by no stretch of the imagination was Meads one of them." Rather he was "mild-mannered", a "modest" and "considerate" man. That was Meads, accepting rather than seeking the spotlight and happiest as a team player immersed deep in rugby – its training, its playing, and its after-match relaxation.

Meeting Meads for the first time, I was struck by his quiet and considerate manner as much as by his physical presence, his solid frame with its eighteen-inch collars and size thirteen shoes. Perhaps meeting him was easier because Meads had not been one of my childhood heroes. He had just been a solid beam in a house I had grown up in, as much an ever present part of life as the 4 Square grocers and the Massey-Fergusson tractors. Colin Meads All Black, that was the way the world was then. Those certainties were what you built your world on when you were a child, for there were many things that were less certain, less secure, ever changing and untrustworthy in their transience.

In his late 70s Sir Colin Meads still lives a busy life, still finds himself in the spotlight. This is a man who has a fan-club as well as a family, whose collected sayings – "too many sweatbands, not enough sweat", for example – are part of rugby legend. Now he has interrupted his morning to help a passing rugby writer he has never heard of. Neither by word nor deed does he give any indication that he might have better things to do, or things he would rather do. He has sold the farm now but still lives in sight of the King Country hills. Pictures of children and grandchildren are scattered around. You sense that his life as both a farmer and a rugby player has been fulfilling, far more so than he could have imagined growing up in this rugged landscape. Then he was a shy country boy, one who'd never heard of things like surfing. Now he is famous, but thoughtful, genial and hospitable, and his wife Lady Verna makes wonderful chocolate tarts.

Meads has been interviewed often enough to know what interviewers need; his answers are straightforward, considered, and quotable. He had wanted to achieve things in life, to be a good farmer and a good rugby player and he surpassed those goals. Now he accepts the responsibilities that come with his greater achievements. There is a private Colin Meads, a family Colin Meads – but that Meads knows that by his deeds he has created a public Sir Colin Meads, an image that he must live up to, and indeed, which will outlive him. As long as rugby is played they will tell the legend of Meads, storming forward with the ball secure in one giant paw or ranging the King Country hills with a sheep under each arm.

His stature was formally recognised in 2009 when he was knighted. In a strange way, Meads had already been ennobled by his humble education–

it has given him a beguilingly self-effacing modesty, and wannabe tough guys will never know the dignity and charm that natural modesty gives a man. "I always regretted not having a good education," he readily admits when the conversation turns to sight-seeing. He was no great sightseer, but joined Whineray's team at Westminster Abbey where he drifted to the back as the "university boys" asked questions, for in such situations his lack of education left him feeling "inadequate". Just as he did on the farm, he began whistling softly to himself and was promptly told off by an attendant. Embarrassed, feeling he had somehow let the team down, the best rugby player on the planet retreated to the team bus to regret his failing. That was the measure of the man.

Meads is now a lion in winter. With Sir Edmund Hillary gone, he stands supreme as the representative of a culture and a way of life that has almost passed. The greatness of the '67 tour is the greatness of Meads, ruthlessly strong on the field, revelling in the running game, modest and straightforward off the field.

Meads was rested for the South of England match, the final regional game before the test match against England at Twickenham just three days later. It had been raining for days in Bristol, the pitch was a sea of mud and there was a howling wind blowing. The crowd were seething and hostile. This was tour rugby as it should be. Yet again the All Blacks ran the ball from the start. Their efforts were regularly halted by the referee, whose last encounter with the All Blacks had been overseeing Newport's victory over Whineray's men. Here he punctuated the match with 41 penalties. The Englishmen threw themselves into the game and provided a solid workout for the tourists, winning the tighthead count by three or four to one. But in the end they went down 3-16 to an All Black side that scored four tries – in today's currency, it would have been 3-24. Lochore, again leading from the front, was everyone's choice for the player of match. But there were differences over Kember's performance at fullback. McLean thought him "Magnificent" with his "complete composure in the face of spirited challenges." Reyburn, apparently watching a different Kember, found him "rather shaky".

Kember was in a difficult position, given the chance to establish himself as an All Black but playing in a position he had barely ever filled. He had no claim at all to be among New Zealand's best full-backs and heard a rumour that in cutting the squad from 31 to 30 the selectors had made that last-minute choice one between Williment and himself. He knew that most of the country would have rated Williment the better full-back and he wouldn't have argued against that judgement. All he could do was give his best.

Kember had grown up in a supportive family with close connections to national rugby administration. His father was an auditor for Wellington and the NZRU, while his godfather was none other than Tom Morrison. He remembered lunches as a young boy where he heard the inside stories of the 1956 series against South Africa, and Morrison telling him to learn to kick with both feet. A schoolboy star with Nelson College, he came into the Wellington and NZ University sides as a ninteen-year-old 1st 5-8 in 1965. The following year he was an All Black reserve for the series against the Lions. But he had a difficult start to the 1967 season and remembers that he saw his chances of national selection "slipping away". Off the field he was fully occupied, taking five units of a law degree and starting full-time work with a law firm. On the field, playing 2nd 5-8, he felt his form had fallen away.

But those whose judgement mattered continued to have faith in Kember. Wellington coach Bill Freeman "allowed me to be in my own space" and the national selectors kept picking him in the Juniors and in trials. Even so, he had only made it into the final trial when Davis was injured and probably only made it thanks to Allen's confidence in his abilities. Now, while no-one ever told him "You're fullback and goal-kicker", it became obvious that he was back-up to McCormick. He had only been a goal kicker for part of a season three years earlier with the

Under-20s and only had soft-toed boots. For the tour, he had a special pair made by O'Brian's in Christchurch that had a hard toe and a steel line through the base to add stability and strength. He had a lot to prove to the public, the team, and to himself. After just two games in the black jersey he had at least convinced the team and much of the public – who are quick to recognise commitment and determination from a player in a difficult situation.

The morning after the South of England match, Allen had the players out on the Clifton club ground for training at 9:15. The team for the test match against England was announced and with the game just two days away there was little time to prepare. The All Blacks had played just five games leading into that first test; Whineray's men had had thirteen games to get their combination right.

There were no real surprises among the fifteen chosen for the test, although there were six changes from the team that played the Jubilee Test. McCormick, already emerging as one of the stars of the tour, was at fullback in place of the absent Williment. Birtwistle, who had been injured for the Jubilee game, came in for Steel on the wing. With McLeod available again, Major stepped down. Laidlaw, another who missed the Jubilee Test with injury, replaced Going. That was a little less of a straightforward choice. Laidlaw was the established half-back, a senior player whose passing game was ideally suited to the sort of running rugby the team sought to play. But Going had been playing well and offered a considerable attacking threat. The competition between them would run and run.

There were two other changes. Kirton was selected for his first test in place of Herewini, a choice made on tour form. His years in the wilderness – post Newport disaster – were now over. As a player, he had improved enormously in that time and his incisive running made him a major attacking weapon for the All Blacks.

That left the selectors one important decision: the replacement for

Nathan. Williams was duly picked. He had been on the path for several seasons, he was the NZ Juniors' captain and was playing well. Picking him was also a tactical decision. New Zealand teams up to that time had almost invariably played left and right flankers. Players like Williams, smaller, faster men whose great skills were in pressuring the opposition's inside backs and snaffling the loose ball on the ground, had generally alternated with their fellow-flanker. But Williams often took the open-side in the Wellington team and Allen had experimented with him in that position against the South of England, with Kirkpatrick playing on the blind-side as he would do for most of his later career. The experiment was a success. For the rest of the tour, Williams played on the open-side at the scrum and at the back of the lineout. That condemned him to a lot of bruises, but his speed to the loose ball was an important part of the team's tactical approach. All Black teams ever since have used that specialised open side player, with men like Grahame Mourie, Michael Jones, and Richie McCaw making it one of New Zealand rugby's greatest strengths.

That Thursday afternoon after training, the All Blacks took the early afternoon train from Bristol Temple Mead to London Paddington and transferred to the Park Lane hotel again. The test players were already in their preparation mode. They don't call them 'test matches' for nothing. The All Blacks were about to be tested by England, and just one week later they would play the great northern rivals Wales. The success of the tour would, to a very large degree, depend on the results of those games.

\*\*\*

CHAPTER SIX

—

# "THIS IS MY ARENA"

At half-time in the first test match of the tour, the scoreboard read New Zealand 18, England 5. As the All Blacks took their five minute break on the Twickenham turf and sucked on the traditional slices of orange, they could rest content. Kirton had celebrated his first test cap with two tries. Laidlaw and Birtwistle had scored one apiece. Bob Lyold had crossed for England just before half-time, but so sublimely had the All Blacks played that the game was in danger of turning into a rout. Kirton's fellow-debutant, flanker Williams, was playing a blinder and the rest of the pack were superb. With MacRae and Davis supreme in midfield, the backline was moving the ball with a sharpness and skill that was everything Saxton and Allen had promised and more. The stunned English crowd could only applaud. On the other side of the world, New Zealanders rugged up against the night listened in wonder as Bob Irvine's commentary on Radio 2YA described the glorious carnage. No sooner had the game restarted than Malcolm Dick scored another try for the All Blacks. Five tries in 42 minutes at Twickenham was paradise gained. It was as good as it got. The new model All Blacks had arrived, and where better to announce it than the home of rugby?

When my mother had escaped the bomb sites and ration books of post-war England and arrived in New Zealand, they would ask her where in the Old Country she had come from? "Oh, a little place on the edge of London" she'd told them. "You wouldn't have heard of it, it's called Twickenham". And they took her ignorance of the rugby game to be dry humour, and they made her welcome.

Historically England weren't the best team in the world, nor even the second or third best. Only once had they beaten the All Blacks, and that had been largely due to an exiled Russian prince, Alexander Obolensky, whose brilliant tries against Jack Manchester's '35 side were woven into the fabric of English rugby legend. But the All Blacks had only scored six tries in four previous tests at Twickenham. Give the Old Country their due, they'd invented the game, or at least invented the mythology of inventing the game. That was good enough to make Twickenham the rugby ground, the Mecca of the game. Just as cricketers in Durban and Dungog and Dunedin grew up dreaming of playing at Lords, so too did rugby-men the world over dream of playing at Twickenham. John Major remembers dreaming that dream: it didn't even have to be in an All Black jersey, just to play there would be enough. He was on the reserve bench now, but he'd lived the dream when he'd trodden that famous turf for Whineray's men against Combined Services.

The best seats at Twickenham were the preserve of the aristocrats, the greatest white-jerseyed players of the past, lords of the manor with double-barrelled names, military men with gold braid on their caps, and former public schoolboys who were 'something in the city'. You wanted to beat England–you had to beat them–but victory wasn't enough to win their approval. To gain that, you had to win – or lose – with style, that indefinable touch of élan, of spirit and flair and grace under pressure. The Springboks never understood that, so they won games there not respect. But Saxton's Kiwis had understood that very British distinction and won immortality.

Yet the Kiwis' aura shone on the past. While there was still "a cache of extreme goodwill from the Kiwis", two decades had passed since then and the grinding All Black wins in '53 and '63 had begun to cloud the memories of the men high in the grandstands. Now Saxton had returned and the Kiwis were reincarnated. The upper echelons of Twickenham, the keepers of the sacred flame, smiled their benediction as the All Blacks ran the ball.

Then it all changed. For the 35 minutes until the final whistle blew the All Blacks laboured and threatened, but scored no more. In the end it was 23-11. The All Blacks had touched glory, held greatness in their hands for 45 minutes before England replied with spirit and determination. At the end of the day there was mutual respect in the handshakes. It had been a fabulous match.

Indeed it had been a match to set before a Queen, and so it had been. Queen Elizabeth was there with Prince Phillip, who was said to have a fair knowledge of the game. Before the match started, the teams lined up, the band of the Grenadier guards played its rousing preludes, and the red carpet – or at least a canvas approximation of a carpet – had been rolled out. Then the Queen, resplendent in a mustard-coloured coat, walked the red line and shook hands with the players and match officials. Lochore accompanied her, introducing each of his men in turn.

It was the first time a reigning monarch had greeted players on the Twickenham pitch. It had been raining for days, and there was still a hint of drizzle from the grey skies above. "Coming from Taranaki you'd know about the rain," she joked with Major. Knowing about farming and horses, she was at home with the players, who bowed or at least inclined their heads if they remembered protocol, or smiled nervously if they didn't. McCormick's thoughts flickered back to Linwood, its tall poplars bending in the crisp winds from the Southern Alps. Meeting the

Queen was an experience he'd remember. This was a reward for all those years of unstinting commitment to the game. And then there was Jack Hazlett, the photographers catching the moment when his giant hands took his sovereign's and therein, as they say, lies a tale.

Budge Rogers was a flanker in the England team that day, the very same Rogers who was responsible for Nathan being in the grandstand with his jaws wired up. A popular man was Waka and as whole-hearted a player as ever wore the black jersey. So it was that when a line-out broke up and the opportunity presented itself, Jack belted Rogers. Fair enough, it might be felt. The trouble was it was on half-way and right in front of the royal box. Now whether the Queen saw the punch or not is nowhere recorded. Perhaps she was reaching for her cup of tea or scratching the ears of her nearest corgi. But Saxton saw it and so did many others, and big Jack was gone. He'd played four of the first six games on tour, but he played just three of the remaining eleven. He never played another test.

Nothing ever seemed to be said, but the man who had replaced Whineray, an integral part of the 1966 forward pack that was probably the best the All Blacks ever fielded, now found himself on the outer. The legend is that Jack's punch had crossed the line that separated tough from rough, the line that Saxton and Allen had drawn in the sand. "No rough stuff," Allen always told them at the end of his team talks. "No rough stuff," Saxton had promised the world. Now, this was rugby and a frank exchange of views between front-rowers was one thing, so too was a sharp reminder of the limits of tolerance when delivered in the dark depths of a ruck. But a punch in the open and a punch in plain view of the Queen— that was high treason.

Nearly five decades later at his home about as far south as you can get in New Zealand without heading for Antarctica, I asked Jack if the legend was true. After all, there were those who judged that Hazlett was simply replaced by a better player. Jack paused for a while, marshalling his thoughts. I waited and his wife Anne watched as I ate more of her shortbread, made infinitely better than ordinary shortbread by the addition of oats. "It did happen," he said finally. "It was on the spur of the moment." And did Saxton or anyone else say anything to him about it, I asked? Again there was a long pause. I felt sorry for asking. Jack was plainly an honest warrior and, perhaps more so than any other member of the side I'd met, he clearly disliked talking about himself. "You know what you've done," he said finally. And that probably was it. Saxton and Allen drew their line in the sand and if you crossed it you were out. Nothing needed to be said and when you were sacrificed to that code you took it on the chin and you never whinged. It was the military way. It was the team way.

It was hard to tell how much Jack regretted that Twickenham moment. Certainly he paid a heavy price for it. But it wasn't done for personal gain, it was done for his teammates and their respect for him endures. That probably matters most to Jack. For all that he was proud of being an All Black, he seemed equally proud of his service to Drummond rugby club and to Southland. If he had burned with ambition to wear the black jersey then that desire remained well hidden. He came from a well-known southern family. An uncle had worn the national colours in the 1920s and become a renowned racehorse owner, another had been killed in Italy during the war and his father had served as High Commissioner in Canberra. There was more to Hazlett than just national rugby, there was family and club and Southland.

There was more than rugby to one of the English players as well. Bob Lloyd was one of rugby's great shooting stars. He had been at Cheltenham College with Danny Hearn and scored against New Zealand in the Midland's game when Hearn was cruelly injured. Now in his debut test, the speedy centre had scored both of England's tries and he would add another for the Barbarians at the end of the All Blacks' tour. Just 24 years of age, he looked set for a long career in the white jersey and was duly selected for the 1968 Lions tour of South Africa. But this was the amateur age and he withdrew to complete his engineering degree. While he toured the Far East with England in 1971, Lloyd never played test rugby again. He worked in Hong Kong for more than 30 years, finally getting to see the Lions in 2013 when they played the Barbarians there.

English rugby takes its role and its traditions seriously. After the honourable defeat to a superior foe, it presented its spoils. There were over 300 guests for the post-match dinner at the Park Lane Hilton. The Grenadier Guards again provided the music before the formalities began with a toast to the Queen. Lochore jotted down notes on the menu as he listened to the RFU President toast his team, and emphasised New Zealand's "new approach" in his reply. In turn, Saxton proposed the toast to the England team. After more speeches, the Dean of St Pauls Cathedral, who happened to be a New Zealander and an ex-22 Battalion man at that, said Grace in Maori. Ironically though, the three Maoris in the '67 side, Nathan, Herewini, and Going, were all on the sideline that day.

So too was the Tongan-born Fijian, Arthur Jennings, who better late than never had just become a New Zealand citizen. He'd never bothered to get a Kiwi passport, travelling to England with the All Blacks on his Fijian passport! But at the reception given for the team by the New Zealand Ambassador, they took the big man to one side, administered the necessary oath and handed him his new passport.

A decent version of the ubiquitous 60s wine, Liebfraumilch, helped to wash down the classic 60s vol-au-vents before the roast beef – or Caneton d'Aylesbury Röti à l'Orange as the menu had it. There was vintage port and fine Drambuie to follow, and cigars in special presentation boxes, black for the visitors, white for the home team. After all, this was a time when Rothmans sponsored the most popular tour guide booklet, although most of the All Blacks took the cigars as souvenirs rather than smoking them.

For those of the team who fancied less hallowed halls and less august company after the conclusion of the formalities, there was the city of

London to enjoy. That night, David Frost observed, "London seemed full of New Zealanders," for there were now several parties of supporters accompanying the side. There were also the itinerants of Earls' Court and Shepherds' Bush. Celebrating an All Black victory at Twickenham brought them out of every basement flat for miles around and many a pub landlord grew much richer by morning.

The Grace given in Maori had been a special gesture. There had been another more spectacular gesture to the Maori side of New Zealand rugby earlier. The All Blacks had performed a pre-match haka, as they would at all the test matches. The tradition had begun long ago, with the remarkable New Zealand 'Native' side. Made up primarily of Maoris on a privately arranged British tour in 1888, they performed a haka before their games as an added attraction for spectators. The All Blacks followed suit from their earliest tours, although they almost never performed it at home games. It was even rolled out before some of their games in South Africa in 1928, although later diplomatically avoided as apartheid strengthened its hold there. Nor, Keith Quinn records, was it performed on the northern hemisphere tour in 1935-36 because the ultra-conservative English RFU of the time considered it a publicity gimmick!

Saxton's Kiwis revived the tradition and even performed it in New Zealand. But usually the haka was only used as a gesture to foreign crowds, who always loved it. It was a big part of their experience of seeing the All Blacks and set the grandstands buzzing with anticipation. But it was nothing like the modern haka. Most players didn't take it seriously and Kiwi expat Reyburn called it "Ragged, entirely lacking in… precision and co-ordination… a third-rate seaside revue." As Sam Strahan recalled, "In retrospect, it was a disgrace." Meads too is among the many who now feel it should have been given more respect. But at the time he was content to use it as part of his warm-up while his opponents watched and shivered. The hefty Muller, no-one's idea of a Kiwi Fred Astaire, remembers that he used to joke that Allen had asked him to lead it.

Williams enjoyed it– it was "A bit of New Zealand"–but another player admitted to having disliked the haka because it spoiled his concentration for the opening minutes of the game.

Rugby historians Chester and McMillan reveal that the 1913 All Blacks in North America practiced the haka daily, while photos show that the 1924 'Invincibles' gave a polished performance of a haka they wrote especially for that tour. But in 1967 there were a couple of run-throughs early in the tour and that was that. The players mostly just watched each other as they tried to synchronize the jump at the end – to mess that up was a ticket to a charge at the team's Sunday court session. They struggled to remember the words. Even Herewini forgot them when he was leading the haka at the West Wales game and called out, "Hey Pinetree, how's it go?"

The haka used on tour was the classic Ka Mate, Ka Mate haka of Te Rauparaha, surely the most majestic poetry to emerge from the Land of the Long White Cloud. The Ka Mate haka was used in the war and by Saxton's Kiwis. But in contrast to today, in the 50s and 60s it was rarely seen in New Zealand outside of Maori cultural performances. Ralph Love taught it to the '67 team with a little help from Herewini and Nathan, who had led the haka when it was performed at the tests on Whineray's tour. They offered a translation of it, although somehow the program for the South of England game printed an entirely different haka, along with an obviously rough English translation. The fact was the haka was a sideshow, a fading echo of Maoridom to stir the crowd. Not until the All Blacks were touring Argentina in 1985 did it change. Wayne Shelford and Bay of Blenty rake Hika Reid get the credit for demanding that it be done right or not at all. It was their demand for proper respect for tradition that began the theatrically orchestrated performances of the modern era. But then they did have a coach on that tour who could both move with the changing times and respect tradition, a coach named Brian Lochore.

\*\*\*

The All Blacks enjoyed a leisurely Sunday after the England game, with the usual court session in the morning. Not until the evening did they board the train to Cardiff where they were delayed on the Welsh border by a train breakdown ahead of them. That gave the veterans of Whineray's tour a chance to chance to ask the more naive of the new men if they had their passports handy, and to laugh at their ensuing panic. Then they were in Cardiff with great Welsh players of the past there to greet them and remind them of what they faced. They were in for a week of deep immersion in Welsh rugby culture. A week in a land where rugby ranked as it did in New Zealand, far above all other sports. And the Welsh could play!

In that era, Wales posed a genuine threat to New Zealand rugby's status. In the first week of November 1967 the record books showed the two nations had met on the rugby field on five occasions. Wales had won three of those games. Whineray's men had eked out a 6-0 win in a try-less encounter four years earlier, but New Zealand was still in deficit. A betting man would have to give the Welsh a decent chance of beating the All Blacks.

If South Africa were New Zealand rugby's greatest opponent, the Welsh were a close second. Their 3-0 victory over the 'Originals' had started a rivalry that echoed down the ages. At the heart of that was the controversy over whether the All Black centre Deans had, or had not, scored a try midway through the second half. The referee, dressed in street clothes and far behind play ruled that Deans had grounded the ball short of the line. New Zealanders were adamant Deans had crossed the line and been pulled back by the Welsh defenders. The incident gave every succeeding game between the two sides a special edge. As a talking point between the respective spectators, it had the great merit of being impossible to resolve, except perhaps by pointing to the scoreboard. The 1924 'Invincibles' had revenged that defeat with a magnificent 19-0 victory, but that game hadn't been played at Cardiff Arms Park – which only added to the lustre of that famous ground. In the 1935 and 1953 tests played there, Wales had prevailed again. Those who had watched the games spoke in awed terms of their glorious intensity and the unique atmosphere of the Arms Park, where the fervour of the Welsh forwards was only matched by the pre-match singing of the crowd. To hear that massive chorus inspiring the Welsh team to greater heights was a highlight of any player's career.

It wasn't just a matter of beating Wales. The regional sides posed a real threat as well. Swansea, where the All Blacks would play West Wales on the Wednesday night, beat the 1935 All Blacks and held them to a draw in 1953. Cardiff in '53 and Newport in '63 had beaten them as well.

Allied to the pressure of history was the pressure of the present. The All Blacks were the centre of attention. Crowds milled around their hotel hoping for a glimpse of the warriors from down-under. In truth, Welsh rugby was at a low ebb in 1967. Their game was still rocked by the defection to the professional code of star 5-8 and 1966 Lion David Watkins. Several other leading Welsh players were injured and Welsh supporters oscillated between defiance and pessimism. But they could dream. Rain was predicted for the test, which they were sure would suit them. That primeval Celtic passion they called the *hwyl* was building. If the Welsh nation could will its men home, then it would win at a canter.

Selecting the team for the mid-week game against West Wales in Swansea on Wednesday, the 8th of November, was complicated by the fact that the Welsh test followed on the Saturday. The selectors wanted to rest as many as possible of the test team. In the end only Tremain, and Meads who was made captain in the absence of Lochore and McRae, were included from that side. It meant a team light on experience. Eight of the All Blacks picked had debuted on the tour, including Wills playing for the first time since Canada. Most significantly, Gray was fit again and included in the front row. That was grounds for general rejoicing.

Whatever the merits of the other prop forwards on tour, Gray was acknowledged as the best in the world. He was one of those rare front-rowers equally skilled on either side of the scrum. Quick, mobile, and technically adept against both tall and short opponents, Gray enjoyed enormous respect for his "awesome" abilities, his "integrity on the field" and indeed his "ruthless" approach to the game. He was, Meads remembers, "The strongest man I ever put a shoulder on." In practice his strength meant that the breakaways and then Meads and the rest of the tight five "could get out of the scrum a fraction earlier than with other props." Those fractions of a second mattered in test matches.

A team man yet not afraid of his own company, Gray did not fit the stereotype of the prop forward. Off the field he was deep: a reader of books, a thinker about issues such as South Africa and the development of New Zealand–China relations. There was an intensity to Gray, a focus that few could match and a sense that he would not fade back onto the farm when his rugby years ended. That he later moved towards politics came as no surprise to his former teammates. For now, they were just hoping he would come through Wednesday's game and reclaim his place in the front row against Wales.

Like all visiting rugby teams, the All Blacks stayed at the Angel hotel, just down the road from Cardiff Arms Park. Such was the Angel's status in the rugby world that the Welsh team were also booked in there. So at the end of the week when the hosts moved in, the teams rubbed shoulders in the elevators and warily nodded "Good mornings" over the breakfast plates.

On the Monday morning after training at the Cardiff University College grounds, the team were guests of the Cardiff Rotary Club for lunch. The speakers included New Zealand Rotarian John Sinclair, who was leading an All Black supporters' tour. Sinclair, a war veteran of the Fleet Air Arm and a Palmerston North businessman, was an Anglophile Kiwi who styled his tours 'Goodwill' visits. He had already made his mark on the social side of rugby, having pioneered the idea of New Zealand schools adopting visiting international rugby teams. Each participating school was allocated a player or two and the pupils would compile scrapbooks of 'their' player's tour. So successful was the scheme that it was adopted by schools in Britain. They closely monitored the members of Lochore's team allocated to them and presented the players with scrapbooks at the end of the tour. Their efforts were much appreciated by the players and most of the All Blacks managed to visit the schools that had adopted them.

For the then tidy pre-decimal sum of £639, Sinclair's party spent 60 days on a world tour that included tickets to most of the All Blacks' games. They were one of four groups following the team, the biggest of which were organised by the New Zealand Truth and Sunday Times newspapers. In all there were about 400 supporters on organised tours. Sinclair's group, limited to 36 participants, had certain privileges. At times they stayed in the same hotel as the players and at one destination the tour brochure suggested that, "You may like to sit around the hotel talking to the All Blacks." Another attraction mentioned in that publicity was that businessmen could make a few calls in the UK that would enable them to claim some of the tour cost as a tax deduction. In an account of the tour in The Diners' Club of New Zealand Digest early in 1968, Sinclair proudly noted that "One enterprising supporter of his own business as well as the All Blacks arranged $60,000 worth of export contracts."

In organising the tour, Sinclair was helped by an old friend of his: Palmerston North Boys' High School teacher and rugby coach Ian Colquhoun. He had played cricket for New Zealand and come close to All Black selection as a member of Cavanagh's Otago side in the '40s. The "Goodwill" tour saw itself as just that: a chance to foster relations with the Old Country, a chance "to go Home with the All Blacks." Their paths often overlapped with Lochore's men. Both tour leaders were friends of Saxton, indeed Sinclair later organised reunions of the Kiwi side which he had seen play. Colquhoun might have had mixed feelings though – he'd played for Wellington in their vigorous victory over the Kiwis.

Sinclair was an enthusiastic character, a self-appointed rugby publicist full of ideas and energy as a tour leader must be. In the manner of the time he waxed lyrical about the joys of flying "In the caressing blue interior of the Boeing Clipper." He was less impressed by both Montreal's "sprawling, uneven" EXPO and by his encounter with the hippies of Haight-Ashbury. "A dirty grubby lot," he recalled. "I found I was scratching myself just looking at them." He found their 'free love' philosophy, "Just pitiful...they seemed to me just indolent escapists." He was clearly much happier to be "home". "We don't see ourselves as South Pacific tourists going to Europe," he told his hosts. "New Zealanders simply say that they are going Home."

Sinclair would have made a fine journalist with his gift for a turn of phrase. He described Muller "Stomping about like something carnivorous" and how, "the forwards crashed and forced their way through opposing bodies like a downhill panic flight through bracken." His summing up of McCormick's character was particularly quotable. The fullback "Corner-flagged like a rat up a pipe" and would "go down in front of an overnight express and be the first to his feet to help with the derailment."

What the All Blacks made of their travelling supporters tended to vary. After all their ranks included men like Jack Finlay and 1950-51 All Black captain Peter Johnstone, whose opinions were valued. Yet while individuals might be popular, the mass of supporters – the 'heavies' as they were known – could be less welcome. There was only so much time you could enjoy chatting with them about their cousin Joe who once played against them years ago. But Sinclair and Colquhoun, like Love, played a useful role fulfilling engagements for which the team, with their cramped itinerary, could find no time. At Saxton's request, they visited Rugby School where the game was founded, and Hagley Hall in Worcestershire to pay their respects to the former New Zealand Governor-General,

Viscount Cobham. They visited more than 30 schools in total and at many of them Colquhoun coached their rugby teams. In Edinburgh they were joined by Allen and eight of the All Blacks on a school visit. Sinclair described how Meads stole that show.

> *Asked to speak, [Meads] ponderously and hesitantly got to his feet. There was a sudden hush, an almost ominous quiet. Then in a deep, resonant voice like an exploding tree stump, he said, "Don't smoke...if you want to be fit...don't smoke." It...must have been worth 5000 cancer campaigns. Every schoolboy who had ever had a puff looked sheepish and you could almost see his shoes [stubbing] out imaginary fags.*

In Wales, Sinclair's group kept alive the legend of 1905, delivering a letter from 'Originals' star Billy Wallace to Willie Llewellyn, the last survivor of the Welsh team from that famous day. Terry McLean caught up with the old man too. In a reminder that there is nothing new under the sun, McLean quoted him as saying that, "You can forget most of the nonsense about our being a great side. I will say this though: we did the simple things well."

There were more sombre tasks as well. Along with a number of the All Blacks, the supporters visited the village of Aberfan. A year earlier a mining slag heap had collapsed and buried a school, killing 116 children as well as 28 adults. They marched too in the Remembrance Day parade in Cardiff and on a side trip to Italy visited the war graves at Monte Cassino, where so many New Zealanders had died in battle. They were, in the main, men of that generation. They were the last New Zealand supporters' tour that could, so explicitly and unselfconsciously, think of themselves as going 'Home'. Britain was about to join the Common Market and cut New Zealand loose in the real world of searching for export markets. As they were cut free of their heritage, New Zealanders increasingly began to regard that land not as Home, but as Away. Signs of that change were apparent in 1967. Men like Sinclair and McLean found a very different Britain to the one they knew in the war, or even as recently as the Whineray tour. Already there were hints that the British found New Zealand's attachment to them just a little quaint.

When the All Blacks next toured the UK in 1972-73, the old closeness between the nations was largely gone. So too was any closeness between the All Blacks and the supporters' tours. Their manager even wrote privately to John Sinclair complaining at any published implication that his All Blacks would attend supporters' functions. But there was a fortunate postscript to the 1967 "Goodwill" tour: another, if tangential, legacy of Lochore's men. Back in New Zealand, John Sinclair offered his suitcase full of tour souvenirs to Tom Morrison for display at the NZRFU. "We don't have a cabinet," Morrison told him. "Go away and start your own museum John. It's not our role to display memorabilia." So Sinclair did just that, and the New Zealand Rugby Museum in Palmerston North today is the result of the efforts he, and others he inspired, made.

***

There were, by the standards of the day, plenty of All Black supporters in the crowd of 40,000 packed into the St. Helen's Ground in Swansea. They at least were confident. There were several internationals in the West Wales line-up, including Llanelli's 1966 British Lion Delme Thomas. They even had an official coach, something revolutionary in British rugby at the time. But Thomas wasn't the legend he became when Llanelli beat the 1972-73 All Blacks and no-one in New Zealand had heard of coach Carwyn James then. His triumphs in 1971 were far over the horizon.

The All Blacks travelled from their Cardiff hotel to Swansea where their coach was escorted slowly through the sea of fans crowding the street. The traffic was jammed up for miles around. Allen chain-smoked nervously. Whineray's men had lost their first game in Wales. His team, and it was very largely his reserve team, was on trial.

With the Welsh test coming up on the Saturday, there was another problem facing the All Blacks. McCormick had torn a rib-muscle. He'd damaged it earlier in the tour but ignored it. Then at training on the Monday he aggravated the injury while, of all things, hauling himself over a fence to retrieve the ball during a warm-up soccer game. Now he couldn't straighten up and the doctors had told him the injury could take six weeks to heal. McCormick reckoned four days would do it. Allen told his fullback he needed him on the Saturday. But McCormick was in agony.

The crowd were in fine voice before the kick-off at St. Helens and McLean described how they ignored the band's timing and sang the Welsh anthem Land of Our Fathers at their own august pace. Reyburn was content to simply award the Pontardulais town band the title of "Most Entertaining". This was Wales and no country has ever combined rugby and song so well, even if the French have the most stirring anthem and the Scots now have the best song.

For most of the local side it was the biggest game of their lives. From the kick-off, they hoed into the All Blacks. Their half back and captain, Clive Rowlands, a former international famed for his tactical kicking, displayed all his old skills. After just ten minutes the young Swansea fullback Doug Rees put his team 6-0 up with his second penalty, this one from inside his own half. The All Blacks were struggling. And then came Thorne.

He'd had a comparatively quiet tour up to that point had Thorne, at least from the public point of view. There'd been a try on debut in Canada, then he'd played the Midlands game without particularly distinguishing himself. Within the team he was living up to his irrepressible image, training hard, studying hard and living hard. Although there were plenty of doubts, a few good judges were already impressed with Thorne. In the trials, McCormick flattened him in a crashing tackle, sending Thorne sprawling onto the ground clutching an injured arm. McCormick then leant over the wounded Thorne and growled, "Get up if you want to be an All Black." The young Thorne promptly got up and staggered back into position. That was good enough for McCormick. But Thorne was a young player, a raw talent taken on tour with the future in mind. Allen rated him, but Davis was the reigning centre. Thorne's opportunities, like those of other raw talents such as Smith, were probably going to be limited. So if he got an opportunity he needed to take it.

Thorne was confident he'd get his chance and confident he would take it. Photographer Mike Tubberty mentioned to Thorne that he wanted a cover photo of the All Blacks in action. Thorne told him to take up a position behind the posts and wait. 27 minutes into the game, Thorne ran onto a long straight pass from Herewini that missed out Cottrell. He was at least 70 yards from the opposition line. Thorne remembers he didn't think – "The moment you think in rugby you're gone" – he just ran, beating man after man on his way to a swan dive between the posts at the other end of the field. The All Blacks had a new threat, a genuine game-breaker. No-one had looked like stopping him. He was in the zone, that sublime space in which the successful conclusion of artistic expression is inevitable. Looking back on it he mused that it was as if, "Time stopped. I got into space and I was in a bubble. I can't explain it. I was free. [It was] a unique experience."

It was also an experience that showed the team that Thorne could deliver. Not that Fred Allen was going to seem impressed. He had a team ethic to foster. He told Thorne in the bluntest of terms that he should have passed the ball. Whether he quite believed that is another matter.

There was another young All Black out there that day who gained a glimpse of the sublime beyond the mundane. Fullback Kember, going down on the ball in front of his own line, was concussed. He played on, as McLean put it, "With exemplary courage, entirely from memory." Within moments of recovering his consciousness, the local side scored from a mistake he made, yet before that he had played superbly. Freed from the self-doubt of his conscious mind, his natural skills came to the fore. After the game when they checked him out at the hospital, Gray congratulated him on his performance, joking that he'd have to give Kember a whack on the head before every game. A seed was planted in his mind. How come, he wondered, "You could play so much better when you weren't conscious of what you were doing?" What if you could call in the freedom of the bubble at will?

With only fifteen minutes to go, the All Blacks were still behind. In the end the ability, fitness, and experience of men like Meads and Tremain was too much for the determination of the local side. They set up another try for Thorne and Going scored another to seal it at the end. 21-14 it finished, but it was a bit closer than that.

Swansea had produced a classic tour game. An unsung local side throwing everything they had against the tourist's reserve side in front of home supporters roaring them on. In the crowd, boys were inspired, men invigorated. This was why they played tour games, they were enduring local landmarks. 'Remember that tackle you made against the All Blacks boyo?' And Swansea was a hospitable place too. The menu for the after-match function at the Dragon hotel was in English and between the contemporary standards of vol-à-vents and sherry trifle there was Welsh roast beef.

Saxton got a particularly warm welcome. On Easter Monday in 1946, shortly after the Kiwi tour, he had accepted the honour of an invitation to captain Swansea against a Barbarians side that included Fred Allen. The programme for the West Wales game had a photo of his team that day, with Saxton and two other members of his Kiwi side proudly dressed in the white jerseys of Swansea. There were still plenty of locals who remembered the day.

Back in Cardiff, the build-up to the Test moved into top gear. Hazlett's demotion to allow Gray back in the team was the main talking point, except that those who knew what was going on weren't talking. There were no other changes in the side, though McCormick remained a major doubt. Wales, however, had six new caps and while their young halves Gareth Edwards and Barry John were considered promising, they were then unproven.

The All Blacks trained on the Thursday and the Friday. No-one was in any doubt as to the importance of victory on the Saturday. But the new style of play required a good victory and if the All Blacks could win at Cardiff by running the ball, that style could transform the New Zealand game.

The All Blacks attended the Lord Mayor's dinner at Cardiff Castle on the Thursday night. That was the social highpoint of the Welsh section of the tour. At least for the 'dirt-trackers'– those not playing the next game – it was a good night. The breathalyser might be cutting a swathe through the social traditions of the land but the Welsh were generous hosts and the All Blacks didn't have to drive home. Such dinners in Wales always contained a welcome portion of former internationals among the invited guests. Great names of the past like Bleddyn Williams and Jack Mathews were there to repay hospitality they had received as members of the 1950 Lions side in New Zealand. Paid up members of the international rugby fraternity were naturally easier company than even the most well-meaning and entertaining dinner-companion from other worlds.

In 1967, the Welsh nation was on a cusp. It was still producing megastars in the field of entertainment; names like Tom Jones, Shirley Bassey, and Richard Burton were famous the world over. Britain was still proud of its National Health Service, prodded into being by that most Welsh of politicians, Aneurin Bevan, a former miner. Wales still had its coal mines and Britain's Labour Prime Minister Harold Wilson still shared beer and sandwiches at Number 10 Downing street with

Miner's Union bosses. Clouds were gathering on the horizon but the future still looked secure. The programme for the Welsh test featured a now poignant full-page advertisement for the National Coal Board Mining Apprenticeship Scheme. It was opposite the pen portraits of the Welsh team, illustrated with a photo of a smiling boy. The caption read: "He's not worrying about leaving school – His future is right here in Wales." The advertisement promised apprentices full pay while training, generous holidays, and sick pay as well as a good wage.

The biggest problem in the Celtic nation seemed to be that their rugby team wasn't at its strongest: it had lost four of its last five games. It was actually entering the doldrums and by the time it regained strength with the great side of the 1970s the rest of the Welsh culture of choirs and mines was in terminal decline. The great days were actually behind Wales. But in 1967 the All Blacks had only to look at the records books to be reminded of the severity of the test they were facing.

Cardiff, a true rugby city, was seething with rugby supporters on the Saturday, its bars overflowing. The passionate fervour of the Celts grew by the hour. When torrential rains arrived, the headline writers kept the phrase 'Celtic storm' at their fingertips. Engelbert 'Ten Guitars' Humperdinck was in town as well, but he wasn't a rugby fan and the All Blacks weren't in concert-going mode, even for the man who sang their nation's unofficial anthem. There would be other chances to catch him in the future. Nearly five decades later when I flew into Wellington to catch up with some of Lochore's men, Engelbert was playing a concert there that night. It seemed like a good omen.

When they left the hotel for the short journey through the rain to the Arms Park, the All Blacks snuck out a sidedoor of the hotel to avoid the crowds. Then in their dressing room under the stand, the team breathed the liniment and prepared themselves for battle. The injured McCormick was strapped up and ready to go. To inspire his side, Allen conjured up the memory of Kiwi soldiers at the Battle of Alamein. They could hear the crowd outside filling the stadium with their anthems, roaring out their songs oblivious to the driving rain and howling winds. They say 99% of sporting success comes from the head. Here, with history and weather massing against them, the All Blacks might have entertained a fatal moment of doubt. It was time for another Fred Allen masterstroke.

Bill Davis went to Parkvale primary school in Hastings, which in the 1950s had a rusting old army tank abandoned just down the road from it. I was a few years behind him and the only lesson I remember is the one I learned on my second day there when someone stole my precious collection of plastic pirates. Davis was in the 1st XV at the High School by then and already had his dreams. In the early hours of a February morning in 1954, he and his father had listened on the radio to the Cardiff crowd singing Now is the Hour at the conclusion of the British section of the 1953-54 All Black tour. "That will be me," he told his Dad.

At eighteen, he was playing centre for Hawke's Bay and scoring eight tries in his first 10 games. The Almanack named him one of its Promising Players of the Year for 1961. He dislocated a knee in '62 and was told he'd never play again, but he did. It just meant he couldn't sidestep. He still had swerve and pace and a convincing dummy pass. Above all he had vision; he was a creative attacking three-quarter at a time when New Zealand rugby produced very few men with such skillsets. Davis was schooled in the necessary discipline by men like Ingpen and "Gentleman Jack" Finlay and being bright and cheerful by nature he made friends wherever he went. They took him on Whineray's 1963-64 tour as a young winger after he'd been pushed out of the Bay centres by the arrival there of Ian McRae. He played fifteen times on that tour but didn't establish himself. Nor did he find much scope as a Whineray winger. Today he laughs as he remembers thinking "Why did I train so hard – you only saw the ball in the last ten minutes."

Davis drifted out of the All Blacks but the extra ten yards of space that backs gained under the new rules of 1965 suited his style of play.

Then, with McRae moved to 2nd 5-8, Davis moved back to centre for his province. The devastating combination of the two was at the heart of Hawke's Bay's Ranfurly Shield attack, they also became firm friends and Allen soon united them in the national side.

Davis was the kind of man who responded to team-talks. They "Fired me up," he remembers. Still as a newly-established international, he feared Allen's caustic criticisms. "When Fred said you went around the corner post, you went around the corner post," is how he puts it. But there at Cardiff, in just his third test match, in the intensity of the dressing-room moments before the biggest game of his life, Allen turned to Davis. "Billy," he said, "We're going to make you the king-pin of our attack today."

When they ran out onto the field to the roar of the crowd, Davis knew, "This is my arena." Sport is about confidence and Allen had proved his mastery of psychology. "Fred knew which string to pull," Davis reflects. "I'd have died for New Zealand that day...there was no such thing as fear." At a crucial point in the game, soon after half-time, McCormick tried a long-range penalty attempt into the wind and Davis gave chase. The kick fell just short of the posts and into the arms of John Jeffrey, a Welsh forward making his debut. Jeffrey dropped it and then panicked as Davis came onto him, desperately trying to shovel the wet ball back to the men behind him. Davis grabbed it and scored. Game over.

At the end of it all Fred Allen, in his polished brogues and dress trousers, rushed out onto the field to embrace his men. He was oblivious to the rain and the mud. Allen had played outside Saxton at Cardiff Arms when the Kiwis beat Wales, now his All Black side were victorious in the 'must-win' game of the tour. All the emotional shades of relief and delight were, for a brief moment, out on display. For all his faults, Fred lived for the team. He was still celebrating at six the next morning when, with a bottle of whiskey in one hand and a jug of milk and two glasses in the other, he woke McCormick up. McCormick kindly helped him toast their victory.

It wasn't a great game, except in as much as any victory over Wales back then was a great game in New Zealand eyes. Some of the old hands like Sinclair and McLean felt the standard of the singing had declined from the Good Old Days while the volume and hostility of the crowd had greatly increased. Perhaps the singing had never been as good as the last time, in which case it must have been pretty good back in '05, for the newcomers still found it spellbinding. Nor was McLean impressed when the local constabulary grabbed a young man who had run onto the field to celebrate John's dropped goal, took him under the grandstand and in full view of various onlookers, knocked him to the ground and gave him a kicking. But the British police of Dixon of Dock Green had always been more myth than reality. A young Kiwi called Blair Peach discovered that a decade later and died of a fractured skull from being in the wrong place at the hands of the wrong police.

There wasn't as much running as they had hoped. But the rain had poured down throughout the game, the field was muddy and there were 32 penalties awarded, so running rugby was hard to play. Instead, the All Blacks had given a superb exhibition of fifteen-man wet weather rugby and totally outplayed their willing opponents. On a dry day, several journalists observed, the Welsh would have been heavily beaten. Instead it had been a reasonably tense match. Up in the main grandstand, Nathan had shouted encouragement with such vigour that he sprung the wires holding his broken jaw together. Wales had won the toss and elected to play into the driving wind. When they held the All Blacks to 8-0 at half-time and Barry John dropped a goal early in the second half, the crowds found full voice. But then Davis scored and New Zealand were always far enough ahead on the scoreboard to survive a Welsh comeback.

There was little consolation for the Welsh. Despite his dropped goal, Barry John was pressured throughout by Tremain and Williams and there was precious little on offer from the other Welsh backs. Their forwards offered plenty of fight, literally so in the opening salvoes, though they were eventually well bested. Several times in the second half their pack was pushed back embarrassing distances as the All Black scrum took complete control. The psychological effect was enormous.

Yet Wales had missed numerous goal-kicking opportunities. In the end, their captain Norman Gale gave up on his kickers and landed a penalty himself, probably the only time a hooker has done so in a test. Then too Stuart Watkins, one of the better Lions in 1966, would have scored a try late in the game but for McCormick's incredible strength in defence. He held the Welshman up to prevent the touch-down despite the pain it must have generated in his wounded ribs. Ultimately the game was a tale of chances taken and chances lost. As for John Jeffrey, suffice to say he never played for Wales again. There are rumours that he moved to North Korea.

It had been a team victory for the All Blacks, yet it was hard not to single out McCormick. Even on the Saturday morning there were grave doubts that he could play. Those doubts weren't held by McCormick. He discovered that if his ribs were strapped up too tightly to move he could still run and he could still breathe. That meant he could still play rugby. McCormick didn't just have a reputation for being tough. He was tough. That was why they picked him, and that was why he played. Wales also had an injured full-back trying to get fit for the test, a young man called Keith Jarrett who'd scored nineteen points on debut against England the year before. Jarrett didn't play, and Wales lost. McCormick did play, and New Zealand won.

There was another All Black with cause to celebrate that night. Bill Birtwistle had scored the opening try of the match, swerving and dashing over in the corner as the cover defence hit him. I remembered murmurs of delight when his name was included in an All Black team in 1966, though he didn't play in the event. But I gathered he was seriously good. Birtwistle was from Auckland originally and he wasn't born with a silver spoon in his mouth. He had an uncle who'd been killed in New Guinea in 1942 and an alcoholic father who'd walked out when Bill was still a boy. He left school after the fourth form and found what work he could. But on the rugby field he could express himself. Playing out of the College Rifles club, he made Allen's Auckland team in a couple of early games in 1961, but he didn't shine and promptly dropped back to the Colts again. Then Birtwistle and a couple of his mates decided to get away from Auckland and try their luck in Christchurch.

Down south it all took off. He found work and established himself on the wing for Canterbury, made the South Island team and the New Zealand trials. Then in 1965 he scored a length-of-the-field try in Canterbury's 6-5 victory over the touring Springboks. A few days later when Dick dropped out injured, Birtwistle was called into the All Blacks for the first test. He scored a try on debut, added another brilliant side-stepping touchdown in the final test and ended the season an automatic choice for New Zealand, with Dick having been moved to the left wing to accommodate him. He was New Zealand rugby's new backline star.

In 1966, Birtwistle tore a hamstring and missed the Lions series. He also moved north to Hamilton where things never quite went as well again. He'd dropped out of the Jubilee test with injury but it was clear that in Allen's mind Birtwistle was his Number One winger. There was at least one very good reason for that. Allen had been famed for his side-step and he was always attracted to players with that skill. Birtwistle's side-step was a thing of wonder. It was instinctive, a step off either foot that left defenders clutching air. Natural side-steppers are rare, most players telegraph their intention but the high-stepping Birtwistle performed in that bubble where he alone had time to think and act.

How did it work, I asked him? "It's all up here," he said, tapping his head. "You can even tell the opposition what you are going to do!" He meant that they still couldn't stop you physically when you beat them mentally. Instinct and confidence, they were beginning to seem fundamental to a good backline.

Birtwistle had scored in both the Twickenham and Cardiff tests. He was comfortable in the stable environment the management had created, was in a team playing the kind of rugby he wanted to play and respected Allen's determination that the team would get it right. He knew the coach had been right to drop him for poor line-out throwing on one occasion. With Allen, he said, "You toed the line."

But it wasn't all good for Birtwistle, and there was worse to come. He'd been laid off work before the tour began and having just changed provinces he couldn't expect much in the way of whip-rounds from his new club. He had recently married Jan and so had a wife to support while he was earning a dollar a day. Nor was it all that simple on the field. Dick had been moved back to the right wing meaning Birtwistle was on the left, a position he wasn't used to. Birtwistle was a confidence player; the vicissitudes of life were nibbling at that confidence. He suddenly lost his side-step, then in that cathartic moment of glory when he scored against Wales, he felt his cartilage tear. It would heal quickly enough to see him back for the final test of the tour, but then it was his hamstring again and the glory days were over.

But for the team, all was shining and as it should be. They had beaten England and Wales. There were still three more tests on the schedule, but for now it was enough that there was victory at Cardiff Arm's Park to celebrate. That was no mean cause for celebration. The Supreme de Volaille Albufera never tasted better.

***

—

# THEIR FINEST HOUR

Before people worried about terrorists, they worried about communists. But communists didn't hijack aeroplanes so airport security usually consisted of an old bloke with a dog strolling around the perimeter. His job was to chase off any plane-spotters who jumped the fence. They didn't have people to stop you getting on an aeroplane if you looked like you knew where you were going. So it was that on the morning after the Welsh test Jazz Muller and Alister Hopkinson boarded a plane for their midday flight from Cardiff to Lyon, in France. The trouble was the plane they boarded was going to America and the rest of the All Blacks were getting on the Lyon flight. Still, it wasn't every day that you could celebrate beating Wales, and you didn't get breathalysed getting on a plane.

Somehow all 30 All Blacks made it to Lyon's Grand Nouvel hotel for the start of their two week sojourn in France. For about half of them, it was their first experience of a land where English was a foreign language. None of the All Blacks spoke French, although Tremain had picked up a smattering and one or two others could read a few words. France was a foreign land, one half-known if at all through faded photographs and the old men's tales of wartime adventures after dark. Now it was the France of the 60s, jazz cool with its art movies and Jet-set hang-outs. Here the stars were Johnny Hallyday and Brigitte Bardot, not the Beatles and Elizabeth Taylor. No English-speaking land could match the sophistication of that France. You had to admit the French dressed better, loved better, and lived better. They certainly ate better. Their match programmes were crammed with pages and pages of advertisements for restaurants where the discerning rugby fan might enjoy a splendid lunch before the match. Meat and potatoes? Boiled vegetables? Unimaginable!

Once they were settled in their hotel, the All Blacks steered their way through the Sunday evening. They managed to delete 278 of the small French bottles of beer with the assistance of McLean and the others accompanying the team. McLean mentioned their enduring a particularly savage court session under Judge Laidlaw, but then McLean wasn't overly delighted to be one of the defendants and fined twice as much as any player. Later still, taking the night air, players discovered streets where exotically dressed – or undressed – ladies whispered "Bon soir, Monsieur" with an implied question mark at the end of the sentence. On K road such things were a lot more discreet. France was indeed a foreign land.

Any levity could only ever last until the next training session. The All Blacks faced three tough matches before the test against France. Quite how tough they would be remained to be seen, but the 1953 All Blacks had lost to a regional selection as well as the French national side, so they had form. At training, Allen duly ran the All Blacks into the ground. There was a good crowd to watch their work out and there were cheers for the bulky Muller as the team went on a tough 'back man catch the front man' run around the park.

The All Blacks were coming up to the half-way point of their tour. For players who had missed selection in the first two tests, the next few games were their big chance to force their way into the test side. Realistically on such a short tour, unless the All Blacks lost in Paris there wouldn't be much chance of changes for the Scottish and Irish tests. First up on the itinerary was a South-East France selection in the Municipal Stadium in Lyon. This being France their team actually included several players with no connection at all to the South-East. Lochore, Meads, and McLeod backed up from the test match while the likes of Smith, Wills, Hopkinson, Steel, and Cottrell were given another opportunity. Cottrell had been no certainty to win selection for the tour but with Kember establishing himself as the reserve fullback, he was fast establishing himself as the mid-field back-up to MacRae.

There was something about Cottrell, a calmness on and off the field. He was one of those reliable players brought up in the classic Canterbury rugby tradition of mastery of the basic skills. The type of player who always does the right thing and very rarely makes a mistake. The sort of player who can become the glue holding a backline together. He wasn't quite there yet, but he was one of those who were developing on just the right lines, demonstrating by his performances and his attitude that he had a future in an All Black jersey.

Cottrell had broken into the Canterbury side as a 1st 5-8 in 1964, and despite the presence in Christchurch of several inside backs who had worn the black jersey, he established himself in the side in 1966. He shone for his province against the touring Lions and later made the NZ Juniors side for their match against the tourists. Proving more adept at 2nd 5-8, Cottrell slipped easily into the All Blacks' culture. As Thorne put it, the Canterbury baker was, "The classic team man". By nature quiet and polite, he had an impish sense of humour and was one of the team's more active tourists, taking every opportunity to see the sights. Never a heavy drinker, he was often found in the company of Sid Going, and he left a good impression on his hosts.

Those hosts in Lyon were enchanted by the All Blacks' presence. The papers were full of praise for the Marée Noire, the Black Tide that was sweeping through northern hemisphere rugby. Now Kiwis can be a little naive in the ways of the world and tend to believe that what is said is what is meant. So when the French praise them to the skies in the weeks leading up to a game there is a tendency, subconscious as it may be, for them to believe their opponents will be easily overcome. Then fifteen Frenchmen with a very different idea turn up and throw the kitchen sink at the Marée Noire and all bets are off.

Certainly the French praise for the All Blacks' new fifteen-man game was genuine, for the French traditionally loved that attacking approach. But recently the national side had adopted a conservative style of play and their fans were not entirely happy. Still, it was working for them. France were the reigning Five Nations champions and had just returned from their tour of South Africa. They only lost the test series 2-1 with another game drawn, and their forwards had matched the Springboks' eight. Their experienced lock Dauga was now a 'reserve' for each of the regional sides the All Blacks would play before the test, giving him plenty of time to work out how to combat them. They didn't really fear the All Blacks at all.

MacRae and Davis, rested for the Wednesday game, took advantage of Lyon's closeness to the Alps. In company with Saxton they enjoyed a day in Geneva, although it included a sobering visit to a village where the Nazis had murdered all of the inhabitants. Other All Blacks took in the sights and sounds of Lyon, with frequent reminders that a dollar a day didn't go far in France. The good news was that they had gained an extra day before the forthcoming French test with the local union agreeing to the South-West selection game being played on the Tuesday rather than the Wednesday before the test. That kind of adjustment was easier then. In amateur days no-one had to worry about broadcasters and their locked-in contracts.

Some touring teams seem to carry the rain around with them. The

1977 Lions were famous for it, and it got them down. Day after day of leaden skies and incessant rain can do that to you. I know because I once hitchhiked across North Africa under a rain cloud that lasted for nineteen days. By the time I got to Tunis, my boots and my attitude had rotted away. So far Lochore's side had been another team of rain-bringers, yet even while that hindered their efforts to play running rugby no word of complaint about the weather ever emerged from the team. They simply got on with it. Of course it helps if you grew up on the West coast.

It was raining again on the Wednesday when the All Blacks defeated the South-East Selection 16-3, scoring four tries to nil. Two of those went to Tony 'Stainless' Steel, the sprint champion on the wing. He hadn't made much impact on the tour before that other than through a propensity to lose things, not least of all his focus. Allen had recently discussed this issue with him in what is diplomatically called a 'full and frank' manner. Steel had got the message.

He had grown up in Greymouth and was related to another West Coaster, Jack Steel, a speedy winger in the 1924 'Invincibles'. Young Tony headed to Christchurch Boys High School where he starred on the track in summer and the rugby field in winter. New Zealand sprint champion in 1965 and '66, he had a meteoric rise in the rugby game, making the Canterbury rep team and serving as an All Black reserve against South Africa in 1965. Injuries to Dick and Birtwistle allowed him to play in all four tests against the '66 Lions and the Jubilee test early in '67. Five tries in five tests proved Steel belonged at that level. Off the field he was reserved by nature, "A different kind of guy", keen to see the sights and happy to pass on what he learned to younger players like Kirkpatrick. If the start of his tour had been unmemorable, this game marked a turning point. Henceforth he was one of the stars.

The South-East match marked a turning point for two other players. For winger Clarke it was the end of the road. His injured leg wouldn't come right and there didn't seem to be much doctors could do about it. He'd tried electric shock therapy in England and in France he tried intensive massage, but nothing seemed to help. Clarke was a personable man, a natty dresser and cheerfully optimistic character although the circumstances dictated that he was something of a loner on the tour. He simply didn't feel entitled to act as a full member of the team, proud though he was of being in it. Saxton and Allen encouraged him as much as they could but "divided between the elation at being in the best seat in the house and disappointment at the injury" Clarke effectively resigned his commission. He came right at the end of the tour but by then he had come to the brutally realistic conclusion that the side had three wingers who were better players than he was. Come to that the centres, Thorne and Davis were probably better wingers as well. He didn't expect to be picked again and so wasn't overly disappointed to miss out. "You take the good with the bad," he reflected. The South-East game was his last appearance on the tour.

Murray Wills, chosen as a fast-moving breakaway, had struggled with injury and failed to find his best form in the three games he'd played so far. After this match he played just twice more on the tour, both times at Number 8, a position he was clearly unsuited to. Wills' problem wasn't just injury, however. He wasn't enjoying the tour and there was a simple reason for that. He didn't get on with Fred Allen.

Wills admired Lochore enormously and found Saxton "A hell of a nice guy." But Allen's sergeant-major approach didn't work with Wills and decades later he remained scathing in his assessment of his '67 coach. Allen, Wills considered, was something unprintable, and "A drunk, cadging cigarettes." I asked him if I could quote him on that. With the honesty characteristic of all the 1967 players I met, he stood by his words.

It was an interesting alternative to the popular view of Allen. The coach is a legend today. Wills, however, is testament to the fact that his methods didn't work with everyone. Effectively written off by Allen early in the proceedings, Wills reached the point where he wanted to give up and go home. He remembers heading to Lochore's hotel room to hand in his notice, then pacing the floor outside in torment. He might have enjoyed telling Allen to go to hell, but Lochore wasn't the problem and already had enough on his plate. So too did Saxton. It was those men who would have had to deal with the repercussions of a player asking to go home. In the end Wills didn't knock on that door.

Players well outside the test team, unless they are satisfied that they are really there for the experience and are having their cards marked for the future, can easily lose focus, or simply become withdrawn and uncertain how to proceed. It had happened to Lochore on Whineray's tour; he knew how it felt. The experienced men, sure of their place in the test side, could only counsel such outsiders to keep battling, to keep training hard, for you never knew when injuries to others could give you a test opportunity. Despite Allen, Wills never gave up hope. Meads remembers him giving 100% effort on the training ground right up to the end of the tour. Wills never lacked motivation, but he never got a break. Perhaps he simply wasn't good enough, but 146 games on the side of the scrum for Taranaki suggests he wasn't a bad player, simply one that Allen couldn't inspire.

Wills wasn't the only one. The search for lock forwards had been a lengthy process. When brother Stan retired, Colin Meads was the only serious candidate with All Black experience. Strahan quickly and convincingly filled the vacancy in the test side and Smith was chosen in the expectation that he'd eventually replace Meads. That left one vacancy at lock and the requirements of the tour meant they needed an old hand, an experienced provincial campaigner for the Wednesday games. Ideally he'd bring some serious poundage to the scrum, some big hands to the line-outs, and a good attitude to the training ground. They must have looked at Karan Crawford, the New Zealand Maori lock from Hawke's Bay. They settled on Arthur Jennings from the Bay of Plenty.

Jennings had been around. His English grandfather was born at sea and settled in the Pacific, marrying a half-Tongan, half-Fijian wife. Born in

Fiji, Arthur had then grown up in Tonga before coming to New Zealand as a twelve-year-old. He'd come into the second row for Bay of Plenty in 1961 and been in the running for Whineray's tour. Now, when he thought his time had passed, he was an All Black. "I'm the luckiest man in New Zealand," he told them when he was picked. On the field he was a strong running player who revelled in the physical stuff. Good value in the rucks and mauls. Enjoyed training. Respected Allen. So far so good.

Jennings made his living as a builder and labourer throughout the Bay, turning out for five different clubs in his time there. He was generally regarded as a good 'happy-go-lucky' sort of bloke, a bit of a character. Allen asked a senior All Black about him before he was picked in the side and was told that Jennings had the ability but controlling him was the problem. "Don't worry," said Allen, "I'll handle that," and they picked him. But once the tour started Arthur proved to be something of a law unto himself. About halfway through the tour the senior All Black, feigning innocence, asked Allen about handling Jennings and how he was getting along with that? Allen's reply was short, blunt, and politically incorrect.

*** 

Their first game in France had given the All Blacks a new respect for French rugby, with their forwards having provided a serious workout for the tourists. 20,000 people had turned out to see the match – they'd had to print an extra 5,000 tickets in the week before the game. But the ground was a mess, with bulldozers having carved up the hill on one side of the ground. As well as Steel, Going and Kirkpatrick had stand-out games and as usual Meads and Lochore were at the heart of the forwards' gradual establishment of dominance over the willing local side. Nine games played, nine games won. Fair enough.

The original itinerary had had the team on an overnight train to

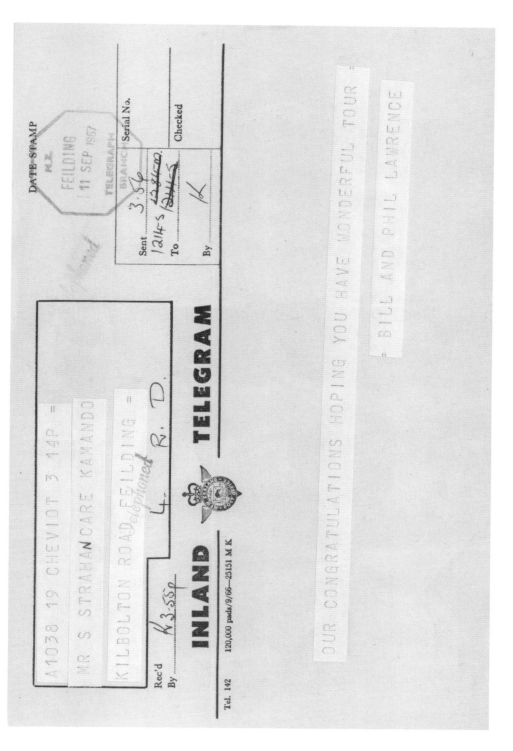

Making the team: the public sent congratulatory telegrams to players on their selection.
Courtesy Sam Strahan.

Another chapter: Colin Meads is ordered off at Murrayfield by referee Kevin Kelleher.

Courtesy New Zealand Rugby Museum.

"You must do it for them": Wayne Cottrell obliges an autograph hunter.

Courtesy Newspix.co.nz/New Zealand Herald

A night off: Allen, Lochore and others at the Moulin Rouge in Paris.

Copyright Agence Presse Sports.

"Swinging Sixties": Roy Ullyett's take on the All Blacks' arrival in London.

Courtesy New Zealand Rugby Museum.

1967 administrators at play: Tom Morrison on attack for the 1938 All Blacks against NSW in Sydney. Charlie Saxton is in the centre of the picture, Jack Sullivan wears jersey number 12.

Courtesy New Zealand Rugby Museum.

## Toast List

**THE QUEEN**

THE NEW ZEALAND TEAM

*Proposed by:*
MR. J. R. LOCKER
(President, Rugby Football Union)

*Reply by:*
MR. B. J. LOCHORE
(Captain of the New Zealand Team)

___

THE ENGLISH TEAM

*Proposed by:*
MR. C. K. SAXTON
(Hon. Manager, New Zealand Team)

*Reply by:*
MR. P. E. JUDD
(Captain of the English Team)

___

THE GUESTS

*Proposed by:*
MR. W. C. RAMSAY, C.B.E.
(Past President and Hon. Treasurer, Rugby Football Union)

*Reply by:*
MR. DESMOND PLUMMER
(Leader of Greater London Council)

---

*The Very Rev. M. G. Sullivan (Dean of St. Pauls) will say Grace in Maori.*

## Menu

Melon Frappé

___

*Seidenhaus "Green Forest" Liebfraumilch 1963*

Vol-au-Vent au Fruits de Mer

___

*Ropiteau's 1962 Volnay*

Caneton d'Aylesbury Rôti à l'Orange
Petits Pois et Carottes au Beurre
Pommes Rissolées

___

Kiwi Surprise

___

*Taylor's Vintage Reserve*

Petits Fours

Café

*Martell Medallion Drambuie*

___

Music provided by the Band of the Grenadier Guards

---

Victory dinner: the after-match function programme from the England test.

Life in France: the team assemble in Biarritz with French Liaison officer Maurice Delbos.
Courtesy New Zealand Rugby Museum.

King Country is Meads Country: Nevile Lodge's classic take on the Meads affair.
Courtesy Lodge family.

## East Wales

| |  | |  |
|---|---|---|---|
| 15 | **D. GRIFFITHS** (Cardiff College of Education) | | FULL BACK |
| 14 | *W. K. JONES (Cardiff) | | RIGHT WING |
| 13 | *T. G. R. DAVIES (Cardiff) | | RIGHT CENTRE |
| 12 | *W. H. RAYBOULD (London Welsh) | | LEFT CENTRE |
| 11 | F. H. WILSON (Cardiff) | | LEFT WING |
| 10 | *B. JOHN (Cardiff) | | OUTSIDE HALF |
| 9 | *G. EDWARDS (Cardiff) Captain | | INSIDE HALF |
| 1 | *J. O'SHEA (Cardiff) | | FORWARDS |
| 2 | J. YOUNG (Harrogate) | | |
| 3 | B. JAMES (Bridgend) | | |
| 4 | I. C. JONES (London Welsh) | | |
| 5 | L. BAXTER (Cardiff) | | |
| 6 | J. HICKEY (Cardiff) | | |
| 8 | *R. E. JONES (Coventry) | | |
| 7 | A. I. GRAY (London Welsh) | | |

\* Internationals

TOUCH JUDGE:
O. P. Bevan (Mountain Ash)

## New Zealand

| |  | |
|---|---|---|
| FULL BACK | 30 | **W. F. McCORMICK** (Canterbury) |
| RIGHT WING | 24 | **G. S. THORNE** (Auckland) |
| RIGHT CENTRE | 21 | **G. F. KEMBER** (Wellington) |
| LEFT CENTRE | 25 | **W. L. DAVIS** (Hawkes Bay) |
| LEFT WING | 27 | **A. G. STEEL** (Canterbury) |
| OUTSIDE HALF | 20 | **M. A. HEREWINI** (Auckland) |
| INSIDE HALF | 18 | **C. R. LAIDLAW** (Otago) |
| FORWARDS | 2 | **K. F. GRAY** (Wellington) |
| | 4 | **B. E. McLEOD** (Counties) |
| | 6 | **A. E. HOPKINSON** (Canterbury) |
| | 9 | **S. C. STRAHAN** (Manawatu) |
| | 10 | **A. E. SMITH** (Taranaki) |
| | 14 | **I. A. KIRKPATRICK** (Canterbury) |
| | 13 | **B. J. LOCHORE** (Wararapa) Captain |
| | 15 | **G. C. WILLIAMS** (Wellington) |

TOUCH JUDGE:
E. M. Lewis (Abertillery)

REFEREE:
F. B. Lovis (R.F.U.)

Honours even: the original teams for the drawn match with East Wales (Raybould withdrew, replaced by John Dawes). Courtesy Sam Strahan.

Toulouse on the night of the game. Again there was a change, with the scheduled seven hour train journey replaced by a more restful short flight to Toulouse and four nights there in the Grand Hotel. Nathan, his jaw still wired up, was amused to find the hotel was also hosting a convention of dentists and wisely steered clear of them. Laidlaw, nursing a muscle strain that kept him out of the first two games in France, received the heartening news that he had been awarded a Rhodes Scholarship to Oxford, an event duly celebrated with teammates.

Rhodes scholarships aren't given out with the cornflakes. The award was a considerable mark of academic and social distinction and a tribute to Laidlaw's ability to balance rugby and scholarship. There was a general rejoicing on his behalf, for Laidlaw was an integral part of the side. He wore his scholarship lightly in camp, and as one of the least educated members of the team put it, "Wasn't up himself at all". But as his splendidly subversive book Mud in Your Eye later revealed, Laidlaw chose not to fully reveal himself to his rugby teammates. Like many a young man trying to fit in better he reluctantly tailored his behaviour to suit his environment. Unlike cricket, rugby doesn't have a tradition of dissenting writings and Laidlaw's book causing something of a stir among his former teammates when it was published in 1973. Kiwis tend to take people as they come and there were those among his friends who were a little hurt to find he had not been all he seemed.

Decades earlier Winston McCarthy, writing about Saxton, had said, "I often wonder will [Saxton] get some youngster with talent, and be able to teach him to pass the ball from the scrum as Jimmy Duncan taught him. If he does, I can tell you this: the boy will be an All Black." It wasn't a bad prediction. Saxton spotted the young Laidlaw and steered him on the path. Now McCarthy could write that, "In 1967, after mature reflection, I was convinced that [Laidlaw] was the greatest half-back in my memory."

Laidlaw was Dunedin born and spent four years in the first XV at King's High School before attending Otago University. Picked for

Otago and the South Island as an eighteen-year-old, he had all the classical skills of the great half-backs and looked set for a long reign in the black jersey. Debuting on Whineray's tour, Laidlaw forced his way into the team for the last test of that tour and established himself in the side against the Springboks in 1965. With Saxton and Allen both rating his play highly, particularly his passing, he was a key figure in the planning for the attacking style of the '67 side. That he had managed to maintain his academic focus through these years was testament to his ability to compartmentalise.

Toulouse was not one of France's more picturesque cities, being an industrial centre of some magnitude. But as the home of the French half of the Concorde project, it offered further insights into what then seemed to be the future of commercial aviation, and a number of the All Blacks took the opportunity to be shown around the factory after morning training. The maiden flight of the aircraft was due in a fortnight and the final touches were being applied as they toured the factory.

France 'B' were the All Blacks' opponents on the Saturday and Cottrell, Steel, Going, Kirkpatrick, Major, and Jennings joined the core of the test players in the team chosen to meet them. At last there was a dry ground and sunshine. A crowd of 30,000 saw New Zealand win a 32-19, five-tries-to-two victory at the concrete oval that was Toulouse stadium. It was a spectacular game, full of running, with the French side briefly turning on one of those periods when they seem to shift into another dimension, counter-attacking in brilliant and unpredictable style. But the All Black forwards were on top throughout and only poor handling prevented them scoring more often.

'Poor handling' was one of the contemporary criticisms of Lochore's men in several of their games and that conjures up images of passes dropped. But we need to remember that in those days the slightest forward adjustment of the ball in taking a pass was classified as a knock-on. Under modern rules, most of that 'poor handling' would have been ignored by the referees and play allowed to continue.

Cottrell, Going and Kirkpatrick were among the standout All Black players in this game and reports in the New Zealand papers were beginning to suggest that Kirkpatrick's form might bring about an almost unthinkable change in the side. Tremain was hampered by an Achilles tendon strain and had yet to hit top form. His test place was now considered at risk. With the resurgent Kirton 'running the cutter' in grand style at 1st 5-8 and McRae and Davis automatic choices in mid-field, there was no vacancy for Cottrell, but Going's form couldn't be ignored.

On that evening after the France 'B' game, the French selectors announced their test side for following weekend. New Zealand selectors might mess up a count to 30, but the French trumped that by forgetting to choose a captain, and took a few days to come up with one. They got it right in the end though, with flanker Christian Carrere proving one of France's best leaders.

From Toulouse it was off to the luxurious Plaza hotel in Biarritz. Along the way, the team pulled into the pilgrim town of Lourdes for lunch at the local rugby club. Catholic Lourdes was host to an endless parade of unfortunates seeking miracle cures for death and all manner of lesser ailments. Nathan got to thinking he could use a little help with the jaw and popped into the sacred grotto to light a candle. True, he wasn't Catholic, but he was from God's Own Country after all. And if Waka didn't actually get a full-blown miracle, well at least he got a good deal. Ten days later he was back in black.

As the coach drove through the late autumn colours of the Pyrenean hill country with its snow-capped mountains above, the team were slowly digesting another problem. New Zealand had devalued its dollar by nearly 20%. That meant that instead of getting thirteen or fourteen French francs for their dollars they were getting anything from eleven francs to as little as nine as the markets fluctuated. Expensive France had suddenly got a whole lot more expensive.

Biarritz isn't a good place to be short of money, unless you get lucky and win some at the casino. In 1967, it was a name that still spelled glamour, although it had passed its peak. But the car parks were still full of sports cars, all reassuringly expensive, and the harbour still housed acres of yachts, none of which needed new paint. Many of Europe's idle rich and a stream of visiting celebrities – 'stars' as they were known then – still came to while away their days on the beaches and spend their nights around the roulette table. You expected to see James Bond there.

One of the delights of European life is a trip across the border–any border will do. You can change countries for the day and be back home in time for dinner. The Spanish border was only an hour from Biarritz so after Monday morning training the team boarded their coach for an afternoon in Spain. They were as keen as any young Kiwi on O.E. to add another country to their collection but like many a young Kiwi before them they were about to get a lesson in political systems. 1967 Europe was still shaped by World War Two. France was a slightly anarchic democracy lead by wartime legend General de Gaulle, while Spain was a fascist dictatorship under General Franco, whose neutrality in the war had enabled him to survive. What you can do in a democracy and what you can do in a dictatorship are two very different things. You don't really understand that when you live in a democracy.

It was the baggage master Richard Walker who broke the rules, not a player. One of the Spanish border guards told the team that he was not to be included in their photos. Walker wasn't listening and took a photo of the side getting back on the bus with the Spaniard right in camera. Dictatorship actually manifests most unpleasantly for most of its citizens, not in dawn raids and torture chambers but in having to deal with petty bureaucrats lacking either humour or tolerance for human nature. Given that even in democracies border guards are not normally famous for their warmth and cheerful good-fellowship, this wasn't Walker's smartest move.

So it was that the baggage man was arrested by the guard, who dragged him off to his office. None of the New Zealand party spoke Spanish. None of the Spanish spoke English. There was no New Zealand consulate in Spain. For a moment there the situation had the makings of an international incident. That it was quickly smoothed over was down to the diplomatic skills of Charlie Saxton, who knew a thing or two about dealing with the uniformed mind, and to Thorne. Walker was actually using Thorne's camera and Thorne, in what McLean called "A grand gesture" – and the Spanish traditionally admire a grand gesture – pulled the film out of the camera and exposed it. Apologies were tendered, explanations were accepted, honour was satisfied, universal brotherhood was invoked, and Walker was released. The All Blacks saw San Sebastian, a rather grim industrial town with a medieval heart, but it was closed for siesta and its lustre was tarnished by earlier events anyway. It wasn't the talking point of the day.

The side to play South-West France the next day looked good on paper, although for the only time on the British section of the tour both Lochore and Meads were rested. MacRae captained the side. For the first time, Tremain and Kirkpatrick were on the flanks. There was a crowd of 18,000 at the Parc de Sports in the rugby town of Bayonne, a short distance inland from Biarritz. It should have been an easy victory, the ground was dry, the sun was shining and the local selection included just one international, although at half-back they had a future star in Jacques Fouroux. But this was Basque country and the Basques are a resilient people who care little for odds against them.

The match ended in victory to the All Blacks by 18-14, three tries to one. The passionately vocal crowd, roaring on their team and roundly cursing the visitors, had much to cheer about as their unfancied side disrupted the efforts of the Marée Noire. At half-time they were in the lead, the first time on the tour that the All Blacks had been down at the break. There was only eight minutes to go when Kember kicked a simple penalty to finally put them in the lead and Tremain scored a try in the dying moments of the game to seal the win. It had been a mistake-ridden performance in which none of the All Blacks really stood out. To add injury to insult, Herewini suffered a dislocated vertebrae that threatened to end his tour.

Particular mention after the game went to the referee, who'd displeased both sides. McLean wrote that he "Gave the impression of having taken the field with certain pre-conceived ideas about the play of the All Blacks and...saw himself as an instrument of correction." The "stinkingly partisan" crowd didn't like him either, especially when he awarded the critical penalty against young Fouroux. At the end of the match, Tremain and local skipper Sitjar walked off on either side of the referee to protect him from the raucous anger of the surrounding crowd. They collected more spit than the Sex Pistols. But it said something for Tremain's sporting instincts that he was there at all, given that as forward captain for the day he'd borne much of the brunt of the referee's assault.

All touring teams have their off-days, which tend to coincide with the absence of the tour captain. Throw in the absence of Meads and perhaps that the All Blacks were due an off-day and you get the recipe for the Bayonne game. But there was a valuable lesson there too. When it was over, Allen was quoted as saying, "We can leave out Meads alone or Lochore alone, but never again both of them together."

Somewhat later that evening, after a reception in a pelota court at the Bayonne club, Allen had more things to say in that vein when he sat with Saxton, Lochore and MacRae to choose the team for Saturday's test. Later still he had something to say in the casino. "Eighteen," he said as he put his money down on the roulette table. "Eighteen" because that was how many points the All Blacks had scored that day. "Eighteen" it was, and was again as he reinvested his winnings. Allen won big. His winnings amounted to "Two or three hundred francs" according to McLean or "close to a thousand francs" according to the much later account of Allen's biographer so perhaps the story grew in the telling. Allen promptly gave his winnings to the team fund. It just about made up for devaluation.

***

Selecting the team for the French test took two and a half hours, the longest such meeting of the tour. In the end they made three changes. Back then players weren't 'rested' or 'rotated'; they were in or they were out. Laidlaw was rooming with Tremain in the Plaza when Allen came in. "You realise you two buggers are out," he snapped. There wasn't much you could say to that. Both players duly put on their best face and congratulated their replacements. But they weren't happy and they vowed to each other they'd be back.

Birtwistle was gone too, replaced by the in-form Steel whose extra pace was needed against the speedy French backs. But it was the introduction of Kirkpatrick and Going that was the talking point. In the case of Tremain, there was sadness that after nine years in black the popular Hawke's Bay skipper was no longer a first choice. Yet Tremain was the first to acknowledge Kirkpatrick was a special player. Reyburn tells of Tremain sitting beside his visiting father in the stands at one of the French games and telling him "This boy is better than I am." The fact was that Tremain hadn't been at his best and Kirkpatrick just kept getting better. He combined well with Going and after playing all three games on the French tour he knew what to expect from their forwards. His selection was half-anticipated.

The selection of Going in place of Laidlaw seemed significant. But it was primarily a tactical decision made with the specific opponents in mind. In retrospect it signalled not that Going was now considered the Number One half-back, but that the All Blacks were expecting a game where Going's strengths would be more valuable than Laidlaw's. In particular, his strong running close in to the forwards was seen as likely to break up the French defensive patterns. 'Create confusion', that was the plan, one Lochore's biography credited to Saxton. Still, it wasn't a simple call. Going had been in great form, but the type of rugby that Saxton and Allen sought ideally required a half-back with the passing skills Laidlaw exemplified. Kirton, whose form had been a crucial part of the team's success on tour, preferred playing outside Laidlaw. Dropping Laidlaw meant breaking up their axis, one that had served the side so well against England and Wales. It was a big call even if no-one in North Auckland had any doubt at all that it was the right one.

Going was the kind of player who demanded you watch him because he was always likely to do something spectacular. The rules of the time allowed the half-back to harass his opposite number. Going stretched those rules to the limit. He'd rob him of possession and tear into the spaces while the forwards were still packed down. Short and immensely strong of leg and thigh, he could bounce off tacklers or throw them off their stride with a check and a step off either leg. Sometimes he simply stood still, looking for the best option. Like all the true champions – Meads remembered Bob Scott as having the same quality – he always seemed to have *time*. When you studied him closely you saw that the time came from his speed of thought. He simply thought quicker than anyone around him. Going's awareness of everyone's whereabouts didn't just give him tactical vision, it meant he never needed to look unless to confuse the opposition. He never telegraphed a move. If he knew it was on he went for it, and teammates around him, brothers Brian and Ken most notably, positioned themselves in expectation of his breaks, while opposition half-backs lived in dread of them. Playing against Sid could be a nightmare.

On the day after the game in Bayonne, the team trained before they headed for the flight to Paris. Soon after the session began, Allen steered his players over to the grandstand where Saxton was waiting. In France, the social pressures seemed even stronger than they had been in Wales and the pressures of constant touring were mounting up. Over the last week or two there had been a few comments that clearly fell under the heading of 'sexist' and a few renditions of rugby songs at inappropriate moments. So Saxton, a gentleman in such matters, addressed the team. He didn't have to say much. "Would you like that if that was your sister?" was one comment that bought it home. No-one wanted Saxton to be disappointed in them. The point was taken. Then they went back on the training ground and Allen ran them into the ground.

They were at home that night in Paris. There was a convivial reception at the New Zealand embassy. The players could catch up on the Trotting cup or how the cricketers were going in Australia and there was mail from home and a chance to get the lowdown on the worth of their money. Later still they went back to France, winding up at the Moulin Rouge no less, or what the New Zealand papers politely called 'the theatre'. Except that the only bare breasted women in New Zealand theatres at the time were in documentaries about jungle tribes and you couldn't drink champagne while you were watching them. It was about that time on a tour when an evening like that is just the way you'd like it. Call it Saxton's day.

Paris has its charms – "My number one beautiful city," Muller called it, and there was a trip to the Palace of Versailles the next day after training. Training had been intense; France were a serious threat. Saxon stepped in to give specialist coaching to Going. Back at their hotel, the test team were into test mode. For the rest of the team there was the Left Bank outside, indeed James Joyce had written part of Ulysses while in the hotel which now housed the team. That kind of history was one of the nice things about touring this part of the world. The hotel had also been home to the commanders of the German Occupation forces, and later to De Gaulle, to say nothing of Picasso.

Around this time, Saxton was alerted to another possible change in the team's itinerary. Britain was increasingly ravaged by a foot-and-mouth epidemic and its farmers were facing ruin. Herds that represented centuries of breeding were being exterminated in an attempt to check its spread. Foot-and-mouth disease is one of those Biblical plagues that spark around the world. With so many of them closely connected to farming, the All Blacks were conscious of its dangers. If it reached New Zealand – carried in the earth on the boots of an All Black or a supporter perhaps – it could destroy the farming sector and hence the New Zealand economy. Naturally Kiwis would support any efforts to prevent that. But there was another country that didn't have foot-and-mouth either. That was Ireland, where the All Blacks were scheduled to play the final games of the tour in a couple of weeks. The Irish were now weighing up the risks of thousands of supporters travelling from Britain to see those games.

***

Not every great achievement brings instant elation. Sometimes the sheer physical and mental effort required to get across the line takes so much out of you there is nothing left to celebrate with. A stranger wandering into the All Blacks' dressing room after the French test would have assumed they'd lost. There was nothing of what Whineray called the "ecstatic chaos" of the winner's room. No grinning and back-slapping, no jokes, just blood-stained players slumped on benches staring at the floor. The All Blacks had given absolutely everything they had – there was only exhaustion left.

It had been a bitterly cold, steam-rising-from-the-scrum sort of day, the skies thick with low cloud while whisps of Gaulloises-scented mist drifted in the air. There were 40,000 impassioned Frenchmen at Colombes stadium cheering and whistling and stamping their feet against the cold. The hip-flasks helped too. There were far more photographers and officials and hangers-on on the field than there were players as the haka and a 63-man police band playing La Marseillaise stirred the blood. Then the ref blew his whistle and it was all on. The All Blacks were in a contest they would remember above all others. This was Test rugby!

Within the first ten minutes, Gachassin had dropped a goal for France, Kirkpatrick had broken his nose in a tackle and Meads had been so brutally kicked in the head by the young French lock Alan Plantefol as to leave even that strongest of All Blacks rolling on the ground in pain. After the game, Meads sought out Dauga to enter a word of admonishment, working on the assumption the massive Frenchmen had been the villain. But Dauga was an experienced enough old campaigner to quickly point out the real culprit.

It was tough enough in the backline where Claude Dourthe, who had been France's youngest ever cap, proved to be an ancient master of the stiff-arm tackle. But French fire was met with selfless resolution. Guys like McCormick loved this stuff, it bought out the best in them. Meads – no stretcher for him – simply got back up and outplayed Dauga. Gray, not a man to cross boundaries with, brought his knee up to the jaw of his troublesome opponent and the scrums henceforth settled down. After Dourthe had done his best to guillotine the Hawke's Bay centre, Davis, uncharacteristically angry, raised a clenched fist and threatened to thump him. Dourthe promptly collapsed to the ground in a crumpled heap. "Hollywood," thought Davis immediately and feared the ref's interpretation. But Davis – and the ref – had missed the action. Dourthe wasn't acting, he was out cold. You might have seen what happened if they'd had slo-mo cameras then. In real time no-one had noticed Bruce McLeod pass by at the critical moment or seen his lightning fast right hook critique of Dourthe's tackling technique.

And then there was the rugby: 80 minutes of fast-moving action on a perfect surface. McLean, who had witnessed 60 or 70 All Black test matches, couldn't recall any where they had moved the ball out to the backline so often. They had plenty of possession, dominating the line-outs not least thanks to a last-minute suggestion from Saxton that they stand farther back from the touchline. That created space to attack at front and rear, confusing the French defence. Going's strong, sniping runs kept the forwards on the front foot. He and fellow newcomer Kirkpatrick were McLean's "heavenly twins" on the day, fully justifying the selector's confidence in them. But the whole team were on song, the old hands in the pack were superb, younger guys like Strahan and Williams shone in this toughest of company, MacRae was at his best, Davis sublime and McCormick was...well, he was McCormick and that was good enough.

The three newcomers, Going, Kirkpatrick, and Steele, all scored tries, so too did Malcolm Dick. Birtwistle remembered New Zealand seemed to have a new star winger every season in those days, himself in '65, Steele in '66, Clarke briefly in '67. Dick had been the star on Whineray's tour and he remained a first-choice wing from that time on. He was one of those players easy to take for granted. If he was fit he was an automatic pick, and when he played he did everything right. He threw the ball into the lineout accurately, tackled effectively, and ran with pace and power despite his relatively small stature. He had vision, he had determination, and he scored tries. The only problem was, he got injured on a regular basis.

Dick's father John had been a good winger too, a teammate of Saxton's on the '38 tour of Australia. Malcolm played out of Ponsonby and from Auckland Grammar made both the Auckland side and the national trials in 1961. He was a 2nd 5-8 or centre then but Allen moved him to the wing where he became one of the stars of the Shield team. By the end of the season he was on the bench for the All Blacks. Making his national debut on Whineray's tour, he established himself in the test side and scored nineteen tries in his 24 tour games.

Dick had been studying accountancy then, but decided to focus entirely on rugby for the tour and skipped the exams that year. He graduated in 1965 and so was suitably qualified to look after the team fund on the '67 tour. Befitting his profession, Dick was neat and well-organised. He was also socially skilled: a mature and sensible personality with a touch of good-humoured charm. And significantly, when they got on the team coach, Dick was one of the back-seat boys. That was a special place, at least in some eyes, and was taken by invitation only. They said that in '67 Dick didn't quite reach the heights of his form on the Whineray tour, but the heart of the team was where he belonged.

The '67 All Blacks kept up the back seat of the rugby bus tradition. When Derek Lever had checked the side into their Cardiff hotel, a certain inside back was missing. Hazlett let on that the player might need Lever's help back on the bus. And indeed he did, having paid the price for trespassing on the back seat he was hiding naked behind a seat. Lever got him a blanket from the hotel.

The French game was something special, a delight to watch. It was also a great All Black victory, one that in the end they thoroughly deserved. France had been good but the All Blacks had been better by a fair margin, whatever the scoreboard said. Tactically, they out-thought the French. Perhaps more importantly, they won by playing fifteen-man rugby. It had been tough; Meads and three others had the stitches to prove it. Yet on reflection, as he told biographer Alex Veysey, the test was "Perhaps, the most complete and satisfying expression of total rugby in which he has been involved."

Lochore played for New Zealand against all comers for nine years. He also rates that French test as the toughest game he ever played in. For the team to play in such a game and to come out of it with victory was something special, something almost beyond words, something transcendent. That was what the long hours of training were for, this "most beautiful feeling". As his biography recounts, in the exhausted silence of the dressing room Lochore felt "The most peaceful feeling you can ever have in your life...to be hopelessly, gloriously exhausted. That is perfect peace. That is utter fulfilment. That is why we play rugby."

That night, at the after-match dinner held in the All Blacks' hotel, there was vintage champagne to wash down the inevitably beef-centred cuisine. There was no toast to President de Gaulle. His star was waning. So many Frenchmen refused to stand and toast his health that it had been dropped. The speeches were short and the musical programme was delightfully up-tempo, culminating in Chansons à Boire, or for the uninitiated, 'Drinking Songs'. But the guys who'd been on the field were mostly in bed at an early hour. They'd passed the supreme test. They were content. This was as good as it got.

\*\*\*

—

# "WE'D RATHER HAVE LOST THE TEST THAN LOST PINEY"

The 1967 tour reached its peak with the victory over France. That was their finest hour. France proved the toughest opponents the All Blacks faced and New Zealand won not by attrition and penalty goals, but by playing fifteen-man attacking rugby. Still, as any mountaineer will tell you, the trouble with reaching a peak is that you have to go downhill after that. The final third of the tour went downhill in many ways, not least mentally. As McLean put it, the team "was now on the defensive." Yet the inherent strengths of the side – its discipline, its unity, pride, intelligence, fitness, and leadership – got it over the line. The All Blacks might have been just hanging on at the end of the tour, but hang on they did in the face of forces that seemed designed to test them to the limits.

The All Blacks left France on the Sunday, flying to Edinburgh for a week in the North British hotel. There's a good book to be written about rugbymen at the North British. It was one of the great rugby hotels of the world. Once, on one of those weekends that lasts until Wednesday, it hosted a couple of dozen Kiwi oil-rig workers down from Aberdeen to see the All Blacks draw a high-scoring game with Scotland. Our mate Pete Howe had had to quit his lucrative off-shore job to be there because his American boss wouldn't give him leave. But his Scottish uber-boss rehired him when he got back from the game. Scots understand New Zealanders' relationship to rugby.

Aberdeen was booming then; its soccer team even won the European Cup Winner's Cup under a young Alex Fergusson, who went onto greater fame with Manchester United. But the expats were more interested in the Oil Blacks, a team of Kiwis and the odd Aussie or Jarpie ring-in who played an annual game against Garioch, a local village side. I'd once made a comeback to play for them, in a game I was also reporting on. It was only for the last fifteen minutes mind, after a pre-arranged injury called for a substitution, but the game was memorable for ending 0-0, a score-line that always leaves you wondering.

The '67 All Blacks were to play two games in Scotland: a Districts side on the Wednesday, then the test match on the Saturday. The District side wasn't up to much on paper–a couple of useful forwards and a young one, Roger Arneil, who became a very good one. Selecting the All Black side was complicated by injuries. McCormick, Dick, and Lochore backed up from the test match, with the skipper moving to lock for the first time on tour while Cottrell played 1st 5-8 and Kember finally got to play at 2nd 5-8. The three players dropped for the French test – Birtwistle, Laidlaw, and Tremain – were all picked and at last Nathan was back, after sitting out eight games with his broken jaw.

In the morning after the French game, the news broke that the medieval plague had won. The Irish section of the tour had been cancelled at the request of their government. They had decided that an influx of people from the UK carried just too much of a risk of spreading foot-and-mouth disease to the Emerald Isles. Now there could be no All Black 'Grand Slam' of victories over the Five Nations. That would have to wait for Mourie's men in 1978-79.

Looking back on it, the All Blacks regret that lost opportunity, although at the time it wasn't uppermost in the minds of the newcomers. For Strahan though, it was a personal disappointment. His father was born in Northern Ireland and Strahan even had an Irish passport to go with his Kiwi one. He'd been there in 1964 with a backpack and would have loved to have made the trip in a black jersey. It was actually questionable whether cancelling the game achieved anything. Muller pointed out that most of the All Black supporters went to Ireland anyway – without taking the disease with them.

Aside from missing the social side of things–for Ireland is perhaps the best destination of all in that regard–the cancellation meant the loss of what was shaping up to be a great game. Ireland had the incomparable Mike Gibson in the backline and they had Willie John McBride, a lock forward of such stature that he may legitimately be mentioned in the same breath as Meads. But while they had some other pretty handy footballers and a ton of team spirit, several of their key forwards were injured. The '67 All Blacks would surely have triumphed over the men in green and won a Grand Slam. But even if the corner flags were ready – Thorne bought one at auction years later – it was a game they'll have to play in heaven. It never happened.

Two games were scheduled in Ireland, against a combined side in Belfast on December 13th and the test in Dublin on Saturday the 16th. In a hasty re-arrangement of the itinerary, those games were replaced by a single match on the Saturday against the Barbarians at Twickenham. This was the traditional tour-ender – though previously played at Cardiff – but had originally been sacrificed to the demands of a shortened itinerary. The new itinerary meant the side would have a week in London before the tour's end. That and the lure of the Barbarians game were at least some consolation for the lost test.

Scotland had its compensations too. Scots and Kiwis find it easy to get on well. There was plenty of Scots blood in New Zealand and the two nations shared a very basic understanding of rugby: you gave it everything, not for yourself, but for the team. Lochore was a good Scots' name; he and his men were welcome. And Scottish rugbymen could look them in the eye, they'd been the only 'international' side to beat the Kiwis, only lost 0-3 to a single penalty goal against the '53 All Blacks and had held Whineray's men to one of those scoreless draws. They're more-or-less extinct in the modern era but draws have the charm of might-have-beens, something cricket understands even if Americans don't.

On the Tuesday morning, the team trained at a public school ground, Jock's Lodge, where there was a poignant reminder of Hearn's injury. Watching from the sideline was David Mercer, an Edinburgh schoolboy who had broken his neck in a scrum collapse and was now in a wheelchair. The All Blacks stopped to chat, signed his autograph book and carried him in his chair up to the pavilion bar for a soft-drink and a bit more of a yarn. They treated him as an equal–it could have happened to them. They didn't leave it there either, but arranged – and it was no simple matter – for him to attend the Districts game the next day, where he sat proudly alongside the dirt-trackers in the grandstand.

At Melrose's pleasantly rural Greenyards' ground in the Scottish Borders, where Scots' rugby is traditionally strongest, 7,000 people awaited the coach that brought the team down from Edinburgh. They had walked through disinfected sawdust to enter the ground, for foot-and-mouth ravaged the land. The weather was surprisingly mild as Lochore led his team out across straw laid down in expectation of snow. The All Blacks won handsomely 35-14, seven tries to one. Birtwistle scored a hat-trick, Thorne crossed for a brilliant solo try, and the returning Nathan drove over for the most popular try of the day. Hopkinson touched down as well. But it was the other try-scorer, Chris Laidlaw, who really stood out. This was Laidlaw's game. He was seriously upset at being dropped and determined to show the management that he should be in the test team. Thus motivated, he played an absolute blinder. McLean doubted whether any New Zealand half-back had ever delivered "So constant a stream of passes of such remarkable quality." Thorne remembers some of Laidlaw's passes reaching him at centre! Certainly they regularly reached Kember at 2nd 5-8.

Tremain, similarly determined to show he wasn't finished, had his best game of the tour. With Birtwistle scoring three tries it was a pretty good day for the discards. It wasn't a perfect team performance but in its attacking intent it was a magnificent display, with barely a touch kick essayed by the All Blacks in the entire game. It was becoming clear that an unbeaten tour, the first since 1924, was a very real possibility.

There was dinner and a dance after the match. The Scots know how to do these things and you can put your watch in your pocket when the evening is in full swing. The team's coach driver had his schedule though and duly headed back to Edinburgh – with a few empty seats. Thorne had been engrossed in discussions about European economic policies – or something – with a young lady and he and Hopkinson had to hitch a lift home from one of the cars departing the car park, while the coach picked up Major, Hazlett, and Jennings the next morning. It was lucky Hopkinson got back that night.

In the selection meeting after the Districts' match, Birtwistle, Laidlaw, and Tremain were all recalled to the test team. Dick had a strained Achilles tendon so Birtwistle moved back to the right wing. Kirkpatrick was still recovering from his broken nose and while he probably could have played, Tremain's return to form meant he wasn't needed. He'd already more than laid down a marker for the future.

But there was one other change in the test team, with Hopkinson coming in to replace Muller. This was something of a surprise, not least to Hopkinson, who'd had no inkling he was in the running until he made it back to the hotel that night. Competition for the front-row positions was strong. The established pairing of Gray and Hazlett had only played together in the first game on this tour, then Gray's injury had seen Muller chosen with Hazlett for the England test. Hazlett was then dropped and the Gray-Muller pairing served well against Wales and France. Now Hopkinson got his chance. Thorne helped him celebrate.

'Hoppy' was a good mate of Muller. The son of a South Canterbury rep, he had started out as a lock with his father's old team in 1962, then moved to Canterbury where he worked as a stock and station agent. He gradually established himself in their rep team over the next couple of years and in 1967 emerged at the head of a group of contenders for a place in the touring side. He hadn't expected to make the team, in fact he was scheduled to be getting married during the time it was away and a hasty rearrangement of dates followed the announcement of the squad. On tour Hopkinson proved to be one of the side's characters, with a quick-witted humour that often served to break the tension. He enjoyed himself immensely and was one of those individuals who seem to be able to get away with anything. In later years, the national management found him hard to handle, but in '67 he was still a young player of considerable promise who was learning the rules that Saxton exemplified.

There was always humour to be found. Hopkinson and Muller were having lunch with the manager of the Bank of New Zealand in London when McLeod came in to cash a cheque. He was informed that without an account that couldn't be done. McLeod pointed out that as an All Black his nation's bank should be able to trust him and demanded to see the manager. The manager duly appeared with Hopkinson and Muller, who were asked to confirm that McLeod was indeed their teammate. Hopkinson's reply was swift: "Sir this man is an imposter. We have never seen him before." It took a while for McLeod to see the funny side of that.

Yet not a man to mess with was Hopkinson. I asked him for his autograph once, while I was wearing my North Auckland ball-boy jersey and he was up at Okara park with the Canterbury team. He signed, but he made it pretty clear I was part of the enemy. I found him the most intimidating player I had ever come across, but maybe I just wasn't in on the joke. Front-rowers have their own sense of humour and the rest of the world doesn't always understand.

Muller could be pretty formidable too. But there was a boyish innocence to him that seemed to carry him through life and he became a favourite of the team. Most of the side had nicknames. Three of the most prominent, along with 'Pinetree' of course, were 'Farmer' Dick from his manner of walking, 'Cutaway' Laidlaw from an incident involving large calf muscles and tight shorts, and 'Jazz', as Muller was already known in Taranaki. Jazz had Swiss parents and was one of a large family. He worked in the freezing works in Eltham and in 1963 he played one match for Taranaki. Not until 1965 did he get another, but he was a huge man by the standards of the time and the word went around that here was a front-rower of serious potential. He added a fair weight of muscle under Allen's coaching regime, and he could eat for New Zealand as well. A massive breakfast would be followed by a couple of pies for morning tea. Meads remembers sharing a room with him and waking up in the night to find him munching a chocolate bar. As lock Strahan put it, "It took a long arm to grip around Muller".

Like Thorne, Muller was a keen souvenir hunter, with his collection worth a museum of its own. Again like Thorne, Muller was one of the practical jokers of the side. He was always quick to slip into a joke shop and emerge with some new trick. Fred Allen didn't always address Muller in the kindest and most complimentary of terms, but Muller would have run into a brick wall for his side and he bit his lip and bided his time. In the final days of the tour, when Allen was looking for a cigarette, Muller innocently offered his pack to the coach. Meads and a few others who were in on it watched with interest. Allen duly lit up, inhaled, and the cigarette exploded in his face. Muller had got him. Allen was incandescent, not least perhaps because war veterans have bad memories about explosions. But you couldn't stay mad at Jazz for long.

They said that Muller slept in his first All Black jersey. He was certainly immensely proud of his team and gave it everything, even if he found the social functions and the school visits a trial. Jazz Muller, All Black, shaking hands with the Queen, running out at Cardiff and Colombes. Not bad for a boy from Eltham. How could you be anything but happy and why wouldn't you give it everything? In his own distinctive way, Muller was as committed as Kirkpatrick and as enthusiastic as Thorne. And if he didn't make the Scottish test… well his mate Hoppy got that one, so he was happy for him. Anyway, after the game Tremain gave him a Scottish jersey to add to his collection. It went with the kilt he had made in Edinburgh and wore with the élan of a true Scotsman. Not bad for a Swiss Kiwi!

The papers that week carried Saxton's criticism of Welsh journalist Clem Thomas, who had claimed that the All Blacks had resorted to "What amounted to brutality" in the French game. Saxton could have used Meads' head wound as Exhibit A. There was better news too, with hints that the 1970 tour would go ahead after talks between South African leader Vorster and New Zealand's deputy Prime Minister Marshall. Marshall wasn't saying anything until he got home and talked to Tom Morrison. But the word was that Maoris would finally be permitted to tour with the All Blacks. That was dramatic progress..

On the night before the Test, the dirt-trackers attended the Watsonian Ball in the MacRobert Pavilion, Edinburgh's premier indoor venue. The musical programme included no less than 24 dance tunes, from Quickstep to Last Waltz. Amidst the Foxtrots and Charlestons and Dashing White Sergeants there was even a Twist to loosen things up a little. The menu – in English at last – was similarly broad. It included everything from Boar's Head to Pheasant, along with the ubiquitous beef. Similarly broad was the wine list, although a glass of vintage port was the only drink listed for less than the All Blacks' daily dollar.

It was a good night, but Fred Allen was preoccupied. He had an odd feeling, one he couldn't quite put his finger on. Perhaps there was something wrong in the stars, but somehow he just felt that something might go wrong the next day. He couldn't shake that feeling.

Princes Street is where it all happens in Edinburgh and the bars were heaving on the Saturday morning. It was grey and overcast but at least it wasn't raining. The Scots had a decent team, full of solid characters. Sandy Hinshelwood was a good winger and fellow '66 Lion Stewart Wilson at fullback had earned a hard-won reputation for bravery under the high ball. There was plenty of experience up front, in a pack boasting the tallest player international rugby had then known, the 6ft 10 (207cm) lock Peter Stagg. Strahan would have to mark him in the line-outs. Scots who liked omens were excited by the half-backs–Melrose combination Hastie and Chisholm. In the ten internationals they had played together – including games against Australia and South Africa – Scotland had never lost. Could they make it eleven?

The bagpipes and drums of the Queen Victoria School band from Dunblane fired up the Murrayfield crowds. This was before *Flower of Scotland* was written, and instead of the calm measured threat that tune conjures up there was the passion of *Scotland the Brave*.

When the two sides ran onto the field, there was one notable change in the All Blacks. Colin Meads, in a typical rugby player's superstition, always ran out last if he wasn't captaining a side. But this time Davis had been getting "last-minute treatment from the physio", which was code for a bathroom nerves call, and he was late getting into the line-up. He ran out after Meads. It was a bad omen. Still, the stage was set for a wholehearted clash. That's what there was, too, but no-one remembers the scoreline because that wasn't the headline.

At 3:40p.m. on the afternoon of Saturday the 2nd of December 1967, with two minutes remaining in the test, Colin Earl Meads, who had received an earlier warning, was ordered from the field by the referee Mr Kevin Kelleher on the grounds of reckless play.

\*\*\*

Kelleher shouldn't have been there. He was Irish and with the foot-and-mouth epidemic his Union would have refused him permission to accept the invitation to referee the game. Knowing that, Kelleher didn't ask permission, he just accepted the invitation and headed for Murrayfield.

Meads shouldn't have been there either. Moments before the incident, Davis scored a good try. At the restart the Scots tried a quick kick-off but the ball hit the ref so the kick had to be retaken. This time the Scots kicked left, where a ruck formed. Meads seemed to enter it from an offside position and was thrown out by one of the Scottish forwards. As that happened, the ball emerged from the ruck and Meads hacked at it with his boot as Chisholm went to gather it. That was the 'dangerous play' that got him sent off, but if the kick-off hadn't hit Kelleher, Meads would have been away from the play.

He shouldn't have been sent off for that in Scotland anyway. Not when the Scots had a fine old tradition of hacking the ball forward soccer-style. "Feet Scotland, Feet, Feet," was an old Murrayfield war-cry. Generations of full-backs had tested their courage at the feet of Scottish packs, which were not renowned for carefully considering the personal wellbeing of said full-backs as they toed the ball on.

There's not much point in the might-have-beens of history. The fact was Meads was the first player sent off in a test match since All Black Cyril Brownlie at Twickenham in 1924 and — at the time of writing — they remain the only All Blacks ever to have been ordered off in tests.

All manner of assault, battery, and mayhem had taken place since Brownlie's despatch with no greater admonishment than a waggling finger and a penalty kick. The stitches in Meads' head, covered for the day in bandage and head gear, were ironical evidence of the violence of rugby in those years.

Meads was not a dirty player, one who kicked or struck defenceless opponents or those who had done nothing untoward. But it is fair to say that he had a reputation as an 'enforcer', one who extracted retribution on behalf of his team for opponents' transgressions. He was not the only player in the '67 team with that reputation, but he was the most prominent of them.

Rugby is a body-contact sport. Gaining physical supremacy is one of the keys to victory. In 1967, as one team's forward pointed out, the struggle up front still involved the "intimidation" of opponents. But long ago there had emerged certain unwritten rules applicable to this inherent mayhem. Two players of roughly the same size might exchange blows without undue censure if the fisticuffs were not overly prolonged. Players obstructing the opposition could, if the referee took no action, be given a firm reminder of the laws. All agreed, however, that the rules, written or unwritten, barred players from kicking or stamping. Players doing that were liable to receive instant retribution. When Going was repeatedly kicked in a ruck in the match at Newport, for example, even Strahan, whom McLean described as "A gentle young man without even elementary knowledge of rugged tactics," was disgusted enough to attack the perpetrators. But it's worth noting that he apologised to Saxton after the game and that Saxton warned him it must never happen again.

There was a fine line between tough and rough in the rugby game. There is no doubt that that line has moved considerably in the decades since 1967. But it is usually unfair to judge people other than by the standards of their time, and in 1967, rugby allowed what we might call the Meads defence: that violent retribution for offending might be permitted for the sake of the team, but not the individual. As McLean put it in his book on the 1953 tour, "If referees will not take action and provided it is done purely in the heat of the moment, there is nothing like a good, healthy punch to clear the air."

The '67 team and its supporters felt strongly that British referees and British rugby in general paid insufficient attention to violence done to the All Blacks. But the problem is that rugby players and fans all-too-frequently see the line as one crossed by the opposition who are dirty players and not by their own team, who are tough and hard. Thus New Zealand rugbymen tell dark tales of the deeds of Irish or Welsh forwards hidden by mist and rain and see French rugby as being as brutal as its foreign policy. But no New Zealand player is ever considered by its public to have crossed the line.

This is of course a myth and perhaps a dangerous one. When, for example, prop Richard Loe, who had a reputation as an enforcer, struck the tiny Australian winger Paul Carozza in the face as he lay defenceless after scoring a try, New Zealanders were collectively forgiving, if not entirely silent. Yet who knows how many mothers on both sides of the Tasman decided at that moment that little Johnny would be better off playing soccer?

As a ball-boy I witnessed, from a distance of perhaps ten yards, one of the 1967 prop forwards deliberately kick Ken Going two or three times after Going had gone down on the ball in open play. Ken was our favourite player. He would say "gidday" when he passed you on the street or saw you in the pool-hall and thus immeasurably raise your status among onlookers, so it was horrifying. Only some vague sense of propriety allied to fear of immediate sacking prevented me running out and confronting the offender myself. Yet that offender – who escaped punishment at least from the referee that day – was not famously violent.

Not that North Auckland were angels. They regularly picked a red-headed prop (what is it about props?) whose propensity for unprovoked violence bordered on the psychotic. Eventually he was picked for New Zealand, who lost the only game he played in. And in the face of increasing scrutiny of violence by both referees and public, it was perhaps this that eventually forced change. The selection of players who failed the Meads defence, those whose repeated assaults were cowardly and symptomatic of innate personal failings rather than loyalty to the team, weakened their side. They gave away penalties and increasingly, they were sent off.

In the end, you might put it all down to public relations. New Zealanders never apologise for incidents on the field. That absence of expressions of regret sustains a brutal image. Whether it was Meads and Watkins, Loe and Carozza, John Ashworth kicking J.P.R. Williams, the tackle that injured Lions' skipper Brian O'Driscoll or any of the other incidents that have caused a media storm, a carefully worded expression of regret for the consequences at the least, along with a few cliques to maintain the image of men hard but fair, could have made an enormous difference. Scotland and Lions back-rower and later coach Jim Telfer got it right in a television interview about his career. Asked if 'hard but fair' was an appropriate description of his playing style, Telfer, in best Scots brogue, growled, "No, I was never fair," and there was laughter all round.

Because a sending off was so rare in rugby union, Meads' dismissal was big news. Soccer referees frequently ordered players off, even if they did tolerate abuse that no rugby player would ever dream of directing at a referee. The soccer-obsessed British papers weren't quite sure how to deal with the Meads story. They knew it was big news in rugby circles but couldn't understand why because rugby seemed inherently violent. J.L. Manning noted sardonically in the *Daily Mail* that, "Violent play in Rugby is much more dangerous than in Soccer. Whole ears disappear."

There were and are members of the '67 side who feel that Meads was used as a scapegoat for foul play within British rugby (although Meads himself has never made that claim).

That would mean there were people at the top of the British rugby tree who realised that if rugby was to increase in popularity and playing numbers, the game's unwritten rules as to what was acceptable violence needed to change. A shift was taking place in society. A war-time generation inured to violence was giving way to a young generation growing accustomed to more gentle lives. People wearing 'peace and love' badges weren't going to cheer what was happening on the blind side of the ruck and down the track they weren't going to let their children play that rough game. There has been a process of change since that time, with touch-judges allowed to intervene for violent play, television evidence used after the game, and so on. But in 1967 that process had not even begun. Clearly to begin it would require that referees used their power to send players off for violent conduct. If top referees did that in internationals then it would slowly permeate to the lower ranks of the game.

Thus might Meads' dismissal have been used – or even pre-arranged – in order to begin cleaning up British rugby and have its players thinking, "'If they'll send Meads off in a test match they won't hesitate to send me off." That it was pre-arranged is a good conspiracy theory that unfolds well in retrospect. It's easy to imagine such a plan unfolding over brandy and cigars in some leather-lined club, with a white moustachioed old colonel harrumphing and muttering, "And if it's that dammed fellow Meads so much the better." Perhaps it happened, probably it didn't.

The facts of the matter are that Meads had been cautioned in the first half for climbing into a ruck, something perfectly normal in New Zealand rugby but frowned upon in the northern hemisphere. He was fully conscious of the warning and was being careful to avoid aggressive play, but trying to kick a loose ball didn't seem problematic. He was in open play, not obscured in a ruck, when he kicked out at the ball as Chisholm went to gather it. Chisholm did take the ball and pass it on. Both he and Meads were off-balance and fell separately to the ground. Clearly it was not Meads' intention to injure Chisholm, nor did the referee infer that. Meads was sent off for reckless play, that is, acting without sufficient concern for the consequences of his action.

In Veysey's biography, Meads remembers Scottish hooker Frank Laidlaw yelling, "Did you see that, ref, the dirty bastard" when the incident occurred, and is convinced that the referee did not actually see what happened but reacted to Laidlaw's cry. Kelleher denies that, although there is a note from Kelleher in the NZ Rugby Museum that seems to imply that he was influenced by the crowd's reaction.

When the referee blew his whistle and spoke to Meads, Chisholm, trotting back into position, touched Meads on the arm to indicate no harm done and no offence taken. It didn't help. Meads was ordered off. He started to walk, paused, then looked back to see if it had really happened. Kelleher reiterated, "You're off." Head bowed, Meads walked from the field.

Lochore had been at the bottom of the ruck and hadn't seen the incident. He quickly stepped in to talk to Kelleher, to no avail. For a moment, no-one in the crowd seemed to realise what had happened. Some witnesses remember a stunned silence, others that a section of the crowd were chanting "Off, off, off" as Meads disappeared down the tunnel.

The last moments of the game passed unnoticed. The teams hastened from the field and Chisholm came into the All Blacks' dressing room and expressed his regret at the sending off. "You were trying to kick the ball," he told Meads. The gesture deeply touched the King Country man, although the Scot's later statements about the incident were more ambiguous. It was a gloomy dressing room. The team's respect for Meads was universal and they were united in the belief that "he hadn't done anything wrong". As Williams put it: "We'd rather have lost the test than lost Piney."

One thing that was universally acknowledged was that Kelleher was a decent, honest and likeable bloke – something that doesn't fit with his being part of a conspiracy. A non-smoking, non-drinking headmaster of a private school in Dublin, he had played for the Lansdowne club before taking up the whistle. He was in his seventh year as an international ref and was highly regarded. No-one doubted that he had simply done his duty as he saw it. The question was whether he made the right call. With BBC television showing the incident again and again, that question provoked considerable discussion. All manner of journalists and former internationals gave their opinion. Clem Thomas, the former Welsh player who had so recently criticised the All Blacks for their "brutality" in the French test, admitted that he could have been sent off dozens of times in his career with such interpretations of the law.

That evening Saxton was interviewed on BBC television and stated that he considered the sending off unjustified. Allen concurred. Reyburn quotes the coach as saying Meads could have been sent off "Dozens of times [in his career]...but not for this trivial thing." Their opinions surely counted more than most. Both men had made a point of strongly condemning "rough stuff". Neither considered Meads' actions at Murrayfield came under that heading. Would they have condemned Meads for a blatant foul? We must give them the benefit of the doubt on that for they were both strong critics of foul play. They firmly believed Meads was innocent.

That night, Meads attended the after-match dinner, although he didn't get the opportunity to speak to Kelleher. He suspects they were kept apart, although the two met years later and regularly exchanged Christmas cards. Still, the mood at dinner was flat; the Scots didn't need this. Later that night Saxton took Meads and some of the dirt-trackers out for a quiet drink. They ensured that Meads did not go thirsty.

On the Sunday afternoon, the team left for Cardiff after the usual court session, with the tension partly alleviated by Saxton and Allen's satirical version of the sending off. Under the terms of the tour agreement, a disciplinary hearing had to be held within 48 hours and arrangements to hold that meeting began. A little later than usual, the All Black selection committee met and selected Meads to play in the following game against Monmouthshire at Newport.

That could be seen as a vote of confidence in Meads' innocence or simply proceeding on the grounds of innocent until proven guilty. But actually the selection was more about the defeat Whineray's men had sustained at

Newport in 1963. Every member of the team who played in that defeat – Meads, Davis, Kirton, Lochore, Tremain, Nathan, and Major– was selected for this game. The only exception was MacRae, who was unfit. But under the circumstances it would have been more diplomatic to have named that old standby, A.N. Other, at lock with Jennings.

Selecting Meads, and Saxton's public defence of him, was criticised for its implicit judgement of the issue. But Saxton's loyalty to Meads, to the team, was complete. He never wavered in standing up for Meads – who as a player was not expected to publically comment.

Naturally the morning papers were more concerned with the Meads incident than the match. In New Zealand, Monday's *Dominion* did lead with a story about a by-election in Palmerston North. But they had Meads' picture on the front page and it was on the front page again the next day, where it jostled for space with the news that the world's first heart-transplant had been successfully completed in Cape Town. Equally prescient was the suggestion from a Mr F.W. Baker of Wellington that appeared on the Readers' Letters page. Meads, he suggested, should be knighted, "To show the world where we stand."

The game itself was forgotten. It had been a close-fought match in front of 60,000 people in which the Scots used short line-outs to maximise the benefit of the giant Stagg. In that and many other ways they did their best to upset the All Blacks' playing patterns. But they created little and Lochore's men were too good for them. Though Kirton kicked more than usual, the All Blacks attacked throughout and scored two tries in winning 14-3. The old hands in the pack had been the main standouts.

At the centre of the storm, Meads was horrified at the thought that he had let down the jersey he had served for so long, horrified that anyone would think he had not been trying to kick the ball. He feared that like Brownlie he would be forever tarnished by the sending off. His wife Verna was in tears at the other end of the phone, so far away. Meads, the family man who loved rugby, who loved touring, who had given so much to the team, was at his lowest ebb.

Inexplicably, the tour agreement specifying that the judicial meeting be a matter between the Scottish and New Zealand Unions was ignored. Instead, the International Board took over. Here perhaps was reason to suspect a conspiracy. Cyril Gadney of the (English) Rugby Union, himself a former international referee, and Glyn Morgan, the President of the Welsh Rugby Union, were appointed to sit alongside Saxton on a three-man subcommittee. The secretary of the International Board was also in attendance.

The subcommittee met and were provided with a copy of Kelleher's report – which has never entered the public domain. Incredibly, they did not watch any film of the incident or interview any players. Nor was Meads called before the committee to speak in his own defence, which was surely unfair by any British standards since the Magna Carta. Saxton had been quoted as saying that Meads had already paid too great a price and should not be subject to any further penalty. But – in what he later called the unhappiest day of his rugby life – Saxton failed in what must have been his best efforts to defend Meads. The statement issued by the committee read:

> *The referee, K.D. Kelleher, of Ireland, having formally warned C.E. Meads, of New Zealand, for foul play and misconduct earlier in the game, making it clear that any repetition would mean dismissal...is supported in the action he took. Meads has been severely admonished and warned as to his future conduct and is suspended for the next two games on tour.*

The committee were clearly concerned to support the referee. Any indication that a referee would be hung out to dry for sending off a player in a test match would send entirely the wrong signal. We can imagine Saxton would have had to agree with that point and even accept for the same reason the patronising warning in addition to the standard caution.

That a referee would not harm his prospects in these circumstances was further emphasised soon after. Kelleher was appointed to referee the opening game of the Five Nations championship, which would commence a month later.

But the suspension was an unexpected blow. It hadn't happened to Brownlie and surely being sent off in an international was enough of a punishment? There was a nasty sting in that suspension. Murrayfield was Meads' 98th game in the black jersey. With just three tour games left the ban meant that Meads could not play his then unprecedented 100th game for New Zealand against East Wales at fabled Cardiff, or in the grand setting of a match at Twickenham against the Barbarians.

In New Zealand, Morrison made no public comment, although he phoned Meads at an ungodly early hour of the morning after the sending off. Nor was any comment issued after the NZRFU had viewed the film of the incident a few days later. We can take it for granted that Saxton did everything he could to support Meads. Of that there is considerable testament and no doubt, although ultimately if the fate of the tour had been placed on the table he would have had to fold. As he told Meads, "I'm sorry. They won't give an inch."

So why was Meads suspended? It wasn't a question I asked any of '67 All Blacks and Saxton is playing the Springboks in that great stadium in the sky. But looking back on it we can imagine several possibilities, including that the British authorities were intent on using the affair to clean up their own game. Perhaps the thought of Meads being honoured at Cardiff or Twickenham for his 100th game so soon after his sending-off was more than Gaffney and Morgan could contemplate. Or perhaps they were concerned with the crowd's reaction to Meads' distinction. Too much cheering just wouldn't do. But neither would booing and while the former seems much more likely, who is to say which would have occurred?

That Sunday night in Cardiff ended with Meads where he could most feel he was among friends, at the home of the great Welsh Lions centre Bleddyn Williams. There, surrounded by All Black old hands, Lions players who had toured New Zealand, and his old friend Williams' family, Meads could relax a little.

In the following days, Meads received sacks of mail and telegrams of support from all over the world. His great fear was that he would be remembered for this one moment, that at home in New Zealand he wouldn't be 'Colin Meads, All Black, and a good one' which is all the personal ambition he would allow himself at the expense of ambition for the team. No, he would be 'Colin Meads who got sent off at Murrayfield'. He feared that it might end his career. The letters and rugby friendships helped but it was only really when he returned to his family and Te Kuiti turned out in force to welcome their man home that he began to lose that fear.

In retrospect, Meads was already a legend when Kelleher sent him off. Where mortals can be felled by a single blow, the lives of legends are measured in chapters. In a career that had already spanned a decade and which would continue into the 70s, Murrayfield became simply one more chapter in the life of Meads. In truth, the man and the myth were bigger than this sad event. Privately scathing about several aspects of the judicial process, Meads rose above it in public. He simply carried on and the chapter was closed. As he says today, "Murrayfield was a point in history. The sending off became a marker."

\*\*\*

CHAPTER NINE

—

# "WE KNEW WHAT WE HAD TO DO"

Having Meads sent off brought Lochore's men even closer together. Part of the ethos of a team is that an attack on one man is an attack on them all. But inevitably the affair distracted from the task at hand. Allen recognised the pressures Murrayfield had generated and the risk that the All Blacks would be distracted or wound up too tightly in the final games. He responded by uncharacteristically taking his foot off the gas. Henceforth, he told the press, "We'll be taking it easy in training." To vary the usual routine, they held a golf tournament on the Monday, the kind of light-hearted but highly competitive event that kept the team together.

One other consequence of the Meads affair was that Saxton was exhausted. It had been an intense tour for all, with hotel changes twice a week before the Scottish sojourn. Managing the team had its own pressures, not least of all the time Saxton had to spend with the various national rugby officials. France, with its different culture and language, added new pressures and Saxton then had to deal with the cancellation of the Irish leg of the tour and the hastily re-arranged itinerary. The Meads affair came on top of that and Saxton had borne the brunt of the administrative workload and emotional strain it added. He had tried to defend Meads and lost in court. The burden of command was heavy. Added to that were worries about his menswear business at home. Saxton quietly took a couple of days off to relax. Many close to the team never knew it and the press respected his privacy. It was never mentioned publically. It's doubtful that even the NZRFU ever knew. Looking back that collective silence seems like a genuine tribute to a much loved man.

The three remaining games were all going to be tough. Two were against Welsh combinations, the other against the Barbarians. Selection for these games was no simple matter. Meads was suspended and the injury list was growing. Clarke was already out and Birtwistle and then Hopkinson suffered muscle strains that ended their tour. Dick, McRae, Herewini, and Kirkpatrick all missed at least one of the Welsh games with injury. Wills was out of favour and didn't play again after the Scottish Districts match. Jennings and Hazlett similarly faded from consideration. Jennings was picked only once in the last six games and Hazlett, the injured Herewini and the unlucky Smith only twice in the last eight games. The All Blacks were effectively choosing their team from 21 or 22 players.

But Gray, Strahan, Davis, and Steele all stepped up and played the last four games on tour. Lochore and McCormick played in each of the last six. That meant Lochore ended up playing fourteen of the seventeen tour matches, an exhausting schedule for a forward in any era. But with the side now stretched to its limits, Lochore and McCormick were proving the old adage: when the going gets tough the tough get going. Each in their own way was indispensable to the team's success.

With the dust barely settled on the Meads affair, the next game was upon them. There was a special edge to this match against Monmouthshire at Newport. In 1945 the Kiwis had been held to a 3-all draw by Newport, although neither Saxton nor Allen played that day. But, as the leading article in the programme reminded them, they were in the Kiwi side that played Monmouthshire at Pontypool and lost 0-15, with a Newport winger scoring a hat-trick against them. Then, although Newport lost to the All Blacks in 1953, they beat Whineray's men 3-0. So there was history behind this encounter and the All Blacks were determined to avenge those defeats. In the West Wales match programme, Lochore was quoted as saying the team were particularly keen to win all the internationals "And the match at Newport". In the black jersey, as he recalled, "history is an enormous influence on how you play the game." So every available player who had suffered defeat with Whineray was on deck for revenge, and none more so than Earle Kirton.

There are not too many second chances in top-line rugby, but Kirton had been determined to come back. Born in Taumaranui, Kirton was schooled in Upper Hutt and at St Patricks' College in Silverstream before heading to dental school in Dunedin and a famed half-back partnership with Laidlaw. The shadow of '63 had blighted his reputation but now he was one of the stars of the tour and playing with confidence and vision. He was ready to face the ghosts of Newport.

The All Blacks were back staying at the Angel hotel in Cardiff. They travelled to Rodney Parade, Newport by coach on the Wednesday afternoon of December 6th. It was fine and even sunny. Meads sat in the grandstand with the rest of the side. The team were joking with him about Murrayfield by now. His old friend Tremain, who they had rooming with him, had taken to calling him 'Sent-off'. But the management and the dirt-trackers were unusually tense as they watched a game they desperately wanted their team to win.

It was one of those Welsh grounds crammed into the town, surrounded by engineering works, offices, and blocks of flats. Spectators were packed into every available inch. Hundreds more watched from the windows of buildings overlooking the arena. A three-wheeler car – presumably owned by a handicapped fan – was parked in the ground just beyond the dead-ball line. There was no shortage of pre-match entertainment, with three separate bands playing. A Scottish band emerged pre-eminent with its pipes and drums, but *Land of Our Fathers* was apparently not part of their repertoire and it was left to the crowd of 20,000 to sing the anthem. The Monmouthshire side included just three Newport players and three internationals, but one of them was Keith Jarrett, the young star who had missed the Welsh test match with injury.

Monmouthshire turned out to be typically inspired Welsh opposition, and the game was still all square with ten minutes to go. It had been all penalties in the first half, but soon after play recommenced Kirton took a pass from Going, moved the ball on to Cottrell, then looped around him to take the ball again. It was a move the All Blacks often used on this tour but never better than on this occasion. Kirton was a long way from the goal-line but he just kept running, breaking one tackle then another, leaving four, five, six or more would-be tacklers in his wake as he raced to the line for the fairy-tale try that locked up and threw away the story of '63. Truth to tell he didn't have a great game, but it was a great try and now Kirton was no longer the guy who lost the game at Newport. Now he was just Kirton, the All Black 1st 5-8.

It wasn't a game for the ages. It took half an hour for the ball to reach Thorne in the centre. But in the last few minutes the All Blacks took control, ending with a 23-12, four tries to nil victory. And if Kirton was the man of the hour, the last try had the whole team smiling. Grey started it with a wild charge that knocked the referee out of the way. Then Lochore snatched up the loose ball and passed it on to Muller who cut inside two would-be tacklers and ran, as the BBC commentary had it, like a "jet-propelled barrel" to score. The try was greeted with great acclaim by his teammates in the stands and, unusually in those undemonstrative days, by those on the field. They say the big Taranaki prop gleefully acknowledged them with a quick thumbs up – or was it a two-fingered salute? But the grainy video of the game gives no hint of that. In the dressing room before the game Allen had singled him out, demanded more effort, demanded a try. Muller had responded. If Kirton had cast a weight from his shoulders, Muller had shown his top gear.

So too had Sam Strahan, who'd been called into this game when Meads' suspension was imposed. He was suddenly the senior lock. Like his 1990s successor Ian Jones, Strahan didn't look like the classic All Black lock. He looked more like an Olympic swimmer. Born in Palmerston and raised in the country, Strahan was unusual in having already been on O.E. before he made the All Blacks. Like most young travellers in those days, he had gone by boat and celebrated his 20th birthday aboard the good ship Northern Star. Strahan's trip had coincided with the Whineray tour and he had been among the crowd for their Scottish and French tests as well as their Southern Counties game. Then there was time to drive around Scandinavia and through Europe, before visiting America and returning home after nine months on the road.

After just three games of senior club rugby in 1965, Strahan was called into the Manawatu side and the following year made the NZ Juniors where he was first coached by Fred Allen. Then early in 1967 he played for Manawatu in a Ranfurly Shield challenge against Hawkes Bay. Allen was in the stand and it was one of those dream days where everything went right for Strahan personally even though his team lost. It became obvious that his sheep were going to need someone to look after them when the All Blacks went off to Britain.

Strahan was still raw when he went away on tour, but he soaked up advice, trained enthusiastically and just kept getting better. The whole team were delighted for him, for the lanky Strahan was a favourite with all. He was as McCormick remembers, a "huge personality", a modest and amusing young man with a gift for getting on with teammates and public alike. He had played in all four tests and now, with the pressure of Meads' absence, he stepped up to the role of senior player.

Eight of the team that had played Monmouthshire remained in the side for the game against East Wales at the Arm's Park on the Saturday. One of them was Thorne, who moved to the wing to fill in for the injured specialists. Herewini and Kirkpatrick returned from injury and Smith came in to partner Strahan in the second row. Chosen as back-up to Meads, he'd had few opportunities until now.

The Barbarians end-of-tour game was traditionally the preserve of the leading players or those with long and distinguished service. About a third of the team could thus be fairly certain that their playing role was either over already or would be after the Saturday. While an unbeaten tour was a powerful motivation for most of the side, the thoughts of some of that third were inevitably starting to turn to home.

In the meantime, the Barbarians were putting their team together. Traditionally they invited the best attacking players from the British Isles but now Irish players were not considered because of the foot-and-mouth disease outbreak, while the idea of inviting French players fell through because the French preferred to keep their men in domestic rugby. Four years earlier, when the Barbarians played Whineray's men, they had honoured All Black prop Ian Clarke with an invitation to play for them *against* the All Blacks. Clarke had been on the All Black tour of the UK a decade earlier and turned out 83 times for New Zealand over the years, although Whineray and Gray kept him out of the test matches on his second UK tour. The invitation, in full accord with the Barbarians' ethos, was a gesture in honour of his long years in the game. Clarke duly played for the Barbarians and in a fairy-tale twist he kicked a goal from the mark, the Barbarians only points in a 3-36 defeat.

Drawing on that precedent, the Barbarians selectors now asked Saxton whether Nathan, who had similarly been out of the test team on this tour, might represent them in the final tour game. It was a mark of respect for a great player. The back row was one area where the All Blacks had a full complement of fit players, so Nathan could be spared by Saxton's injury-hit side. The offer to Nathan was also one to strike a chord with

Saxton and Allen. After all, Allen had captained the Barbarians in their 1945-46 victory over a Swansea side led by Saxton. The following day Allen played another game for the club, which ended in a 6-11 defeat to Newport. Several other members of the Kiwi side had also turned out for both the Barbarians and Swansea as well as various other teams around the country.

Despite those precedents, Saxton apparently decided not to release Nathan, who was included in the All Black team for the match. Saxton's felt the competitive nature of the game would be threatened if Nathan played for the opposition and that the All Blacks had to retain their group identity. But in retrospect, it was surely a mistake. Aside from the fact that it meant Williams, who had played in all of the tests, couldn't be fitted into the side for the final game, it deprived Nathan of a very special honour. Perhaps if Saxton had not been under such pressure he might have made a different call. But then there is some doubt about whether it was his decision. Reyburn attributes it to David Brookes, who was to manage the 1968 Lions in South Africa and wanted a Barbarians team entirely made up of candidates for that tour. As it was, Nathan and Colin Meads were to be presented with Barbarians jerseys as a token of the esteem in which they were held, while Lochore was made an honorary member of the club.

On the Friday before the East Wales game in Cardiff, it began to snow heavily. That afternoon about a dozen of the 'dirt-trackers' headed to Port Talbot to visit what is variously remembered as a sports club or an entertainment centre. It was owned by actor Richard Burton's brother, who proved a popular host. The players got snowed in and couldn't make it back to Cardiff that night. Instead, they spent a wonderfully informal night relaxing in the Valleys. For Wills it was, "The best thing that ever happened to me on the tour." There was a visit to a bingo hall at one point, where Birtwistle received a good natured booing from 400 women for having had the temerity to score a try against Wales, while Major found that Burton's brother knew the family of his Welsh fore-fathers. The players ended up on hastily arranged beds in the club and made it back to the team hotel in time for breakfast. That a break from the constraints and discipline of touring brought such relief was indicative of the mounting pressure the team was under.

That Saturday morning, Cardiff Arms Park was covered in a foot of snow. The ground itself was protected by eight tons of straw and tarpaulins and when they were removed the playing surface was in good condition. But the snow had covered the seats and terraces. In those days of brooms not hot-air blowers, there was no possibility of clearing them in time for the scheduled kick-off. The authorities had to call the game off, at considerable financial loss to the Welsh Rugby Union.

The match against the Barbarians was scheduled for the following Saturday, with the All Blacks due to travel up to London on the Sunday and spend a week there before that final game. But when the decision was made to call off the East Wales game, Saxton offered to reschedule it to the Wednesday. The offer was gratefully accepted and so yet again the itinerary was altered.

There was a precedent for this. In 1953, the All Blacks match against an English South-East Counties side was called off because the ground was frozen and they had to come back a month later. Ironically that return was, as McLean's book on the '53 tour notes, "Primarily a gesture toward Mr Cyril Gadney, who was most anxious to propagandise Rugby in a Soccer district." Gadney had been, McLean wrote, that team's "faithful knight, the perfect friend", who hosted no less than three parties for the '53 team. But the '67 team had a rather different opinion. It was the same Gadney on the disciplinary committee that suspended Meads!

The All Blacks stuck to their usual match day schedule despite the cancellation of the game, although with added beer. Williams and Smith built a snowman on the halfway line and the team wandered back to the hotel. But the day improved. Although the East Wales game was called off, the after-match function wasn't and it was a great occasion. The success of the party had some wondering if it was necessary to play rugby. Couldn't they just have the after-match functions?

Lochore was ensuring Meads kept his spirits up. As his biography recalls, the two men crammed into the back of Jackie Mathews' Mini-Minor and headed to the home of Rex Willis, where they were joined by McCormick, Bleddyn Williams, and Cliff Morgan the brilliant Welsh 1st 5-8 of the 1950s. Things got a little blurry. It was Monday before they were back on deck.

The All Blacks decamped to London, back to the Park Lane hotel and the Mayfair pub. Sacks of mail were still arriving for Meads, a continuing reminder of the events of the previous Saturday. With the tour finale imminent, many of the team went into major shopping mode. In 1967, New Zealand had extensive import controls and British products like Pringle knitwear, Burberry coats, or Scotch whisky were subject to taxes that rendered them rare and esteemed gifts. Hopkinson, with his re-arranged marriage awaiting him, was particularly acquisitive. As always, however, it was Jennings whose shopping exploits were supreme above all others.

Tuesday afternoon saw the All Blacks take the opportunity to watch one of the highlights of the British rugby calendar: the Oxford-Cambridge match at Twickenham. They weren't impressed. It was a grim struggle which Cambridge won 6-0 with a single try. It seemed pretty dull to a team that had so enthusiastically embraced the running game. But then the Oxbridge match is a tribal war. For most of the players it's the biggest game of their career, one they focus on for months. I had an old uncle in London who would speak in awe of watching the fervour on the faces of the Oxbridge players running out at the start of the game. What business was it of the All Blacks how these tribes played? But things would change—Laidlaw was watching and soon he'd be a member of one of those tribes.

Chapter Nine

The All Blacks couldn't arrange suitable accommodation in Cardiff for the Tuesday night. So they stayed in London and on the Wednesday morning took the train to Cardiff for the East Wales game. Then it was onto a coach for the journey of a few hundred yards along the crowded street that led to the Arms Park. On paper they were a strong side, ten of the team had played at least one test on the tour. But their preparation had been poor, their focus too frequently blurred by acts of God and end-of-term blues. In truth the All Blacks were just hanging on now, not enough players mentally or physically fit. "The wheels had fallen off," as Thorne put it. But they were still unbeaten and there remained two games that would decide how the team was remembered.

If they won this game in Cardiff they'd be the first All Blacks to get through Wales unbeaten since the 1924 'Invincibles'. East Wales were keenly aware of their responsibility. Coach and former Welsh flanker Dai Hayward had been preparing for them for weeks. Meads' biography tells of how when the game was cancelled their hooker Jeff Young was in tears at the thought of missing his chance to defeat the All Blacks. They were totally up for it. Their side was built around the strong Cardiff team of the time. It included seven players with Welsh caps and three others who would later become internationals. Gareth Edwards, Barry John, Gerald Davies, and last-minute inclusion John Dawes would go onto star for the 1971 Lions in New Zealand, Dawes as captain. They were not a team to underestimate.

40,000 people crowded into the Arms park on an overcast day. The ground was soft and slippery underfoot but instead of a forward battle the Welsh side tried to out-run the All Blacks. None of their opponents had really tried that before and the All Blacks response was uninspiring. Herewini had been passed fit and was keen to play, but his selection was something of a risk and it didn't come off. Nothing went right for him that day. In contrast, Edwards and John began to reveal their talents to New Zealanders, talents largely hidden when they had played in the

Welsh test. East Wales came close to scoring on a number of occasions and deserved to win. But with their kickers missing numerous chances, their only points came from a try mid-way through the first half when John sliced a drop-goal attempt and Cardiff winger Frank Wilson won the race to the ball.

With ten minutes to go, the All Blacks looked down and out. But as they have so often shown, winning rugby is about taking your chances, upping gears physically and mentally in that critical instant when a chance appears. And it's about more than that. It's about believing that those chances will come and being fit enough to take them and above all *determined* enough to take them. That determination was strong in the '67 team because the selectors had sought out players with just that quality. They had picked them, provided the example of excellence in leaders like Saxton and Lochore, trained them to exhaustion and fluency under Allen's coaching, and trusted them to deliver. Now, when the pressure was on, that all paid off. There were still enough men standing who had the right stuff.

It was—and it's tempting to say inevitably—Lochore who started the crucial move. As Hazlett and the other forwards drove to around half-way, Lochore dropped off and threw a long pass left to Davis – or was it Kember? – who fed Steel. Steel had a long way to go and one, two, three tacklers came at him on the way. Sprinter's speed, strength, and determination carried him on. The last tackler seemed to have him. He stumbled, regained balance and made it to the corner. The triumph of determination, the triumph of the will.

That try tied it at three points apiece. McCormick, human at last, failed to win the match with his conversion attempt. Then in the last play of the game Barry John failed to win it for his side with a drop-kick. Four years later he'd make up for it with the Lions. For the day it was a draw. The All Blacks were still unbeaten, but the Welsh had the consolation of having preventing them from making a clean-sweep through the Principality.

In a poor All Black performance, Alan Smith stood out over the 80 minutes. Smith had a tough early life. His mother died young and his father, wounded by a sniper in Italy, was a stranger to him when he returned. But steeled by his experiences, the Taranaki lock made his provincial side as a nineteen-year-old in 1962 and been part of their Ranfurly Shield era. Like Thorne, with whom he'd once been billeted during a youth cricket tournament, he'd probably rather have played cricket for New Zealand and he did open the bowling for Taranaki.

When he was picked for the '67 tour, Allen told him that he was being groomed to take over from Meads. So he understood this was a learning tour and being a straightforward and honest young man he set to studying. He was intelligent and learned well, but perhaps that sense that he was not yet being given full responsibility imposed a ceiling on his immediate ambitions and hindered the expression of his learning. Or perhaps it hindered his communicating the desire to show what he could do. Whatever the case, Smith had had a quiet tour. Before this match he played just four of the fifteen games. Now, with Meads unavailable, Smith stepped into his shoes and showed that they weren't entirely too big for him. He left it a bit late, but like Cottrell, Kember, Thorne, Williams, Hopkinson, and Kirkpatrick, the newcomer earned the tick in the selector's notebook for the future. They'd all be back in black.

For three of the team it was their last game for New Zealand. Along with Herewini and Hazlett, it was the end of the road for John Major. In 1968, they decided to blood a younger player, although they might have taken Major again because he was, as Lochore put it, "Good value." Like his Taranaki teammate Smith, Major's early life wasn't easy. He had lost both his father and his mother by the time he was ten, but he progressed through Waitara High School first XV and Inglewood club to the Taranaki side in 1961 and was part of the Ranfurly Shield era that followed. In 1963, he made Whineray's tour as the reserve hooker to

Dennis Young. In the years that followed he was reserve to Bruce McLeod, who leap-frogged him in the rankings in 1964. In those days before injury replacements, he sat on the bench through fifteen internationals before he finally won his solitary cap in the Jubilee test. He then sat on the bench for the four tests on the '67 tour to add to his earlier spells there. In the modern game of regular replacements he would have won nearly twenty caps.

Being a regular reserve behind an established player in a specialised position requires certain qualities. Foremost of those is naturally playing ability. Major was inevitably described as "hard-working", which in a sphere not renowned for its slackers is a good reputation to have. Years hooking the Taranaki scrum had seldom seen him bested. But certain personal qualities are necessary for the bench too. The ability to suppress the ego and dedicate yourself to the team is paramount, to be the kind of guy who trains hard, supports the man in front of him, guides the young guys and gives 100% on and off the field. And from that it follows that he will be a good bloke, someone whose company is welcome in any corner of the team room. Major had those qualities. He was the kind of guy who'd help out the baggage man for something to do and visit a school when no-one else wanted to go. It was that quality of giving to the team – and getting on well with his hosts – that made Major what they call 'a good tourist'.

He played seven games on tour, after playing sixteen games with Whineray. Unlike his speedy Taranaki teammate Wills, he found the wet northern hemisphere grounds suited him. They gave him that timeless moment in which he could anticipate, be in the bubble. The *Almanack*, honouring him as one its Players of the Year for the 1967 season, noted how important the tight-heads he'd robbed in this game had been in relieving pressure on his side. He'd done his job. Now he'd go back to the farm.

\*\*\*

Returning to London after the chastening draw with East Wales, the selection committee chose its team for the Barbarians game. There were no real surprises given that selection for this game was something of a reward. That meant the experienced Laidlaw rather than the disappointed young contender Sid Going. He had played just one match after his starring role in the French test and felt he deserved more. It also meant Tremain and Nathan rather than Kirkpatrick and Williams on the side of the scrum. Dick was fit again so he was in and Muller was back in the front row.

The Barbarians team included seven Englishmen, six Welshmen and two Scotsmen, thirteen of whom had already played against the All Blacks in their national colours. With a Lions side to be chosen to tour South Africa this was a good chance for their players to impress (although only seven of them made it).

Most of the All Blacks' dirt-trackers were now what soldiers calls 'demob happy'. They were like passengers when a plane lands, workers five minutes from knock-off time. It's a perfectly natural human state of mind. After a long period of focus on one aspect of the world, the brain embraces imminent change to a broader experience of life, family and friends. No matter how good the experience may have been, the mind knows it's over and time to move on. So most dirt-trackers didn't join the likes of Meads and Kirkpatrick on early morning runs. Instead they took the chance to see the Black and White Minstrel Show, the Natural History museum, a game of soccer at one of the big stadiums, or just took a taxi around "the sights of the Monopoly board".

There were still official invitations to fulfil. One of the more sought after was to BBC Television 'Sports Review of 1967' at the Shepherd's Bush studios on the Thursday night. The All Blacks were in the running for the Team of the Year award and Kiwi driver Denny Hulme was a contender for Sports Personality award. They didn't win but for the team it was a chance to mingle with the likes of Personality winner boxer Henry Cooper and round-the-world yachtsman Sir Francis Chichester, who presented the award. Nathan, Herewini, and Going, along with Smith who was one of the few who took the haka seriously, got up on stage to perform it proudly for the invitation-only crowd.

The show was something of an eye-opener for the All Blacks. It would be years before the media and the NZRFU worked closely together. New Zealand had had its Sportsman of the Year award since 1949 but the committee were notoriously reluctant to give it to an All Black. Only Ron Jarden, Don Clarke, and Wilson Whineray had been honoured and none of the '67 side ever got the award. In fact it didn't go to rugby again until it was given to the 1987 World Cup winning team. There always seemed to be a feeling in their homeland that the All Blacks got enough recognition. Yet their media profile was remarkably low compared to the new breed of international sports star that was starting to emerge in the 60s – men like Pele or the jet-setting skier Jean-Claude Killy. Star quarter-back Joe Namath was being interviewed in Playboy, George Best was soaking up champagne and bedding Miss Worlds, and Arnold Palmer had been on the cover of Time Magazine. The cover of Sports Digest was about as big as it got for an All Black.

\*\*\*

At the start of the 1967 tour, 30 young men had set out with the intention of enjoying a successful rugby tour. Now there were fifteen men left to seal the '67 All Blacks' reputation with a final victory. Not since 1924 had an All Black side toured unbeaten through the northern hemisphere and neither Springboks nor Wallabies had ever done so. This was a powerful motivating factor, dispelling fatigue, driving them forward to one more effort.

The traditions of Barbarians' rugby required touring sides to adopt their ethos of playing attacking fifteen-man rugby. That had troubled a few sides, notably the dour 1960-61 Springboks who'd lost their unbeaten record trying that style. But Lochore's men were playing fifteen-man rugby already so that was not a problem. Nor was history—Whineray's men had entered into the spirit of things brilliantly and enjoyed a big win. But then Whineray's side had nothing to lose. They weren't defending an unbeaten record as Lochore's men were. That record brings an additional burden, the fear of failure starts to take over from the feeling of confidence. The occasional loss isn't such a bad thing especially if it's early in the tour and in a match of no great consequence, meaning preferably not in Wales!

Yet that level of pressure, defending an unbeaten record against a tough final opponent with tactics dictated by the opponent, is something that winners ultimately enjoy. After all the training there is a mental level above the physical, summoning up the sheer willpower necessary to go on at your absolute best, bringing out reserves of strength that the individual barely suspected they possessed. As Laidlaw recalled in his book, while he, "Aged ten years" in that last week, it was nonetheless an "intense and stimulating" time.

There were 40,000 people at Twickenham on December 16th, a good crowd for a match arranged at short notice. It was a fine day. The sun even appeared and the All Blacks received a long round of applause as they took the field for the last time. If McLean was pardonably exaggerating when he said they'd remember this game until, "The sands of the desert grow cold," it was a wonderful game full of running rugby from both sides. There were really too many mistakes for it to be a great game, but it had the crowd constantly leaping to their feet and climaxed in an amazing finale.

It was 3-3 at halftime after a dropped goal apiece. Early in the second half the Barbarians scored a try from a kick ahead by John. Barbarians captain Stewart Wilson missed the conversion and five other shots at goal, kicks that could have put his team out of sight. Bob Lyold scored their try. In a testament to the efficiency of the All Blacks' defence, only ten of their opponents had managed to cross their line, and only England and France 'B' had done so twice. Remarkably, Lyold scored four of the twelve tries notched against them.

The All Blacks efforts were spoiled by poor handling. McCormick remembered "We had the incentive to win [but] we struggled, we just couldn't finish." With a minute to go they were down 3-6. The Barbarians had two clear chances to score tries to seal victory. Both times they were ended by the indomitable McCormick. Allen had picked McCormick because he judged him a player who would give everything down to the last whistle. He had already repaid that trust many times over. Now that the very last whistle was imminent, his determination to reward their faith in him became something more, something legendary. The Barbarian wingers were speedsters, Keri Jones sprinted for Wales in the Commonwealth games, Gerald Davies had both pace and extraordinary elusiveness in his running. On paper, McCormick could never catch them when they had a start on him, but rugby isn't played on paper.

Jones got free with 40 yards to go, McCormick had to turn and chase him. It should have been history, but it wasn't. McCormick's willpower triumphed over Jones' speed. He tracked him, cut off his angles of escape and broke his confidence. Jones kicked as he was flattened in the tackle and Davis was first to the ball over the line. Problem solved.

Then Gerald Davies had his chance. He had a clear run to the line, with a man in support. The All Blacks had McCormick. He was running at Davies on the angle, trying to cut him off at the corner flag but the winger looked certain to score. Then something happened, just when Davies should have been diving for the line, he threw a pass inside to his support. It was a wild and misdirected pass; the ball went loose and the All Blacks cleared. What happened was a triumph of McCormick's will. As he ran at Davies, McCormick's commitment went into overdrive. He began screaming at the flying Welshmen. It was pretty explicit stuff. Davies, given the option of maybe scoring in a tackle that was going to shatter him into a thousand pieces and bury them in the Twickenham turf, or of getting rid of the ball, sensibly chose the path of self-preservation. That is what mortals are programmed to do. McCormick never even needed to make the tackle, the threat of it was enough to do the trick. "Oh, I reminded him that if I got him I'd kill him," said McCormick laconically when I asked him about it, before giving the credit to Allen for the way the coach's training sessions had improved his speed.

The All Blacks were still behind on the scoreboard. Then in the last minute of scheduled playing time, they ran a penalty from inside their own half. McCormick took it up and from the ruck they ran the ball to the right. Steel came through from the blind-side wing at full pace. Tacklers bounced off him until he was almost at the line. He was held up but he flicked the ball out and there was MacRae to take it and dive over; it was 6-all.

Just as in the East Wales game, McCormick had the chance to win the game with his conversion. As at Cardiff, he missed. The two misses were the only serious blemish on his tour record. But it wasn't all over yet. There were a few minutes of injury time to be played for this was in the days before the clock stopped when a player was injured. It was still an unscientific matter of the ref saying, "OK fellas, three minutes of injury time".

Great leaders don't waste words. McCormick doesn't remember Lochore saying anything as the All Blacks took up their positions to field the Barbarians kick-off. "We didn't need to speak. We knew what we had to do," he says. The All Blacks ran the ball, then Laidlaw kicked and Wilson, the Barbarians fullback, had only to find touch to end the game and end the tour. Still an unbeaten tour, but draws in the last two games would take the gloss off it. Wilson kicked, but he failed to kick it out of play.

Inevitably – for now we can say inevitably – it was Lochore who fielded the kick 45 five yards out from the Barbarians line. He ran, passed to Kirton who straightened, then it was Steel, tearing down the left wing, taking the pass and running the All Blacks into immortality. Kirton, Nathan, and Meads were in support as he touched down. This time McCormick converted to bring up a personal tally of 100 points on the British tour. He had succeeded with 44 out of his 90 goal attempts on tour, which was about par in that era. The ball disappeared into the crowd. It was all over. They were going home unbeaten.

Lochore was chaired off by his teammates, exhausted joy and satisfaction shining from his face. The weight was off his shoulders and on theirs. The crowd sang *Now is the Hour* and *Auld Lang Syne* and Bill Davis was there just as he had promised his father all those years ago. The All Blacks had won. The tour was over.

The accolades began, and they were many and rich. Saxton and Allen had made a promise: the '67 All Blacks would win by scoring tries. That promise had been fulfilled. They had scored 71 tries in seventeen games, with thirteen in the four victorious tests. By comparison, the 1953 and '63 sides between them managed nine tries in ten tests, only seven of which were won. The '67 side had averaged 17.75 points per test against their two predecessors' average of 6.8 points. Their three top try scorers were wingers. The old days were gone. New Zealand rugby would never go back to ten-man rugby. The spirit of the 'Kiwis' had triumphed under their old captain.

The celebrations ran long into the night. At the after-match dinner in the Savoy hotel the champagne flowed. No training run in the morning. The All Blacks could finally relax. In fact, morning saw the All Blacks, hangovers not withstanding, dressed in their Number Ones. Saxton, Allen, Lochore, MacRae, Ralph Love, Derek Lever and Richard Walker were all formally thanked by a different player and presented with a token of the genuine esteem in which each were held. Then it was back to last-minute stuff, muscle applied not to scrummaging but to closing suitcases crammed with gifts and souvenirs.

One thing they didn't pack was their boots. The foot-and-mouth epidemic meant they had to leave them behind. Even their ordinary shoes had to be washed and presented for inspection when they arrived back in Auckland. Wills wasn't too pleased. He'd worn out his last pair of boots in the final trial and borrowed the pair he took on tour from his brother-in-law. Now he had to throw those away and buy replacements for himself and his brother-in-law! Boots made an awful mess of a week at a dollar a day.

The team flew out of London on the Monday afternoon, hopping across the world on a Qantas flight that stopped in Rome, Teheran, and Delhi before it reached Hong Kong the following afternoon. Qantas had recently carried the Kangaroos, the Australian rugby league team whose tour coincided with the All Blacks visit. The airline was sparing in their provision of beer. Rumour had it that the Kangaroos had drunk them dry and hadn't been the most pleasant of guests. That meant the All Blacks soon had to switch to spirits, which is always a trap for young players. A night in the luxurious Mandarin hotel swept them up.

An overnight flight to Brisbane followed, with former All Black Des O'Connor arranging a breakfast reception for them at the airport. Australia was waking up to the news that their Prime Minister, Harold Holt, had drowned during a dip in the surf the day before. They named a swimming pool after him.

Then the team flew on to their sixth stop, in Sydney. Finally, at 6:30 pm that afternoon, to the strains of Nathan and Hazlett singing Green Grass of Home, they touched down in Auckland. It was three days, give or take time changes, since they had left London but they were home for Christmas.

The tour was over, the players dispersed. There were connecting flights to Wellington and Christchurch and wives and families waiting. The farmers returned to their farms, the others to their jobs or in Birtwistle's case to study the 'situations vacant' column in the local paper. Kember and Davis were off to do national service. And of course, homecoming is never quite what you imagined. McLeod discovered things hadn't gone well at home in his absence. Thorne learned that while he was away his parents had sold his Ming blue Triumph MG sports car and replaced it with a humble Humber 80, which wasn't really a Thorne kind of car. Life went on. The players, having served the team, went back to their ordinary lives.

***

CHAPTER TEN

—

# "LIFE IS BROADER BECAUSE OF RUGBY"

The accounts presented at the NZRFU annual meeting in April 1968 show the 1967 tour cost the Union $21,577 – and three cents. The biggest expense was the trials, which cost $7,667. Then there were the manager's expenses, outfitting and accommodation costs, souvenir silver fern badges, insurance, the farewell dinner and luncheon, and presentation rugs to include. At a dollar a day the players themselves collectively earned a grand total of just over $2000. That was the amateur way. But Lochore could be forgiven a wry smile at the news that in 2009, his tour jersey – long since gone to another – had sold at auction for a 1,000 pounds sterling.

What those accounts didn't show was the immeasurable goodwill the tour generated from the team's embrace of fifteen-man rugby. By adopting a style of play with wide popular appeal, the team ensured the future for New Zealand rugby, although the new style gradually permeated through the national game rather than immediately flooding into it. As Meads commented, the players needed to go back to their local teams and "spread the gospel" of running rugby. Allen certainly saw the new approach as a process, not an event. His comments in the New Zealand Weekly News Christmas edition obliquely acknowledged criticism that the running game of the '67 side did not allow for individual flair. He pointed out that:

> *What I will say very firmly is that there is another stage of development to be exploited. This is the stage when players, and especially backs, become so effective in their mastery of basic skills that they are able to make use of their individual genius… This is the stage to be developed in the next year or two.*

This suggests Allen saw a decisive role for creative players like Thorne and Going if the Springboks were to be defeated in 1970. But by then one of the greatest strengths of the '67 team had been cast aside.

Despite Saxton and Allen combining so successfully, Saxton's role ended when the team returned to New Zealand. By tradition, managers were only appointed for a single tour. It would be someone else's turn next time. So the best manager of his era went back to work in menswear and being an ordinary member of the NZRFU Council, although rewarded with the Presidency of the Union in 1974. Looking back, sidelining Saxton seems extraordinarily stupid, but many things look that way in retrospect. Did we really wear flares and spotted ties in the 70s? Back then that was just the way it was. Saxton had had his turn: thank you and goodnight.

When the team returned home, the start of the new season was only months away, and it was to be no ordinary season. Indeed, many strange things happened in 1968, not least in New Zealand rugby. A Japanese winger scored four tries against the New Zealand Juniors and wound up as an Almanack Player of the Year. Three different players captained the All Blacks in five tests. And Fred Allen quit as coach.

The All Blacks played two tests on a twelve match tour of Australia (and Fiji), and three at home against France. The selection panel was unchanged yet despite the success of the '67 tour, the 25-man team for the Australian tour included seven new players, although in the first test team only flanker Tom Lister had not been on the '67 tour. Thorne and Cottrell graduated to the test team. When Lochore broke his thumb in the first test, Kirkpatrick came on as the first replacement in a modern test match and celebrated with three tries.

The injured Lochore missed the next two tests. MacRae missed the tour completely, and Laidlaw got his chance to captain New Zealand in the second test when they scraped home courtesy of a controversial penalty try at the death. He kept his place in the side but Tremain took over the captaincy for the first test against France before Lochore returned for the last two. All three tests against the French were won, meaning New Zealand had played 37 matches since Allen became coach in 1966, with 36 wins and a draw. Whereupon, despite the lure of the South African tour scheduled for 1970, Allen quit.

Although he had served a three-year term, Allen's resignation was a matter of some controversy. The catalyst was his allowing respected Wellington journalist Alex Veysey to sit in on his team-talk before the first test against Australia. When Veysey's report duly appeared in the Dominion, Tom Morrison phoned new All Black manager Duncan Ross (who had agreed to Veysey's presence), and told him to pass on to Allen his extreme displeasure at this breach of convention. Allen was furious both at the reprimand and the fact that Morrison hadn't spoken to him directly. The incident seems to have convinced him to stand down.

It wasn't actually the first time that Allen had allowed outsiders into his team talk. David Brooks and Ronnie Dawson, who were to manage and coach the 1968 Lions side, sat in on the Murrayfield team talk as had one or two others close to the team on various occasions. In any case, Veysey's report was in no sense anti-rugby. It was an 'atmosphere piece', giving away no tactical secrets while offering considerable insight into Allen's genius. But it was typical of NZRFU relations with the press at that time that the idea of a journalist attending the team talk seemed outrageous to them. It did to Terry McLean too. He claimed he would never have accepted such an invitation, although perhaps that was a journalist's sour grapes at being scooped!

But Allen had already recognised his mortality as national coach. In the Weekly News Christmas edition he said he had "Made it plain" to Morrison that, "If there is a feeling in New Zealand Rugby against me I want to be told, so that I can slide out and avoid the embarrassment [of being sacked]." As Allen told his biographer, his great ambition had been to take the team to South Africa in 1970. But ultimately he couldn't handle the "interference and pettiness" of "a small group of top administrators."

That inability to ignore his critics might suggest that there was a basic insecurity about Allen, something stemming from his tough childhood or the defeats of '49. But perhaps it was his impulsive nature, the same character that enabled him to cut Williment with a pen-stroke also enabled him to simply toss it all in and step away rather than continue to fight political battles. It's hard to believe that the 'drop Meads, Gray, and McLeod' story was his only grievance against the administration, for that was a battle – if it was a battle – that he had won. No doubt there were older enmities at work. Perhaps without Saxton to deal with the administration Allen simply found it just didn't work for him.

Whatever the case, it meant that by the end of 1968 Saxton and Allen were both gone. Perhaps coincidentally Morrison also stepped down and was succeeded as NZRFU Chairman by the much less conciliatory Jack Sullivan. The players, however, mostly carried on. Lochore lead the All Blacks to South Africa in 1970 with 18 of his 1967 side in the 30-man squad, and twelve of them played in the first test. It would have been thirteen but Meads, in career-best form, had his arm broken by a cowardly stamp in a ruck. As usual, no penalty was inflicted for assault *on* Meads.

1970 was intended to be the culmination of the process of developing an All Black side that would be victorious in South Africa. But the dreamed-of victory didn't happen. Despite being unbeaten in the provincial matches and playing some spectacular rugby, they lost the test series 3-1. Something was missing. Perhaps key players were past their peak, perhaps they were just unlucky with injuries, or referees, or the bounce of the ball. Or perhaps they needed Saxton, who was back in New Zealand, and Allen. In an extraordinary waste of talent, their old coach was leading a supporters' tour of South Africa. Instead, under a manager who failed to inspire or connect with his players and a coach who wasn't the best, even if he was well-liked, they lost the series. It was a sad end to the hopes of a generation. Saxton and Allen had found glory in the UK with the Kiwis and the All Blacks, but South Africa in 1940, 1949, and 1970 defeated their dreams.

***

There the 1967 side might rest in the archives. One of the best teams ever sent overseas. A side that enjoyed an eventful tour and successfully re-introduced the running game to New Zealand rugby. But a side that failed to lay the groundwork for victory in South Africa.

Yet relating the 1967 team to the 1970 tour is unfair. The leadership of Saxton, Allen, and Lochore was fundamental to the success of the 1967 tour. With Saxton and Allen gone and far less talented men replacing them, Lochore had an almost impossible task in South Africa. That was a tougher tour anyway, not least because of its blatantly home-town refs.

In any case, it was their re-introduction of a fifteen-man game that really made the '67 side a great one. Its precise place in the top rungs of the ladder of great All Black sides is a debate for the ages. What is hard to imagine now is how fundamentally the team's style transformed the national game. Allen saw the tour as the "Summit of my coaching career," precisely because they "sustained the attempt to play balanced, fifteen-man rugby." Laidlaw at least sees the credit as due largely to the forwards and the law changes allowing backs more space were an important factor. But Saxton and Allen were the drivers of change. They made it happen.

Selection was a big part of making that change. Players like Thorne, Going, and Kirton were statements. They were never going to stuff it up their jumpers and drive it forward a couple of yards, then stand around chewing their fingernails while the scrum was set.

Perhaps the team's approach was overly optimistic at times. Kember made the point that it could be a little naive to attack before their forwards got on top. But as David Frost pointed out, the team, "Showed that there was no need to be constantly searching for second phase possession [as] a high proportion of their tries were scored by the backs direct from set pieces." That ability to create tries by well-timed passing, along with basic loop movements and the fullback as the extra man, was a hallmark of the great teams of any era.

One easily-forgotten aspect of their success is that on all the big calls the selectors – and Allen was the main man – got it right. They started by choosing the perfect captain when there were more obvious contenders and they took McCormick, Kirton, and Kirkpatrick on tour when they could easily have gone with alternatives. They made Kember back-up fullback and that worked. They took a punt on Thorne before he had even played for Auckland and he too repaid their faith. On the tour itself, choosing Going and Kirkpatrick for the French test was a masterstroke and using Williams as a specialist open-side flanker was another good call. Allen's ability to see the potential in a player, and in a man, was second-to-none. He knew the style of play he wanted, the type of player who would blossom in that style, and the type of man who would step up when the going got tough. He got what he wanted and in terms of character that was the type of guys he'd have wanted beside him in the Kiwis, and in the darkest days of war.

Yet even judging the 1967 side on its own terms is no simple matter. The fact that they kept winning means they were never tested by defeat. It's a lot easier to have a happy and united team when you keep winning. The team fell behind on the scoreboard in each of their last seven games yet kept running the ball and kept coming back to win. Allen's comment that the side couldn't afford to leave out both Lochore and Meads suggests a lack of depth up front and they were undoubtedly hanging on in the last games. Many felt they would have struggled on a longer tour. Meads' biography tells us that:

> *The 1967 team for all its wonderful record and its fine reputation came unstuck after twenty-two or twenty-three players... I believe that had that tour been of twenty-six or twenty-seven matches... it would have cracked. There was an element in that team which tossed it in, threw it away, and had we been playing, say, another ten matches those players would have been needed. They had no dedication in anything except their own social activities as the tour went on...*

It is a harsh criticism from one with the highest standards. Earlier itineraries included many easier games than the succession of regional sides Lochore's men played and players had much more time to relax and stay mentally fresh. The compacted nature of the '67 tour made it an extreme test of physical and mental endurance, beyond that required of any earlier tour. The disruptions to the itinerary further hindered proper preparation, most obviously against East Wales. Furthermore, had the tour been longer, replacements would surely have been called in. The injection of a couple of experienced tourists like Watt and winger Ian Smith, or new men like Panther, Sutherland, and Finn would surely have helped reinvigorate the side.

Some of the new players – Kember, Thorne and Cottrell in the backs,

Smith and Kirkpatrick in the forwards – had stepped up and were capable of anchoring the mid-week team. The reserves at half-back and hooker were top class and with Nathan restored to fitness, to say nothing of Wills who was crying out to play, the back-row was immensely strong.

There is no doubt also that, as he had done in France, Saxton could have stepped in again after the Murrayfield dust had settled and reminded the players of their responsibilities. The mental and physical fortitude of the side was certainly tested, but not necessarily to the limit. Meads himself would have gone on, presumably until long after the cows came home. Men like Lochore, Davis, and McCormick were at their very best at the end of the tour and Laidlaw, Steel and Tremain had just reached their peak. Perhaps Meads underestimated the side.

But we can also take his statement as an example of the extreme honesty in self-appraisal that is an outstanding characteristic of the '67 players. They were their own harshest critics. And that honesty is part of what made this team something more than just a legendary side. They were a group of individuals whose lives were immeasurably enhanced not only by rugby in general but by the example of Saxton, Allen, and Lochore. It is given to few men – or women – to manifest the ultimate quality of leadership, the bringing together, the welding of disparate individuals into common cause. And that cannot be done through division, inflexibility, or with anything less than complete and innate honesty. Those were qualities its leadership brought to the 1967 team and reinforced in its players.

How the players lived their later lives owed an immense amount to their leaders. Without exception, the players I met held Saxton and 'BJ' Lochore in the highest regard as men of a character to emulate, men who had influenced their lives. And Allen's biographer noted how the old coach had valued comments "From the All Blacks themselves, many of whom made a point of telling him later in their lives just how much his discipline, hard work, attention to detail and personal motivation had meant to them."

None of the players can confidently answer the question of why so many of them were successful in later life. But many of them reached the peak of their career form on that tour and were brought to that peak at least partly by the example of the team leadership. They remember the "discipline" and "high standards" set by the leadership group and those lessons stayed with them.

Having seen how diverse the personalities of the players were, I began to see that if honesty and personal example were key factors in leadership so too is the sensitivity of the professional dog-walker, keeping a dozen breeds all moving happily in the same direction. It's not a grand metaphor like helmsman or pilot, but it helps us understand how Saxton and Lochore led the side so successfully and how they and Allen guided the players to success not just in rugby in 1967, but in their lives that followed.

When we look back at any given All Black side they often contain a man like Tom Morrison who rose to the top of rugby coaching or administration, or an individual like Sir Wilson Whineray who went on to a prominent and successful life in some other field of achievement. But there has never been an All Black team, indeed a rugby team anywhere, that produced so many individuals whose later lives were so successful both in terms of measurable achievements and in character as did the 1967 squad. That alone makes them a great side.

Former All Blacks often become regional beacons, stalwarts of their club or provincial structures enjoying the respect of their peers and their community. Like Whineray and Meads, many of them take an active role in supporting the less fortunate members of that community, they remain givers, not takers. Accustomed to hard work and discipline they tend to be successful in their worldly endeavours. So it is no surprise that most of the '67 side later served their clubs, with around a third of them going on to representative or national rugby positions.

Their contributions to the game were formally recognised. Allen, Lochore, and Meads were knighted for services to rugby, while Terry McLean was knighted for services to sports journalism. Others including Saxton, Meads, Lochore, Kirkpatrick, and Going were awarded OBEs or MBEs and had Tremain lived he would probably have been honoured as well. But it was not just a matter of players giving back to the game or being ennobled for services to it. What is unique about the '67 side is the number who rose to prominence in fields outside of the world of rugby.

In the business world, for example, the immaculate and successful farms run by those who worked the land testify to their abilities in that field. Indeed Going, Strahan, Smith, and Lochore were all still active on their properties when I called. My conversation with Going took place against a background of rumbling engines as a fleet of earth movers dug out a new dam on his property. Others such as Dick, a successful chartered accountant specialising in tax law, and Davis, who runs a flourishing outdoor and sporting goods shop in Rotorua, are also still active.

Then there was Jack Hazlett, who found his future on the '67 tour. Near Yeovil in Somerset he visited a business that collected and processed still-born lamb and calf skins into quality leather. That got him thinking. As his rugby career wound down he set up a tannery at Thornbury out of Invercargill and began the systematic collection of unwanted skins. He paid due credit to the rugby connections that helped him get established and develop a multi-million dollar business, Slinkskins Ltd., which supplies quality leather to some of the world's great fashion houses. As he showed my wife and I around his tannery I got the feeling that he was proudest of this achievement above all others in his life. He'd created a successful business to pass on to his children, one that provides a decent workplace – and I've seen plenty of terrible ones to judge it by – for people in the local community. He played rugby for nineteen years. "I got it all back," he said, and he was grateful.

The achievements of the players cannot be divorced from the lessons and the confidence they gained from rugby and from the example set by Saxton, Allen, and Lochore. Biographer Veysey records how McCormick's "Life is broader because of rugby," and that applies to the team as a whole. Rugby gave them opportunities and most of them took those opportunities, some modestly, some in full measure. As Veysey lamented:

> *It is a human failing in New Zealand that we tend to hail great players for what they have done for rugby, while not paying due tribute to the game for what it has done for many of its players.*

***

What, I asked the players, had they got out of the tour? A time "Living and breathing rugby" and being "on tour with 30 guys who love the game you love" were what Smith and Lochore remembered, but at the individual level it was also a personal journey. As Dick put it, there were "30 guys learning where you fit in the world." At the end of it, as Thorne remembered, "You looked in the mirror and you were different, not least from having added six or eight kilos of muscle!"

With added muscle came added confidence. Many young men lack confidence, particularly those who lack a supportive family or fail to shine at school. They become quiet and withdrawn or compensate by acting tough or overconfident. The need to fit into a team and the constant social life of a rugby tour tended to bring out those who were withdrawn and smooth out those who compensated. Shy young men suddenly found the dinner table of high and mighty or the lounge table of young and pretty were interested in them, listened to what they said, treated them as worthy of respect. That could be a revelation. McCormick in his biography credits rugby with giving him the confidence to speak in public, and to "Deal with businessmen or politicians with confidence." Meads' biographer made a similar point: that confidence didn't just help the players in their future lives either, it had a knock-on effect. Sharon Williams observed that, "It let Graham allow his children to achieve their goals as well."

Friendship was something most of the players mentioned as a treasured benefit of the tour; friendships with people met on the tour as with MacRae and Hearn, but also friendships with teammates. In a happy team there was a sense of belonging. Inevitably there were those you didn't particularly like. But collectively you were teammates, and there were those you became especially close to and who became life-long friends – Nathan and Kirkpatrick, for example.

Being part of a team was something many of them identified as character forming in the best sense. Kember noted the great satisfaction he got from the experience of the individual being part of a team and placing the team first, that wanting, as Smith remembered, "To be the best for the team". They all wanted to contribute and regret it if they couldn't. Men like McCormick and Nathan singled out the enjoyment of shared experiences and the sense of being there for each other. As Nathan put it, team members "Became like family". Several players identified the '67 team's style of play as contributing to that, with backs and forwards able to express themselves equally.

Then there was the joy of touring. What stood out was not the sightseeing but the social occasions, so different from those in New Zealand, nights singing in Wales, the different vibes of France, or the grand traditions of England and Scotland. Those formal dinners might have seemed formidable at first but they became wonderful memories. Strahan loved the "Great insight into how things operated – to see the Old Starched Shirts, fine gentlemen, but upper-crust, [and how they] did things with panache."

There could be drawbacks to this wider world though. As Clarke admitted, "You're put in a position you didn't ask for. They all want to know you." You could get cynical about your new appeal. Thorne remembers a girl who'd turned him down suddenly wanting to go out with him when he became an All Black. Clarke was used to trusting those around him in the Air Force. Having to be a little cautious about what people might want of you, or why they wanted it, was something new. But most of the players learned a certain caution in their dealings with the world. They gained the confidence to say 'No' as well as 'Yes'.

Laidlaw pointed out that the "Hardest thing for a 'great' Rugby player is to become, after it is all over, accustomed to being ordinary again." That can take time. Being an ex-All Black isn't always a positive status, there is always the Tall Poppy syndrome. As Hazlett put it, you can feel "branded", unable to be ordinary again.

Overall though it was an overwhelmingly positive experience, one that "opened doors" and "shaped their lives". As Williams said, there was "Great satisfaction in achieving a lifetime goal." For Clarke, "It gave me a platform...and it was up to me what I did with it. I could die happy, knowing I'd done something." They had all put the effort to be there, yet each thought, "how fortunate I was to play for the icons" – or to coach them. As Allen told his biographer:

> *I don't believe any other team... had as much fun as they did... during the long tour of Canada, Britain and France. Those players possessed all the qualities I could wish for in a team. They had discipline, self-respect and a strong belief in themselves – and it didn't happen all by chance... without that splendid attitude we would not have achieved what we did.*

The commentators agree the 1967 team's behaviour off the field left a good impression on their hosts. The Welsh journalist and former international J.B.G. Thomas for example, tended to be critical of New Zealand rugby. But he acknowledged that this side "Were always well turned-out; maintained punctual attendances at official functions, and gave little or no trouble to hotel managements or travel authorities." The team "mixed more freely than several previous sides" and were, he concluded, second only to the Kiwis as the most popular tourists since the 1905 side.

The media were a lot less intrusive in 1967. They diplomatically turned a blind eye to goings-on that would make headlines in today's world. Just as obituaries in those days used a particular code – 'confirmed bachelor' meant gay, 'convivial' meant a confirmed drunk, and so on –rugby writers only discreetly hinted at players' transgressions or personality defects. But even reading their accounts with code book in hand, the '67 side seem to have generally been well-behaved and a good number of the players were clearly popular guests. Alan Smith remembers the British workers they encountered – doormen and the like – loved the egalitarian Kiwis because they treated them as human beings rather than servants. Yet Laidlaw's book gives a different impression. He wrote that:

> *A 1967 All Black had a fight with a London publican and had to be restrained by police… By the following morning the case was forgotten…On that same tour, there were clobbered waiters, insulted managers, felt waitresses, outraged wives, and many a flattened night porter. All this and more, but with little fuss and no more than the occasional word of restraint on the arrival of morning and sober sanity.*

Certainly not every incident reached the ears of management. Muller, for example, recalls hooker McLeod being chased down the street by a Chinaman on the North American section of the tour while the abstentious Going was sometimes embarrassed by some of his hard-drinking teammates. Perhaps it is safest to conclude that it was a different era, with different standards, and the behaviour of the players was within the parameters allowable to and accepted of young sportsmen at the time. The war-time generation judged by different standards to those that operate today.

***

The 1967 team didn't just change New Zealand rugby, it changed British rugby too. Sensing they were in danger of being left behind, northern rugby began to appoint coaches throughout the game. They started to develop forwards with ball skills, to increase the competitiveness of their club rugby, and to plan for success. The seeds of the 1971 Lions' success in New Zealand were planted in 1967. McLean noted that South of England's John Pullin was "Certainly the best hooker the All Blacks encountered on their tour." But other future Lions stars like J.P.R. Williams, Mervyn Davies, and David Duckham were still making their way in the game.

The '67 tour impacted in another area too: the British public consciousness. The Test match against England was the BBC's first rugby international broadcast in colour. Even if the jerseys were black and white and the sky was grey, at least the grass was green and the spectacular rugby on show was a wonderful advertisement for the game. In NZ, the sole television station only broadcast in black and white, but the future was clear.

Can the modern game learn from the 1967 All Blacks? Probably not much, for it is a different New Zealand today, more equal in issues of gender and difference, more urban, more, dare we say it – soft? And there are only two things history really teaches us – don't invade Russia in winter and don't invade Afghanistan at any time. But perhaps of 1967, like 1987 and 2011 or 2015, we can say that All Black rugby is at its best when it represents all of New Zealand society and when the game is led by men who are honest, open, and inclusive. And when our game reaches its greatest heights, as it has in those years, it is the game that the Originals played in 1905, the Invincibles played in 1924, and the Kiwis played in 1945; honest, open, and inclusive.

But the differences between rugby in 1967 and rugby today are enormous. Apart from obvious things like five point instead of three point tries, it is tactically an almost entirely different game. Defensive formations today leave far less space for the three-quarters to move in. There are also far fewer scrums and line-outs than there were then, but scrum-collapses were almost unknown in the 60s. And when players took off their long-sleeved shirts there were no six-packs or Popeye-like muscle bulges, there was just core strength. The fearsome rucking of the old days is also long-gone. "You'd be ordered off for rucking today," mused Hazlett.

There are other changes that stand out to the players. Meads now smiles at the old idea that you didn't drink water during a game. He followed the advice of Arthur Lydiard, the great running coach, who said an athlete's last drink should be three hours before they performed. Even drinking after the match has changed. Verna Meads pointed out that teams used to sit together with their opponents. Now they sit with their wives and partners on separate tables to the opposition and rarely mix. Forming friendships isn't a big part of touring now; there's no time for that. Being an All Black isn't as exceptional as it used to be either. Now it's sometimes just a stepping stone that adds a few noughts to a contract to play in France or Japan.

The frequency with which the All Blacks play and the constant use of replacements means many more players now become All Blacks. In the period from 1964 to '67 the All Blacks used fewer than 30 players in the sixteen tests they played. The British Lions side that toured Australia in 2013 used 30 players in three tests. And you can get to see the All Blacks play a test in New Zealand now, which wasn't easy in the earlier years. In ten seasons from 1967-1976, the All Blacks played just sixteen tests at home and people would camp out the night before tickets went on sale to be sure of getting one. No longer is a test match a grand event that stops the nation. Now it's more a part of a range of possible evening entertainments.

Several writers have pointed out that New Zealand sides tended to be easier to pull together in the 60s because while player's personalities could be very different, their backgrounds and interests were similar. As Lochore pointed out to his biographer:

*Those were the days when rugby was everything to rural communities. It bound people together. It made neither judgements nor distinctions. It created no divisions. It was the game for all the people.*

In some ways that hasn't changed, and the respect in which the All Blacks are held today owes much to the direction in which the '67 team took the game. But the whole structure around the side has now changed and there will be more changes down the track. What we see happening in other professional sports such as soccer and league will inevitably happen in rugby. In a world where nationalities are blurred, the lure of playing for your country will not be the same. Players will aspire to play for the jersey, the franchise, or the company, but these are all moveable according to the dictates of the market. The future might be the China Airways All Blacks playing at home in Hong Kong. Their starting fifteen will include a majority of players born in the Pacific Islands and players will wear high-tech protective helmets that prevent concussion. Every year a number of players will be suspended for the use of performance-enhancing or recreational drugs and several others will face court for various offences off the field. Only a handful of the players will drink alcohol, however, and several will be vegetarians.

The game will commence with a version of the national anthem as striking as Jimi Hendrix's version of The Star Spangled Banner. Television will demand both sides do a haka. Play will comprise four twenty-minute quarters with ten-minute advertisement breaks in between. The scoring of points will be celebrated by thanks to various gods, cartwheels, fist-pumping, and group hugs. The opposition will be largely ignored at the end of the game while the team gather for more hugs or perhaps prayers, although Hansie Cronje's great legacy has been to discredit team prayers for everyone short of the Vatican XV.

But somewhere out of the back of Invercargill or on a muddy field in Whakatane, fifteen blokes will still shake hands with their opponents, thank the ref, and trudge off to have a beer together after 80 minutes of giving their best for nothing but the love of the game. The last time I was in the Rugby Museum in Palmerston some schoolboys testing themselves against the scrum machine broke it off its moorings. New Zealand rugby is in safe hands.

\*\*\*

CHAPTER ELEVEN

—

# WHERE ARE THEY TODAY?

Of the 32 members of the 1967 side, 23 were still alive when this book was completed, the official photograph of the 1967 All Black team can be found on page 264. Inevitably, as the years pass, their ranks grow thinner.

**Charlie Saxton** died in 2001. As his obituary in the New Zealand Herald put it, "Saxton did not die a millionaire, but he did leave thousands of friends throughout the rugby world." **Fred Allen,** knighted in 2010, died in 2012. Although he later coached many youth teams, notably – with Sid Going as his assistant – the New Zealand Rugby News touring sides, his first-class coaching career ended in 1968. He remains a legend of the national game and perhaps his legacy is all the better for his quitting when they asked 'Why?', rather than when they asked 'Why not?'

**Ken Gray** welcomed the Springboks to his farm in 1965. He was a good friend of Andy Macdonald, the prop in that '65 side who later fought off a lion but later still was murdered by guerrilla fighters. Yet while he didn't announce it publicly, Gray was not prepared to tour apartheid South Africa and retired from top class rugby after 1969. He went into local politics and in 1992 was selected as the Labour candidate for Western Hutt at the next elections. But soon after selection, despite having a recent full medical examination, he died suddenly of a heart attack.

**Kel Tremain's** All Black career ended in 1968. The dynamic Hawke's Bay captain then built up a successful real estate and tourism business. Manager of the Bay side in 1985-90, he joined the NZRFU Council and was considered a future Chairman before the cigarettes caught up with him. He died in 1992. One of his sons played for Hawke's Bay, another is now an M.P.

**Alister Hopkinson** last played for New Zealand in 1970. He coached Canterbury in 1992 and died in 1999. His teammate **Wayne Cottrell,** the ultimate team-man who retired at 28 to focus on the family business, died in 2013. **Mac Herewini,** a northern Maori selector after his retirement in 1971, suffered a series of strokes and died in May 2014. **Jack Hazlett,** who retired from playing after the 1968 season, died in December 2014, soon after I interviewed him.

There was one member of the '67 team who didn't prosper in life. **Bruce McLeod** is the exception that proves the rule. He grew up in South Auckland, another product of a broken home, and after Otahuhu College he made the Counties side in 1962. He didn't make the Whineray tour but in 1964 became the Number One hooker. He kept that position into the 1970 South African tour. A tough, abrasive, and mobile player, McLeod was one of the characters of the '67 side, with Hopkinson "the song and dance men." Wills remembers that even as an automatic choice in the test team, McLeod was "One of the boys. He got on well with everyone, dirt-trackers included." He had a sardonic sense of humour. After a tub-thumping team-talk from 1970 coach Vodanovich that invoked the battles of Cassino, Alamein, and Passchendaele, McLeod murmured, "And remember the Alamo!"

Some men, most men even, can drink steadily all their lives yet never lose their way in life. But a few are destroyed by alcohol. The 1967 side contained a fair number of heavy drinkers. Call it the culture of rugby or just the culture of New Zealand and a good many places beside. But only one of the 1967 team suffered from alcoholism. That was McLeod. There were other issues involved: isolation, tales of regular drug treatment for some unspecified condition, a marriage breakdown. One teammate said it was schizophrenia, but whatever it was the grog made it worse, and the grog took over. He was found dead in his Foxton batch in 1996. McCormick remembered the last time he'd seen him, when he was with his '67 teammates and said, "I know there's people [here] who will look after me." That was the problem, says McCormick; "People around him didn't look after him." Hazlett provided his epitaph, "There's one thing I know about him," he said. "McLeod was a bloody good hooker." It's an epitaph he'd have been proud of.

One player could not be interviewed. **Tony Steel**, whose last minute tries twice preserved the All Blacks' unbeaten record, retired early due to injury. He went into teaching, firstly at Brisbane Grammar School and later back in New Zealand he became headmaster of Hamilton Boys' High School. He also served two terms as National party M.P. for Hamilton East. Sadly, the memories of his All Blacks days have now faded from his mind.

\*\*\*

The remaining players I was able to interview are now scattered throughout New Zealand, with one living overseas. There was a reunion of sorts at Petone in the early 80s, but these days the players usually catch up at a general All Black reunion held annually to coincide with a test match. They are not so much a band-of-brothers circle as a chain of friendships, with each man still in touch with at least some of the other links in the chain. News passes along the chain from one link to another.

**Fergie McCormick** grew up with two balls: a cricket ball in the summer and a rugby ball in the winter. He also had the kind of balls you need to get a reputation as the toughest full-back in the business. Full-backs weren't supposed to be extra wingers then. They were supposed to stand rock-solid under the high ball as eight angry forwards converged on them at maximum speed, then bounce back up after they were flattened and take out any winger with the temerity to approach their line. Fergie did all that and more for his club and his province, and finally he did it for Fred Allen and the All Blacks. The '67 side didn't really have a star, but let's just say that if they hadn't had McCormick the sky would have been a heck of a lot darker.

He spent his working life with the Canterbury Frozen Meat company. They were a good employer who looked after him and he liked the fact that most of the blokes he worked with were good honest men. McCormick still reveres Saxton and particularly Allen, who "Saw me as a person [and a person] that he wanted in a team...and I never forgot." He remembers the "thrill" he got from doing his job, kicking the vital goal, making the try-scoring tackle. McCormick's still active these days, still coaches women's rugby, still supports Canterbury rugby. He's learned to be at home in the spotlight and he tells a good story—he's comfortable in himself. And if you were in the trenches, he's still the guy you'd want beside you.

**Phil Clarke** headed to Australia at the end of 1968 and turned out for NSW Country. He even played rugby league as an amateur and remarkably found their training sessions even tougher than Allen's! There was a lot of sand hill running, something New Zealand rugby then considered slowed you up, but it got Clarke fitter than ever and he played Senior B rugby after his return to New Zealand in 1976. He became the first Sport and Recreation officer in Blenheim in 1977-81, then resigned and joined brother Adrian in his cray-fishing business. Later he managed a hotel and then a motel. He eventually started a brewery, but retired after a heart murmur. He treasures a logbook from his days flying Harvard trainers along with his All Black jersey and he remains a positive personality, "Very fortunate [to have lived] a good life."

**Bill Birtwistle** finished playing first-class rugby in 1970, then played Golden Oldies until he was 49 and loved it. He loved coaching too and often found himself quoting Fred Allen. He's retired after working for a bank and later as a driver for the Child-Youth-Family department. He still looks fit and he and his wife's suburban garden is in good shape.

**Malcolm Dick** was working in his office when I met him. He still jogs and like so many of the '67 side looks much fitter than the average. Dick stayed involved in rugby after he retired following the 1970 tour. Auckland union president in 1981-83, he was part of the administration and financial planning through the eventful years of the 1981 Springbok tour, the founding of Super Twelve and the rebuilding of Eden Park. In 1987, he managed the All Black team to Japan and he served on the NZRFU Council from 1986-92.

Dick still has a sharp, analytical mind, you can imagine him out-thinking an opponent or understanding the real consequences of a balance sheet. He is gifted with the ability to correct without giving offence; he'd have made a good teacher. He is one of the first All Blacks I met and I was struck by what I later find they have in common: an honesty of thought that when spoken can only be taken as something properly assessed. You might not agree, but the opinion is forensic and should be treated seriously. Dick is another of the '67 side who have succeeded in life, and he happily points out the photo of his father's 1938 All Black team.

**Grahame Thorne** isn't about retire either and he probably never will. He's got too much energy to be pensioned off. After the '67 tour, Thorne moved into the test team as a winger and went on to tour South Africa in 1970. Soon after – to the delight of the tabloids – he left his New Zealand fiancé and returned to South Africa to marry a lady he'd met on the tour. There he turned out for Northern Transvaal and Natal and collected a Currie Cup winners' medal, although the Springbok selectors were never going to let an ex-All Black wear their colours. But in time his son Bruce – now deceased – made the Junior Springboks side while playing for Transvaal and the two

Thorne's even played a game of rugby together in 1995.

By then he'd moved back to New Zealand and remarried. A spell on the Auckland City Council was followed by three years as National M.P. for Onehunga before he moved to Marlborough in 1997 and planted a vineyard. Others followed and now he has a vineyard in the golden hills outside of Queenstown. It hasn't always been easy – his son David was badly injured playing rugby – but Thorne has served as a City Councillor in Nelson and had two cooking shows on New Zealand television: Thorney's Cooking Canterbury and Thorney's Cooking Central. He remains a fine host, an ebullient personality with a complicated life, and is the antithesis of the stereotype All Black of the era – a stereotype he helped to change.

Thorne was probably born out of time. He'd have fitted right into the Kiwis team and if he was playing today his agent would be a busy man. His picture would rarely be missing from the gossip columns. He's the nearest thing the All Blacks have ever had to a glamour boy, probably the only one who wouldn't have been out of place in a Playboy interview. But he was never a dilettante, never just there for the ride, as much as he enjoyed it. He gave it everything and that commitment to whatever he focuses on stands out above all else. A guy so nervous he regularly threw up before the games and yet so determined he earned the respect of men like McCormick. In a team of extraordinarily diverse personalities Thorne still stands out, and as his teammates ruefully recognise, he always will.

**Bill Davis** went on the South African tour in 1970 and retired from rugby at the end of the following season when the need to earn a living finally had to take priority. But giving up the sport didn't come easy, so he "wound down" by playing softball, and playing it well enough to represent New Zealand. He made three tours with the national side, including one to Africa. These days he runs an outdoors and sporting goods shop in Rotorua and he and his wife live the New Zealand dream in their comfortable home at the water's edge. They are people people, good-humoured, enjoy company, hospitable and wide-ranging conversationalists. It's a long way from Parkvale primary, but the journey's been a good one.

Davis's old friend **Ian MacRae** also ended his All Black career in 1970 and he retired after the 1971 season. He was in real estate for a while, but went into the construction business and was happier there. After serving as Chairman of the Bay union he was talked into standing for the NZRFU. In 2013, he became President of the NZ Rugby Football Union. Once again you have to acknowledge Allen's ability to see the talent in a man.

MacRae doesn't stand on ceremony and speaks his mind as honestly as any of his teammates from '67. Like them he "Was happy to play in my era, I think we had the best of it." But he is pleased that today's All Blacks "have adopted a lot of what we did – they are seeking the perfect game as Saxton and Allen did...so it takes a generation to soak through." His admiration for those men still shines through, those "immaculate people in their own lives" who set the example of how success was achieved. Admiration remains too for Tremain, who exemplified those virtues of hard work and disciplined pursuit of a goal.

I asked MacRae whether he felt that New Zealand neglects its old stars, in contrast to Australia where sports grounds are invariably named after a local hero. But that wasn't a recognition they wanted; "All you want is to be respected by your peers, that's what matters most to players," he said.

Of all the journeys members of the '67 side have made through life, none have gone in such a stereotype-defying direction as **Gerald Kember**. He was a valued member of the side, "Quiet and good to meet" as Meads remembered and Lochore was quick to testify to the contribution he made to the team's success. Handed the short-straw as reserve fullback, Kember "stepped up". While managing to keep up his studies in his spare time – he passed two units of his law degree while on tour – Kember proved he was All Black class, and after devoting 1968 to his studies, returned to the side for the South African tour in 1970. After that he focused on his career as a corporate lawyer. So far a perfectly normal upwardly mobile C.V.

Kember today looks a decade or more younger than he is, the very picture of the health-conscious modern urban professional. But he has actually left the corporate world far behind. Today he is a life councillor, essentially seeking to enable people to perform at their best by freeing themselves from the restraints that can be imposed by their normal thinking. Finding the right means by which that freedom may be found is a part of the counsellor's role, and Kember's enquiries into the nature of consciousness have sometimes led him into areas far from the conventional.

His experiences as an All Black contributed to Kember's journey. He saw himself as having a personality totally unsuited to playing fullback. Playing at 5-8 he was "in the moment", able to react on instinct, to be in the bubble. Yet at fullback the fear of making a mistake that could cost his side the game hindered him. The experience of being concussed and playing so well on instinct when his conscious mind was removed made him wonder, "How come you could play so much better when you weren't conscious of what you were doing?" His life-long interest in the fundamental questions of life began to focus on the conscious and unconscious mind.

**Sid Going** played for New Zealand until 1977, and coached North Auckland from 1993-96. Outside the secular world, Going also reached great heights. He became President of the Church of Jesus Christ of Latter Day Saints (or Mormon), Temple in Hamilton, the faith's New Zealand centre where believers make their covenant with God. Church and family remain the most important things in his life. Brother Ken died in 2008 and Sid now spends much of his time in Hamilton serving his church. But he gets north sometimes and remains active on the farm.

Going's old sparring partner **Chris Laidlaw** became a city councillor in Wellington after serving as a Labour M.P. He also served as New Zealand's High Commissioner to Zimbabwe, and in effect to southern Africa and then New Zealand's Race Relations Councillor. Later he hosted the NZBC Sunday morning radio programme for thirteen years and he has written two incisive books on rugby. He still lives in Wellington. So too does **Earl Kirton**. I only caught up with him on the telephone as he planned another overseas trip. An All Black selector in 1988 and again from 1992-95, he is now retired from his career as a dentist but still wears his characteristic scarf. While their political views might be polar opposites he and Laidlaw are old friends, and both are still men who speak their minds.

The '67 tour was just the opening chapter of **Ian Kirkpatrick's** rugby career. It set him on the path to greatness and – as many had predicted – in 1972-73 when the All Blacks returned to the northern hemisphere, 'Kirky' was the captain. He was an All Black until 1977 and retired from playing two years later. The Manager of the 1986 Cavaliers team, he has also lead rugby supporters' tours.

He remains incredibly fit, with his long-distance cycling exploits a thing of wonder to his old teammates. This is a man who played more than 250 first-class games and never left the field injured. He dominates the chair he sits in. Straight-forward, honest, Kirkpatrick looks back on '67 with the wide vision of a long-serving All Black, isolating the team's discipline as its outstanding characteristic. He still enjoys the reunions with his teammates from that era; "You pick it up ten years later just as it was," he says. He's particularly close to Nathan.

1967 was the end of **Waka Nathan's** big rugby. He was a New Zealand Maori selector from 1971-77, managed the 1982 Maori side that toured Wales, and was President of the Auckland union from 2003-04. He is still cheerful and easy-going, instantly putting you at ease. But his memory isn't as sharp as it used to be and has worsened since I met him. He was still a fine-looking man and I had to see him in the morning because he was off to meet up with old friends and watch the Melbourne cup in the afternoon. He and wife Jan are never short of friends.

Loose forwards take a lot of head-knocks. The memory of fellow-flanker **Graham Williams** isn't great now either, and his fingers bear the marks of rucks and three dislocations. After 1967, he struggled to get time off from the family automotive business and wasn't available for the 1970 tour. He also struggled to keep his business going and if William's rugby status opened some doors perhaps it also left him subject to the tall poppy syndrome. But he focuses on the positives, thanks to rugby he "Got me a good lady" – which sounds great until Sharon laughingly protests that, "No I was already there!" Williams made it to Ireland eventually, on a private trip with Sharon. They went on to France where the locals wouldn't let them go when they found Williams had been an All Black. "Good days they were," he says thoughtfully of '67.

**Murray Wills** had a bad tour – there's always one. He's retired back to Taranaki now. He and wife Marilyn were doing up their new house when I visited. It's in a state of emerging elegance. He'd love to have toured South Africa, got a chance to show his pace on their hard grounds rather than British mud. He's honest about how he saw the '67 tour—honest with a touch of bitterness. He felt left out, hated Allen, and came home to find out he'd been ripped off by his farm manager. But things went better with Taranaki, 132 games between 1962 and 1972, the last two seasons as captain. And anyway, Wills was an All Black, and people still write and ask for his autograph.

**Alan Smith** was groomed to inherit Meads' place in the All Black scrum. But Meads was still playing when Smith retired. These days he has one of the best views in Taranaki above farmlands of Irish green. He's strong, active, and open, the kind of guy you trust on a handshake. Again as we talk, I find myself scribbling a note about the extraordinarily honest self-appraisal these players possess. He enjoyed his time in the sun, recognises the status he gained from it even then, and considers how much more difficult it is in the modern era for a player to retire from such a public world. His wife Christine is from Norfolk. She's as fit and positive as he is and she can hold her own. Alan once scored 165 not out and took seven wickets for eleven runs in a club cricket match, only to find the evening sports paper that day had headlined her breaking eight Taranaki athletic records!

**Sam Strahan** still lives on his farm too and it's another immaculate operation – the dogs look contentedly well fed. He couldn't always take time off from the farm and so missed the 1972-73 UK tour and retired from national rugby aged just 28 after the 1973 season. He has been the President of the Manawatu Union since 2003 and is a patron of the New Zealand Rugby Museum in Palmerston. Strahan recently lost his wife Rose, the lady the Indians would call his 'life's partner'. But he is still the Strahan they talked about on the '67 tour, a man whose company is always welcome, quietly dignified, a gentleman of self-deprecating humour, reasoned and helpful. He remembers the '67 tour with particular pleasure. "There wasn't one bad apple – they were a good bunch," he says fondly.

**Sir Colin Meads** is a legend, universally respected as a player and as a man. It will be impossible to write a proper history of New Zealand that does not mention him. His All Black career ended in 1971 and having managed King Country he became an All Black selector in 1986. He also coached the unauthorised Cavaliers side to South Africa that year and after a period of suspension for that role served on the NZRFU council in 1992-96. He was All Black team manager in 1994-95. As this book went to press he was living with cancer, and Te Kuiti had commissioned a statue of him. He was the greatest rugby player of the 20th century, but just happy to be remembered as "An All Black, and a good one".

**Arthur Jennings?** It took a while to find him. The Hazlett's had visited him in Fiji but he'd moved on. Everyone seemed to have a different idea of where he was. California was a strong rumour, while web-searches seemed to hint at Hawaii. He'd married a Swiss lady, or perhaps a princess. Turned out she was American and that's where he is now based. But by email he tells me he is still proud to be a "Coconut Kiwi", one for whom the "Best part [of the tour] was just sharing a beer with the local people – although to be honest I think I skipped out to enjoy the locals perhaps a few times too many."

Jennings entered parliament in Fiji after his rugby career ended and he was Shadow Minister for Youth, Sport and Public Works for five years.

The poacher turned game-keeper in 1986 when he selected, coached and managed – "mothered and fathered" –a Fiji Barbarians team on a seven country tour. That led to a call from Dannie Craven and a job managing the South Pacific Barbarians team to South Africa. That didn't work too well for him. It got him a life ban from rugby – rescinded a few years later – and the South Africans reneged on the promised $30,000 per man payment after the rebel tour generated a wave of bad publicity for the apartheid state!

But he finds himself full of tears remembering how it felt to make the All Blacks: "I can honestly tell you when I heard my name after the Wellington final trials… I sat down and cried to myself, thanked God, thanked my family, thanked every teammate I ever played with, every coach that ever coached me, every referee, every person that gave me work, I thanked the game itself for making me the man I was and still am."

Taranaki prop **Jazz Muller** is another of the '67 All Blacks whose larger-than-life personality has become legendary. He stayed in the All Blacks through to the end of 1971 and worked at J.C. Hutton's freezing works for 24 years. Stories attach themselves to Muller just as they do to Colin Meads. Meads with a sheep under each arm. Muller trimming his hedge with a lawnmower.

I heard that Muller was a recluse, which is not quite true. But he certainly doesn't seek the limelight and he takes a bit of tracking down. The time I spend with him is not so much an interview or a conversation as an insight into his world. With his Swiss heritage, I believed him when he said one of his uncle's fought for Germany in the war– at least until he told me another one fought for Japan! Muller reduces complexities to the minimum. Cut it back, sort it out; he's a kind of Kiwi backwoods' philosopher. That there is another side to him is apparent from the artworks he creates from found objects. They say the role of an artist is to make us see things differently. Muller does that.

His collection of rugby memorabilia is renowned. He is proud of his All Black cap – number 656 – and enjoyed seeing different places and meeting different people, including some of the supporters. He joined a supporter's tour that followed the All Black tour of Ireland in 1974. Life has gone in different directions since then, but one thing is certain: modern rugby won't produce men like Brian 'Jazz' Muller. He didn't come out of a mould and he remains a unique, larger-than-life character. Whether in the news or staying well out of it, Muller remains alive, passionate, warm, irascible and funny; a genuine 100% original.

**John Major** is in a wheelchair these days, the victim of an inherited condition. He doesn't act like a victim. He's too busy being alive and he just gets on with it. He makes coffee and laughs warmly at the tour memories, tells stories like the one about the mural of Uzzel's kick on the Newport club wall. He finished farming back in 1989 and he and wife Rae moved into town. Like so many of the side he is still closely involved with his old club, proud to be a member of Inglewood as well as the All Blacks. And the four Taranaki members of the '67 side still share a special closeness: they're in touch. Major is a part of a good community and his warmth and equanimity in the face of handicap are inspirational. He's the kind of guy that when you leave, you feel better for having met him.

One thing has not changed since 1967; **Sir Brian Lochore** – the man the players all call 'BJ' – remains the trusted leader of the team. He's still farming in the Wairarapa. He last played for New Zealand in 1971. He moved on to coaching his club Masterton, then coached Wairarapa, and from 1985-87 he coached New Zealand. It was Lochore who brought together players divided by the South African rebel tours and turned them into a team that won the first ever Rugby World Cup. Later he was campaign manager when the All Blacks reached the final of the 1995 World Cup and he was on the panel of respected New Zealanders who selected the range of possible new flags in 2015. Fame has not affected him at all.

\*\*\*

Mr C. K. Saxton (Otago)
(Manager)

Mr F. R. Allen (Auckland)
(Assistant Manager)

B. J. Lochore (Wairarapa)
15st 4 lb; 6ft 3in; Age 27; Farmer
Number Eight          Captain

W. F. McCormick (Canterbury)
13st   1 lb;   5ft   8in;   Age   27;
Slaughterman          Fullback

M. J. Dick (Auckland)
12st 13 lb; 5ft 9in; Age 26; Com
Secretary          Threeq

P. H. Clarke (Marlborough)
12st 11 lb; 5ft 9in; Age 25; Insurance
Agent          Threequarter

W. M. Birtwistle (Waikato)
11st 12 lb; 5ft 11½in; Age 28; Sales
Representative          Threequarter

A. G. Steel (Canterbury)
12st; 5ft 11in; Age 25; Secondary
School Teacher          Threequarter

W. L. Davis (Hawke's Bay)
13st; 5ft 11½in; Age 24; Sales
Representative          Centre

G. S. Thorne (Auckla
13st 7 lb; 5ft 10in; Age
Student

I. R. Macrae (Hawke's Bay)
13st 11 lb; 6ft 2in; Age 24; Timber
Company    Executive    Five-Eighth
(Vice-Captain)

W. D. Cottrell (Canterbury)
12st 2 lb; 5ft 11in; Age 23; Baker
Five-Eighth

G. F. Kember (Wellington)
12st 12 lb; 5ft 11½in; Age 21; Law
Student          Five-Eighth.

E. W. Kirton (Otago)
12st 10 lb; 5ft 10in; Age 26; Dental
Student          Five-Eighth

M. A. Herewini (Auckland)
11st 3 lb;   5ft 6in;   Age 27;
Proprietor          Five-E

C. R. Laidlaw (Otago)
13st; 5ft 9in; Age 24; Arts Student
Halfback

S. M. Going (North Auckland)
1st 8lb; 5ft 7in; Age 23; Farmer
Halfback

I. Kirkpatrick (Canterbury)
14st 12 lb; 6ft 2in; Age 21; Farmer
Number Eight

W. J. Nathan (Auckland)
14st 3 lb; 5ft 11in; Age 27; Sales
Promotion Officer          Siderow

M. C. Wills (Taran
13st 10 lb; 6ft; Age 2
Farmer

G. C. Williams (Wellington)
13st 7 lb; 6ft; Age 22; Automotive
Machinist          Siderow

K. R. Tremain (Hawke's Bay)
15st 10 lb; 6ft 2in; Age 29; Stock
Agent          Siderow

C. E. Meads (King Country)
16st 6 lb; 6ft 4in; Age 31; Farmer
Lock

S. C. Strahan (Manawatu)
16st 3 lb; 6ft 4½in; Age 22; Farmer
Lock

A. E. Smith (Tarana
15st 6 lb; 6ft .3in; Age 24;
Lock

A. P. Jennings (Bay of Plenty)
15st; 6ft 4in; Age 27; Contractor
Lock

K. F. Gray (Wellington)
16st;   6ft 2in; Age 27; Farmer
Prop

B. L. Muller (Taranaki)
17st;   6ft 1in;  Age 25;  Freezing
Works Employee          Prop

E. J. Hazlett (Southland)
14st 13 lb; 6ft 2in; Age 28; Farmer
Prop

A. E. Hopkinson (C
15st 13 lb; 6ft 2½in; A
Agent

J. Major (Taranaki)
14st 4 lb; 5ft 10in; Age 26; Farmer
Hooker

B. E. McLeod (Counties)
15st; 5ft 11in; Age 27; Compan
Representative          Hook

# ACKNOWLEDGEMENTS

In his book *Mud in Your Eye*, Chris Laidlaw wrote that while it was easy to write an ordinary tour book about the "jumble of assorted incidents" along the way, "[it] is quite another thing to relate the whole to an analysis of the social environment in which the action takes place." That is what I have tried to do here, and I alone am responsible for its accuracy and its opinions. But without the help of the surviving players themselves, this book could not have been written. I am immensely grateful to all of them for taking the time to talk about the 1967 tour. Often it was a case of their interrupting work, family commitments and even holidays. But they were invariably hospitable, kind to a novice rugby writer, gave freely of their time, expressed their opinions honestly, and asked absolutely nothing in return. I thank them all.

Where I have quoted players directly, or have noted or cited other published works on the tour and about the players themselves, I have indicated that with double quotation marks.

While it is a little unfair to single any individual players or their families out, the project would never have got off the ground without the good wishes of 'BJ', (Sir Brian) Lochore. My particular thanks to him and to Lady Pam. Bill and Barbara Davis and Jack and Anne Hazlett offered hospitality well beyond the call of duty, as did Thorne who has been a regular source of encouragement and ideas. Laidlaw and particularly Sam Strahan have helped with follow-ups, as have Jennings and tour secretary Derek Lever. Thanks also to Jazz Muller for showing me around his extraordinary museum gallery and to his nephew Roger and to John Major for getting me there.

I am pleased to acknowledge Christine Thomson at New Holland Publishers and her enthusiasm for this work, and I am grateful for the resources of the National Library in Wellington, the Central Library in Auckland and particularly The New Zealand Rugby Museum in Palmerston North. At the museum, the support of Director Stephen Berg has been invaluable. Thanks also to rugby historian and mine of information Bob Luxford for his advice, and to Ian Long at the New Zealand Rugby Union.

A special thanks also to my niece Cirran Payne for pointing out the reference from Moana Jackson, old friends Dave Macfarlane and Danny Shaw for their comments on the project, to Colin and Marcia Wylie for their hospitality and Terry Lehane, Jim and Caroline Carver and Mike Copeland for their various supporting efforts. To Rona and Ian Ramage and Mary-Jane and Brian Handyside and their families also, many thanks for your hospitality and clanship. Finally, I thank my wonderful wife Jeri McElroy for her constant support, understanding and encouragement.


Alex McKay

# BIBLIOGRAPHY

Allen, Fred. 1970. *Fred Allen on Rugby*. Auckland; Cassell & co.

Ambrose, Stephen E. 1992. *Band of Brothers E Company, 506th Regiment, 101st Airborne from Normandy to Hitler's Eagle's Nest*. New Jersey; Simon & Schuster.

Burke, P.S. (ed.) undated. *All Blacks can Laugh*. Taranaki Newspapers Ltd.

Chester, R.H. & N.A.C. McMillan. 1984. *Centenary. 100 Years of All Black Rugby*. Auckland; Moa publications.

Chester, Rod, Ron Palenski & Neville McMillan. 2000. *Men in Black. Commemorative 20th Century Edition*. Auckland; Hodder Moa Beckett.

Frost, David. 1968. *The All Blacks 1967 Tour of the British Isles and France*. London/N.Z.; Wolfe publishing/Whitcombe & Tombs.

Howitt, Bob. 1978. *Super Sid: the story of a great All Black*. Auckland; Rugby Press.

Howitt, Bob. 2004. *75 New Zealand Rugby Greats*. Auckland; Moa, Beckett.

Jackson, Moana. 1998. 'Snapshots from a Boyhood Album', in Witi Ihimaera (ed.), *Growing Up Maori*. Auckland; Tanden Press.

Knight, Lindsay. 1979. *Kirky*. Auckland; Rugby Press

Knight, Lindsay. 1982. *Shield Fever*. Auckland; Rugby Press.

Laidlaw, Chris. 1973. *Mud in your Eye*. Wellington; A.H. & A.W. Reed.

Laidlaw, Chris. 2010. *Someone stole my game*. Auckland; Hachette

Lawrence, Richard. 2007. *Unshaven Jaws. Sixty All Black captains 1903-2007*. Privately published.

Lewis, Paul (with Jock McLean). 2010. *TP. The Life and Times of Sir Terry McLean*. Auckland; HarperCollins.

McCarthy, Winston. 1947. *Broadcasting with the Kiwis*. Wellington; A.H. & A.W. Reed.

McCarthy, Winston. 1953. *Rugby in my time*. Wellington; A.H. & A.W. Reed.

McCarthy, Winston. 1968. *Haka! The All Blacks Story*. London; Pelham books.

MacKenzie, Morrie. 1969. *Black, Black, Black*. Auckland; Minerva.

McKenzie, J.M. 1960. *All Blacks in Chains*. Wellington: Truth (N.Z.) Ltd.

McLean, Terry. 1954. *Bob Stuart's All Blacks*. Wellington; A.H. & A.W. Reed.

McLean, Terry. 1959. *Great Days in New Zealand Rugby*. Wellington; A.H. & A.W. Reed.

McLean, Terry. 1960. *Beaten by the 'Boks : the 1960 All Blacks in South Africa*. Wellington, A.H. & A.W. Reed.

McLean, Terry. 1968. *All Black Magic. The Triumphant Tour of the 1967 All Blacks,* Wellington; A.H. & A.W. Reed.

McLean, Terry. 1987. *New Zealand Rugby Legends*. Auckland; Moa.

Murray, Bruce & David Wood. 2011. *Arthur Carman's Suitcase*. Tawa; Tawa Historical Society.

Palenski, Ron. 2008. *All Blacks Myths and Legends*. Auckland; Hodder Moa.

Quinn, Keith. 1999. *Legends of the All Blacks*. Auckland; Hodder Moa Beckett.

Reyburn, Wallace. 1968. *The Unsmiling Giants: The Sixth All Blacks.* *London;* Stanley Paul.

Rogers, Warwick. 1991. *Old Heroes; The 1956 Springbok Tour and The Lives Beyond.* Auckland; Hodder and Staughton.

Ryan, Greg. (ed.)2005. *Tackling Rugby Myths: Rugby and New Zealand Society 1854-2004.* Dunedin: University of Otago Press.

Saxton, Charles. 1960. *The ABC of Rugby.* Dunedin; The New Zealand Rugby Union.

Sayers, Alan & Les Watkins. 2011. Fred the Needle. *The Authorised Biography, The Untold Story of Sir Fred Allen.* Auckland; Hodder Moa.

Smith, Andrew. 2006. *Moondust. In Search of the Men who Fell to Earth.* London; Bloomsbury.

Thomas, J.B.G. *1968. Rugby in Red and Black.* London; Pelham books.

Tillman, H. 1957. *Great Men of New Zealand Rugby.* Christchurch; Lancaster Press.

Turner, Brian. 2002. *Meads.* Auckland; Hodder Moa Beckett.

Verdon, Paul.1999. *The power behind the All Blacks: the untold story of the men who coached the All Blacks.* London; Penguin.

Veysey, Alex. 1974. *Colin Meads All Black. Auckland;* William Collins.

Veysey, Alex. 1976. *Fergie.* Christchurch; Whitcoulls.

Veysey, Alex, Gary Caffell, Ron Palenski. 1996. *Lochore. An Authorised Biography.* Auckland; Hodder Moa Beckett.

Whatman, Mike. 2005. Khaki All Blacks; *A Tribute to the 'Kiwis' – the 2nd NZEF Army Rugby Team.* Auckland; Hodder Moa, Beckett.

Zavos, Spiro. 1979. *After the Final Whistle.* Wellington; Fourth Estate Books.

**PERIODICALS**

The Listener

The Dominion

New Zealand Herald

New Zealand Weekly News

Sports Digest

The New Zealand Rugby Almanack.

The Diners' Club: New Zealand Digest, Feb/March 1968

Rothmans Pall Mall Rugby Almanack; Rothmans NZ Ltd, 1967.

**WEBSITES**

www.rugbymuseum.co.nz

www.scrum.com

www.youtube.com (footage of various 1967 All Black games)

**FILM**

The Making of an All Black, written, produced & directed by Michael Scott-Smith, NZBC television, 1969.

**INTERVIEWS**

W.F. McCormick, W.M. Birtwistle, P.H. Clarke, W.L. Davis, M.J. Dick, G.S. Thorne, G.F. Kember, E.W. Kirton (telephone), I.R. MacRae, S.M. Going, C.R. Laidlaw, I.A. Kirkpatrick, B.J. Lochore, W.J. Nathan, G.C. Williams, M.C. Wills, A.G. Jennings (email), C.E. Meads, A.E. Smith, S.C. Strahan, E.J. Hazlett, B.L. Muller, J. Major.

# INDEX OF RUGBY PERSONALITIES

UK: £16.99